Guadalajara

Olivier Jacques
Esteban Cadena

Travel better, enjoy more

ULYSSES

Travel Guides

Offices

CANADA: Ulysses Travel Guides, 4176 Rue St-Denis, Montréal, Québec, H2W 2M5, ☎ (514) 843-9447 or 1-877-542-7247, ⇌(514) 843-9448, info@ulysses.ca, www.ulyssesguides.com

EUROPE: Les Guides de Voyage Ulysse SARL, BP 159, 75523 Paris Cedex 11, France, ☎ 01 43 38 89 50, ⇌01 43 38 89 52, voyage@ulysse.ca, www.ulyssesguides.com

U.S.A.: Ulysses Travel Guides, 305 Madison Avenue, Suite 1166, New York, NY 10165, ☎ 1-877-542-7247, info@ulysses.ca, www.ulyssesguides.com

Distributors

CANADA: Ulysses Books & Maps, 4176 Saint-Denis, Montréal, Québec, H2W 2M5, ☎ (514) 843-9882, ext.2232, 800-748-9171, Fax: 514-843-9448, info@ulysses.ca, www.ulyssesguides.com

GREAT BRITAIN AND IRELAND: World Leisure Marketing, Unit 11, Newmarket Court, Newmartket Drive, Derby DE24 8NW, ☎ 1 332 57 37 37, Fax: 1 332 57 33 99, office@wlmsales.co.uk

SCANDINAVIA: Scanvik, Esplanaden 8B, 1263 Copenhagen K, DK, ☎ (45) 33.12.77.66, Fax: (45) 33.91.28.82

SPAIN: Altaïr, Balmes 69, E-08007 Barcelona, ☎ 454 29 66, Fax: 451 25 59, altair@globalcom.es

SWITZERLAND: OLF, P.O. Box 1061, CH-1701 Fribourg, ☎ (026) 467.51.11, Fax: (026) 467.54.66

U.S.A.: The Globe Pequot Press, 246 Goose Lane, Guilford, CT 06437 - 0480, ☎1-800-243-0495, Fax: 800-820-2329, sales@globe-pequot.com

Other countries contact Ulysses Books & Maps, 4176 Rue Saint-Denis, Montréal, Québec, H2W 2M5, ☎ (514) 843-9882, ext.2232, 800-748-9171, Fax: 514-843-9448, info@ulysses.ca, www.ulyssesguides.com

Canadian Cataloguing-in-Publication Data (see page 8)
© December 2000, Ulysses Travel Guides.
All rights reserved Printed in Canada
ISBN 2-89464-250-4

Guadalajara, Guadalajara;
Guadalajara, Guadalajara.

Tienes el alma de provinciana,
hueles a limpia rosa temprana;
a verde jara fresca del río;
son mil palomas, tu caserío.

Guadalajara, Guadalajara,
hueles a pura tierra mojada.

Guadalajara, Guadalajara;
Guadalajara, Guadalajara

Yours is a provincial soul;
you have the sweet perfume of a spring rose;
from the bed of grass of a cool stream;
your roofs are like a thousand doves.

Guadalajara, Guadalajara,
You smell of pure, moist earth.

Mariachi song by Pepe Guízar

Table of Contents

List of Maps

Map Symbols

	Park	▪▪▪▪▪▪▪▪	Footpath
✪	National capital	▬▪▬▪▬	Trail
✈	Airport		

Symbols

🚢	Ulysses's Favourite
≈	Air Conditioning
bkfst incl.	Breakfast Included
⊗	Fan
⇆	Fax Number
ℨ	Fireplace
⊘	Fitness Centre
◼	In-room Safe
K	Kitchenette
≠	Mosquito Net
P	Parking
pb	Private Bathroom
≈	Pool
ℝ	Refrigerator
ℜ	Restaurant
△	Sauna
sb	Shared Bathroom
☎	Telephone Number
tv	Television
⊛	Whirlpool

ATTRACTION CLASSIFICATION

★	Interesting
★★	Worth a visit
★★★	Not to be missed

HOTEL CLASSIFICATION

$	$20 or less
$$	$20 to $40
$$$	$40 to $70
$$$$	$70 to $100
$$$$$	$100 or more

The prices in the guide are for one standard room,
double occupancy in high season.

RESTAURANT CLASSIFICATION

$	$5 or less
$$	$5 to $8
$$$	$8 to $12
$$$$	$12 to $16
$$$$$	$16 or more

The prices in the guide are for a meal for one
person, not including drinks and tip.

All prices in this guide are in US dollars.

Authors
Olivier Jacques
Esteban Cardena

Editor
Stéphane G. Marceau

Publisher
Pascale Couture

Project Coordinator
Jacqueline Grekin

Copy Editing
Eileen Connolly
Jacqueline Grekin
Anne Joyce

Translation
Danielle Gauthier
Renata Isajlovic

Page Layout
Typesetting
Dena Duijkers
Anne Joyce
Visuals
Isabelle Lalonde

Cartographers
Bradley Fenton
Patrick Thivierge
Yanik Landreville

Computer Graphics
Stéphanie Routhier

Artistic Director
Patrick Farei (Atoll)

Illustrations
Richard Serrao
Josée Perreault

Photography
Cover Page
Anne Rippy/
Image Bank (Catedral
de Guadalajara)
Inside Pages
Tibor Bognár/
Reflexion
M. Daniels/
Megapress

Thanks to: Jacques R. Dubé, Eric Bélanger, David Chávez, Michel Jacques, Secretaría de Turismo del Gobierno del Estado de Jalisco, particularly the staff at the information office.

We acknowledge the financial support of the Government of Canada through the Book Publishing Industry Development Program (BPIDP) for our publishing activities.

We would also like to thank SODEC (Québec) for its financial support.

Canadian Cataloguing-in-Publication Data

Jacques, Olivier
   Guadalajara
   (Ulysses travel guide)
   Translation of: Guadalajara.
   Includes index.
   ISBN 2-89464-250-4
   1. Guadalajara (Mexico) - Guidebooks. I. Titles. II. Series
F1391.G9J3213 2000   917.2'3504836   C00-941744-3

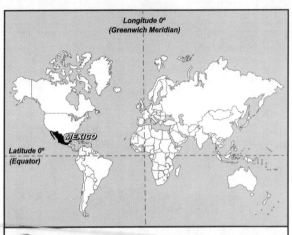

Where is Guadalajara?

©ULYSSES

Guadalajara
(21°N 103°E)

Mexico	
Capital:	Mexico
Population:	96,000,000 inhab.
Currency:	Mexican peso

UNITED STATES

Hermosillo

Chihuahua

Monterrey

Gulf of Mexico

La Paz

MEXICO

Mazatlán

Puerto Vallarta

Mexico City

Guadalajara

Cancún

Bahía de Campeche

Veracruz

Taxco

Pacific Ocean

Acapulco

Oaxaca

BELIZE

Puerto Escondido

Huatulco

GUATEMALA

Write to Us

The information contained in this guide was correct at press time. However, mistakes can slip in, omissions are always possible, places can disappear, etc. The authors and publisher hereby disclaim any liability for loss or damage resulting from omissions or errors.

We value your comments, corrections and suggestions, as they allow us to keep each guide up to date. The best contributions will be rewarded with a free book from Ulysses Travel Guides. All you have to do is write us at the following address and indicate which title you would be interested in receiving (see the list at the end of guide).

Ulysses Travel Guides
4176 Rue Saint-Denis
Montréal, Québec
Canada H2W 2M5
www.ulyssesguides.com
E-mail: text@ulysses.ca

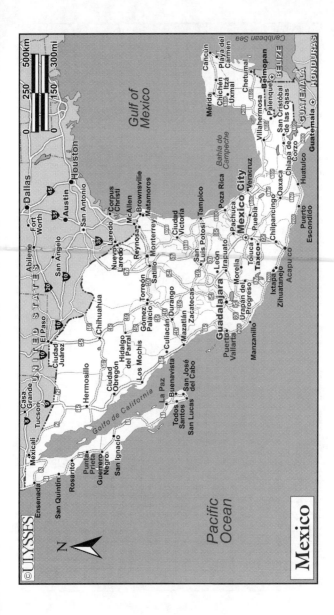

Mexico

State of Jalisco

Portrait

E ndless stretches of tropical beaches, mysterious Aztec pyramid builders, Andalusian-style colonial cities, Mexico City in 1968: the mere reference to the word "Mexico" evokes a kaleidoscope of images.

This country of light, bright colours and diverse landscapes appeared to Europeans for the first time in the 16th century as a fabulous goldmine of inexhaustible resources. Mexicans, heirs of a new civilization born from Spanish and indigenous cultures, have rapidly transformed themselves to face the challenges of today's world. No other country in the "New World" offers visitors as many wonders.

Guadalajara, Mexico's largest city after Mexico City, was once the starting point for explorers searching for hidden treasures and the legendary El Dorado. Today, this metropolis owes its fame to its commercial development, folklore and the hospitality of its residents. Two symbols identified with Mexico throughout the world—mariachis and tequila—also originated in this region.

Located in western Mexico approximately halfway between Guatemala and the United States, Guadelajara enjoys an excellent climate where it is never cold and bougainvilleas flower year round. By exploring this city, nicknamed *perla del Occidente*, visitors will discover the charm of its ancient quarters dating from New Spain, the great wealth of local crafts and even a small pyramid at the centre of the region's most important excavation sites.

Geography

Greater Guadalajara stretches into the Atemajac Valley, 1,561m (5,121ft) above sea level. Including the large suburbs of Zapopan and Tlaquepaque, it is home to approximately 6 million residents. Located near the centre of Jalisco, one of the 31 federal states that form the Mexican Republic, this region is traversed by the Sierra Madre del Sur mountain chain and bordered by the Pacific Ocean to the west. Asides from the famous beaches of Puerto Vallarta, some of the geographic attractions of the state of Jalisco include the Cola de Caballo falls (150m or 492ft) and the Lago de Chapala (bigger than Lake Leman), a winter refuge for migratory birds escaping the cold of the north.

Flora and Fauna

The variety of Mexico's relief is the result of the great diversity of its climate and soil. The vegetation in the northern part of the country thus features species of cactus found in the desert, while the south offers exuberant tropical flora. Located in between these two contrasting regions, the high central plateau (where Guadalajara is located) enjoys a spring climate. As early as the beginning of the 19th century, the famous German scholar Alexander von Humboldt conducted important scientific studies here that revealed Mexico's extraordinary biodiversity to the world.

Orchids

Portrait

Currently, 15% of Mexico's flora and fauna is considered unique in the world.

Flora

In the past, Mexicans cultivated dahlias, orchids, valerians and *tzempazúchitls* (a type of golden daisy) with care. For them, flowers symbolized life in its ephemeral state, a concept masterly presented by Pierre de Ronsard: "how truly cruel nature is, with each flower living only from morning to night." Extraordinarily diverse, Mexican flora includes around 30,000 species. Among the edible plants originating in Mexico are cocoa, tomatoes, avocados, corn, peanuts and vanilla, which are appreciated the world over.

The roses that adorn practically every park, garden and traffic circle in Guadalajara gave the city its nickname "the city of roses." On their arrival, visitors will be struck by the ubiquitous bougainvilleas (Bougainvillea glabra) with their purple, red, orange or white flowers. The floral setting is crowned with tall trees, jacandras *(Jacaranda mimosaefolia)* and

tabachines *(Deloniz regia)*, whose blooms add to the different seasonal colours of the city.

Fauna

The country's permanent plethora of animal residents include the jaguar elephant, the prehistoric-like iguana and parrots of every colour of the rainbow. The turkey originated in Mexico.

Jaguar

In addition to Mexico's own fauna, the country is also visited by many migratory species. The monarch butterfly *(Danaus plexippus)* with its orange, black and white wings, has captivated scientists and butterfly amateurs alike for ages. After a summer stay in southeastern Canada, these fragile winged creatures undertake an extraordinary trip, travelling over 4,000km (2,485mi) to finally arrive at the Santuarios de la Mariposa Monarca, east of the state of Michoacan (between Guadelajara and Mexico City), in early November. Other species that add to the impressive list of migratory fauna include whales from the coastal areas of British Columbia that swim along the Pacific coast to spend winter in warm Mexican waters. The beautiful seaside near Puerto Vallarta takes on a unique dimension thanks to the presence of gentle humpback whales *(Megaptera novaeangliae)* that swim in these waters from November to March. Migratory bird species liven up the natural habitat of Lago Chapala (over 20), including white pelicans *(Pelecanus erythrorhynchos diazi)* which are extremely sought after by amateur ornithologists, as are Canada geese *(Chen caerulescens)*, which migrate to Lago Sayula.

Urbanism

In order to better understand Guadalajara's urban fabric and keeping its historic past in mind, the city can be divided into six zones. They are briefly described below, even though these zones do not completely coincide with tourist itineraries.

Zone 1: Historic Guadalajara

This zone is the cradle of Guadalajara and includes the centre of town and the first district built in the ancient capital of New Galicia. Among the remarkable monuments located in the heart of this area are the cathedral, Palacio de Gobierno and the Museo Regional.

Zone 2: Popular Guadalajara

Located east of the ancient districts of San Juan de Dios and Analco, this zone stretches all the way to Tlaquepaque. A belvedere offers a spectacular view over the Barranca de Huentitán at the end of the Calzada Independencia.

Zone 3: The Avenues of Guadalajara

Organized around pretty traffic circles, this residential and commercial zone includes the famous Minerva, one of the city's symbols, and the Plaza del Sol, with its shopping centre.

Zone 4: Industrial Guadalajara

The Zona Industrial and the popular neighbourhood of La Cruz del Sur are located in this zone, south of the city.

Zone 5: Zapopan

Once built around the Virgen de Zapopan basilica, this ancient, picturesque suburb is today part of Greater Guadelajara. It includes residential neighbourhoods, as well as important industrial and commercial establishments west of the city.

Zone 6: Tlaquepaque

Once a peaceful potters' village, Tlaquepaque became famous for its village setting housing elegant craft shops. Today, it neighbours popular districts east of the city.

History

The First People

The first sedentary inhabitants of the Atemajac Valley (whose name is derived from *atlemaxak*—"place where stones cut through water"—in Nahuatl, language of the Aztecs) are said to have arrived over 6,000 years ago. But it is during the classical period (second to the fourth centuries AD) that a civilization with its own characteristics, independent of other pre-Columbian Mexican cultures, developed. A seigneurial system similar to that which developed in Europe in the Middle Ages was the method of social organization. Like all Western peoples, the indigenous

residents of the Atemajac Valley had a simple way of life. Their religion revolved around two axes: the belief in the existence of a correlation between humans and the forces of nature, and the cult of ancestors. They dug graves in which they buried their dead along with statuettes of human figures performing daily activities. Among the graves listed in Guadalajara, an interesting document dating from the 18th century that describes, in rather great detail, one of these burial sites, which was discovered at the time the Civil Hospital was being built. In 1978, a worker discovered another in a residential development in Zapopan. How many have yet to be unearthed?

The apparition of tribes from the high central plateau around the seventh century AD radically changed the lives of the modest Western culture. Graves were replaced by other types of burial places and pottery from the era illustrate the influence of the great Teotihuacana civilization, creators of the Sun Pyramid near Mexico City. Religious centres were built, the cult of Quetzalcoatl (feathered snake) spread and other gods venerated by the Aztecs and Mayas. The pyramid construction of El Iztepete, south of

Important Dates
in the History of Mexico

Towards 1200 BC
Birth of the Olmec civilization, the first great pre-Columbian culture, which preceded the Maya, Aztec and other ancient Mexican peoples.

Between 300 BC and AD700
Golden Age of civilizations considered to be classic: Teotihuacán (Sun Pyramid), Gulf of Mexico civilizations (El Tajín), the Oaxaca Valley civilization (Mitla and Monte Albán) and the Mayas of the Old Empire (Tikal, north of Guadalajara, and Palenque, in Chiapas).

Towards 940
The Toltecs, who preceded the Aztecs, first settle in Yucatán, where they establish a new Toltec-Maya empire (construction of Chichén Itzá).

1168 Fall of the Toltec capital Tula, located in the heart of Mexico. It is at this time that the Aztecs first appear.

1325 Founding of the Aztec capital Tenochtitlán on the islands of a lake, where Mexico City is currently located.

1519 Conquistador Cortés lands on the Gulf of Mexico and founds the city of Veracruz.

1521 Fall of Tenochtitlán, death of Moctezuma II and Cortés's conquest of the Aztec Empire.

1522 Founding of Mexico City, the start of the evangelization of New Spain and of the birth of the *encomienda* system.

1810 Start of the War of Independence, led by a group of Creoles under the leadership of Father Miguel Hidalgo.

1821 Treaty of Córdoba, proclaiming Mexico's independence.

1822 Coronation of Agustín, emperor of all Mexicans.

1846-1848
   War between Mexico and the United States, loss of half of Mexico's national territory: Texas, New Mexico, Arizona, Colorado, Nevada and Upper California.

1857   Promulgation of a new constitution establishing a civil government and confiscation of Church property; start of the Reform War.

1858   Benito Juárez, Mexico's first indigenous president.

1861   Landing of French troops at Veracruz and the beginning of French intervention.

1864-1867
   Second Empire, rule of Maximilian Hapsburg, archduke of Austria, sent by Napoleon III.

1876-1910
   Presidency of Porfirio Díaz, period of imposed stability marking the beginning of the industrialization of Mexico.

1910-1917
   Revolution rocks the country.

1929   Founding of the one-party system, with the PRN (Partido Revolucionario Nacional), which became the PRI (Partido Revolucionaro Institucional).

1934-1940
   Presidency of General Cárdenas, important land reform and the nationalization of oil companies.

1938   Mexico is one of the few countries that does not recognize Hitler's annexation of Austria.

1942   Mexico declares war on Germany.

1945   Mexico takes part in the liberation of Manilla.

1961   Mexico is the only Latin American country to maintain diplomatic relations with Cuba.

1968   Political crisis and riots in Mexico City; Olympic Games in Mexico City.

1985   Earthquake destroys part of Mexico City.

Portrait

1988   Presidential election. Carlos Salinas is elected under questionable circumstances with 50.36% of the vote. Nine million of 38 million eligible voters go to the polls.

1992   Mexico signs NAFTA, establishing a trading partnership union with Canada and the United States.

1993   Salinas renews diplomatic relations with the Vatican, which had been severed since the Revolution.

1994   The Zapatista rebellion under the leadership of sub-commander Marcos erupts in Chiapas, illustrating the government's instability and the inequality in Mexico. Luis Donaldo Colosio, the PRI presidential candidate, is assassinated during the electoral campaign and, shortly thereafter, Francisco Ruiz Massieu, the party's secretary general and brother-in-law of President Salinas, suffers the same fate; Ernesto Zedillo is elected following a serious crisis at the heart of the official party (PRI); new devaluation of the peso.

1999   President Zedillo welcomes Pope John Paul II, who greets 3 million faithful during a mass held in a stadium in Mexico City.

2000   Right-wing opposition leader Vicente Fox wins the presidential election.

Guadalajara, dates from this post-classical era.

The City's Founding

Events leading up to the founding of Guadalajara began a few years after Cortés conquered the Aztec Empire in 1521. Nuño Beltrán de Guzmán, one of the cruelest conquistadors, landed on the Gulf of Mexico in 1527, near what is today Tampico. He was first named governor of the coastal territories he conquered and later president of the Audience of New Spain. But driven by his unbridled ambition, Cortés's rival sought to expand his domain towards the Pacific in order to consolidate an enormous province between the two oceans over which he would rule—the

Portrait

future New Galicia. Leaving westward from Mexico City two days before Christmas in 1529, he passed through Michoacán, where he stopped the poor Calzontzin, the last Tarasquian king. He stole 10,000 measures of money, some gold and other significant riches, tortured him and burned him alive.

Shortly thereafter, Nuño Beltrán de Guzmán arrived in Tonalá, chef-lieu of the indigenous seigneury ruling over the Atemajac Valley. Native queen Cihualpilli greeted him despite the mistrust of some vassals who revolted. Helped by those loyal to the queen, the Spanish crushed the revolt and undertook the evangelization of the indigenous peoples. Nuño left, but ordered Juan de Oñate, one of his captains, to found a city that would serve as a starting point for new conquests. Wanting to please his commander, Oñate founded the Villa del Espíritu Santo Guadalajara and named it after Nuño's home- town, the name of which comes from the Arabic *wad-al.hid-jara* or "river be- tween stones."

Caravel

Development

The new colony was fa- voured by the emperor of Spain, Charles V, who gave it city status by granting it the shield it still holds today. Despite this privi- lege, which enabled it to rival Compostela, then the capital of the kingdom of New Galicia (name of the western province of Mexico at the time), the city was ceaselessly attacked by the region's indigenous people. Due to these circumstances, the Spaniards moved it three times before finding its permanent location. They ended up founding it in the middle of the valley, on the western shore of Río de San Juan Dios on Febru- ary 14, 1542. Events related to the founding of a diocese favoured the future of the new city. In 1546, the first priest of New Galicia, Mon- signor Pedro Gómez Maraver, had to get to the capital and passed through Guadalajara on the way. Finding Compostela in an appalling state, he refused to set up his residence there and asked the king of Spain to move the capital of New Galicia to Guadalajara. His request was granted and the city de- veloped slowly.

Two centuries after it was founded, the city counted approximately 8,018 Spaniards, Creoles, Mestizos and mulattos loyal to the Catholic church, not counting the indigenous people.

The founding of the port of San Blas on the Pacific coast in 1778 benefitted New Galicia. This opening gave the city access to the lucrative trade route that had been developing in the Pacific basin since the 16th century. Following the *ruta de kis galeones*, the famous nao of China, a Chinese vessel, left the harbour of Manilla (Philippines) for New Spain, loaded with goods, including gold and jewellery, cinnamon and pepper, silk and china, and carved ivory from India.

During the final 20 years of the colonial period, a series of events significantly contributed to the prestige and grandeur of Guadalajara. The Civil Hospital was built thanks to the devotion of Fray Antonio Alcalde y Barriga, a bishop from 1771 to 1792. This noble Domican, with an extremely virtuous and social-minded spirit, went beyond his ecclesiastic role and created public infrastructure for city residents. He even built public housing at his own expense. His influence was a decisive factor in King Charles IV bestowing the charter creating the Real Universidad de Guadalajara. In addition, the Palacio de la Audiencia, which had been destroyed in an earthquake, was rebuilt, and printing was introduced to the city. The Real Consulado de Comercio (the chamber of commerce) was founded, thus putting an end to the monopoly Mexico City had enjoyed for over 200 years. The Casa de la Misericordia, a magnificent jewel of neoclassical architecture that is today known as the Hospicio Cabañas, also dates from this era.

Independence

New Spain and New Galicia enjoyed relative stability after their founding. Towards the end of the 18th century though, the wave of liberal European doctrines began to have its influence felt among unhappy Creoles, dreamers of freedom, equality and brotherhood. With the scene set, Napoleon's invasion of Spain unleashed internal quarrels and it is in this context that renowned priest Padre Miguel Hidalgo gave the signal for the start of the War of Independence on September 16, 1810. In less than a month, Guadalajara was in the hands of the rebels, who had set up an independent government and had taken in Padre Hidalgo. The rebels' first newspaper, El *Despertador Americano* (the American waking), appeared just before Christmas that same year. A month later though, royalist troops reclaimed the city and it was only on June 13, 1821, in the suburb of Tlaquepaque, that the independence of New Galicia was proclaimed. Victorious general Itrubide was crowned Agustín I, emperor of all Mexicans. Unfortunately for him, his reign was short-lived, as Guadalajaran authorities founded the free state of Jalisco in 1823, a year before the first constitution of the Republic was drafted.

Industrialization

The opening of textile factories towards 1840 put an end to a 300-year-old administrative, commercial and agricultural tradition and marked the beginning of the industrialization of Guadalajara. The immigration of farmers increased the number of residents to 68,000 in 1856 and the first tramway company was established shortly thereafter. Cultural life was enhanced by the construction of the Degollado theatre, inspired by Milan's famous opera house, La Scala.

Diplomatic relations with France were reestablished during the political stability of the regime of Porfirio Diaz (1876-1910). Economic development spread throughout the country and the London Bank of Mexico and South America opened a branch in the city. The railway linking Guadalajara and Mexico City was inaugurated in 1888, and the line was extended to the port of Manzanillo 20 years later. By thus consolidating the prominent role of the city in the important Pacific trade, the railway made Guadalajara the true metropolis of western Mexico. It is during this period that the face of the city was beautified. The will to make the "pearl of the West" the most beautiful city in the country fuelled the construction of several buildings and elegant Edwardian-style residences, several of which still stand on Avenida Vallarta and its surrounding areas.

Finding few sympathizers in Guadalajara, the Mexican Revolution (1910-1917) swept through the city without causing too much disruption. The social structure did not undergo great changes and life went on practically as before. Nevertheless, public education and unionism benefitted from the revolution. In the years that followed, the

The French Intervention

In 1848, after suffering defeat in a war against the United States, Mexico lost over half its original territory. The expansion of this powerful English-speaking republic was worrisome to other world powers, including Napoleonic France. This led French emperor Napoleon III to attempt to offset U.S. forces with a Latin empire on the American continent. Using President Benito Juárez's moratorium on foreign-debt payments owed to France as a pretext, he sent the French fleet to Veracruz at the end of 1861. Although the Mexicans won a stunning victory in the Battle of Puebla on May 5, 1862, French troops entered Mexico City in 1863 and Guadalajara in January of the following year. Napoleon III then established his authority on the North American continent by making a Catholic prince, Archduke Maximilian Hapsburg of Austria, along with his wife, princess Charlotte of Belgium, emperor of the new empire. But the new puppet regime was short-lived. The War of Succession soon enabled the United States to help Juárez win back power. Under pressure from the United States and with a growing desire to consolidate his position in Europe, Napoleon III pulled his troops out of Mexico. Left high and dry, the unfortunate Maximilian was over-thrown and executed by firing squad.

university, which had been closed since 1826, was re-opened, the Guadalajara Symphony Orchestra was founded, and a zoo was opened in Agua Azul park.

The city grew in all direc-tions and soon new neigh-bourhoods bordered those of Zapopan and Tlaquepaque.

Even though a poorly led modernization effort initially resulted in the destruction of a part of its urban heritage, Guadalajara is today a beautiful metropolis whose core attracts visitors from around the world.

Politics

The two most famous modern Mexican political figures are certainly Zapata and Pancho Villa, nicknamed by many the "Mexican Robinhood." These two colourful men personify the popular image of the Mexican Revolution, which exploded in 1910 and lasted seven years. This violent period is remembered in many songs of the unique *corridos de la revolución* style.

Nine years after the Revolution, anticlerical measures adopted by the government upset the conservative stratum of society. A new rebellion, the *revolución cristera*, was unleashed in the western part of the country. A one-party system, endorsing socialist ideas popular at the time, was established in 1929. The PRI (Partido Revolucionario Institucional) supplied all of Mexico's presidents until Ernesto Zedillo. Even though every other party was completely excluded from power until the last 15

years, this system provided the country with the stability necessary for its development, which is rare in Latin America.

Since 1985, however, the system has shown signs of weakness. After years of relative prosperity, the economic crisis that unravelled in 1982 due to the fall of international oil prices politicized a significant proportion of the generally apolitical population. Also, the rigidity of the system no longer corresponded to reality. And so, Carlos Salinas was elected in 1988 with 50.36% of the vote, with a large proportion of the population abstaining (nine million votes out of 38 million eligible voters). Seeking the approval of his fellow citizens, he launched Solidaridad, an ambitious social-work program and initiated diplomatic relations with the Vatican.

But on New Year's Day 1994, a revolt in Chiapas, the country's poorest state, shook Mexico and made international headlines. Led by an independent army with sub-commander Marcos at the helm, the rebellion denounced corruption and the misery suffered the indigenous population of this isolated region on the southern border. Unfortunately, despite some progress in social order, a

Portrait

satisfactory solution to the problem has yet to be found.

The situation was worsened by the political crimes attributed to Salinas's inner circle. In 1985, internal quarrels led to the assassinations of Luis Donaldo Colosio, a PRI presidential candidate, and a few months later, Francisco Ruiz Massieu, secretary general of the PRI. In 1996, the older brother of former president Carlos Salinas was imprisoned for corruption and drug trafficking.

Despite the existence of nine parties, political life in Mexico currently revolves around three parties: the PRI, representing the now weakened centre-left; the PAN (Partido Acción Nacional), representing the powerful right, a party extremely influenced by the Catholic church; and the PRD (Partido de la Revolución Democrática), which is benefitting from increasingly popular leftist trends.

In the 2000 presidential election, Mexicans wrote a new page of their political history. The leader of the PAN, Vicente Fox, won the election and ended the PRI's 71-year domination of the country. Fox won 43% of the vote compared to 36% for PRI candidate Fran-

cisco Labastida. The new president promised to quash corruption, restart the economy and invest in education. Despite several fraud allegations, these are considered to be the most democratic elections in Mexico's history.

More aware of their role in a Latin-American context, Mexicans now, more than ever, see a future for themselves in the 21st century.

Economy

Mexico today shares first place in economic importance in Latin America, along with Brazil and Argentina. After quite a long period of transition from an economy based on agriculture and mining to a more modern one, since the 1950's, Mexico has enjoyed dynamic industrial expansion. Its growth was boosted 20 years later with the discovery of oil within its territory and the spectacular rise in prices on international markets. The economy enjoyed significant growth, but the miracle did not last long. Soon after, the dramatic collapse of prices made this mirage of inexhaustible resources disappear. Mexico also failed to diversify its economy. Marked by devaluations, galloping inflation and an out-of-proportion foreign debt in 1982, the country suffered its worst crisis since the Revolution.

But the peso and cheap labour had a favourable effect on two sectors: tourism and manufacturing. Seeking to stabilize the situation and contrary to commercial trends at the time, Mexico adopted a protectionist policy aimed at promoting national industry. Outdated industrial infrastructure, unproductive subsidized agriculture and a nationalized (bureaucratized) banking system, however, held the country back and the nation slipped into an economic slump.

Making a 180° turn in 1992, President Salinas negotiated the country's entry into NAFTA (North American Free Trade Agreement). Mexico, however, was not prepared to take part in an international trading agreement as an equal partner with its Canadian and American counterparts. The will to access the lucrative North American market was not enough to spare Mexico a second devaluation in 1995. The current metamorphosis of the globalized world economy has made recovery slow and Mexico's buying power is obviously much lower than that of North America, with the former's GDP per citizen at $8,370.

Nevertheless, Mexico leads Latin-American economies and is often considered a model for developing countries. The stability of the peso, the end of the PRI's hegemony and an annual growth rate of 4.5%, the strongest in Latin America, is encouraging. Guadalajara has not been outdone. Today, this Silicon Valley of the South employs 70,000 people in electronics. The region exported $10 billion worth of electronic products last year and is replacing Asia as the main supplier of the United States.

Population

With approximately 95 million citizens (48 citizens/km^2 or 19/sq mi), Mexico is Latin America's second most populated country after Brazil. After a demographic explosion that began in the 1960s, the annual population growth rate is currently at 1.8%. Unlike other North American countries, more than half of Mexicans are below the age of 20. In this young country, 28% of inhabitants live in a rural areas and 12% of the population is illiterate. Guadalajara's metropolitan area counts 6 million inhabitants.

The composition of society is extremely particular. Indigenous peoples, direct

Tapatíos

In Mexico, Guadalajarans are commonly known as *tapatíos*. This patronymic term comes from the Nahuatl (the language of the Aztec) word *tapatíotl*, which denotes the concept of three-way trade. In pre-Columbian times, local indigenous peoples adhered to this tripartite trade system. After the Spanish conquest, they made small leather pouches containing three cocoa beans, a form of currency, known as *tapatíotl*. Over time, the word became *tapatío* and, through association with Guadalajara merchants, came to describe its inhabitants.

descendants of pre-Columbian peoples, make up around 15% of the population. These people live mainly in rural areas in the southern part of the country, where they preserve their language and traditions (Nahuatl, the Aztec language, is still spoken by 1,200,000 people). Most Mexicans are Mestizos (Spanish and native ancestry) and make up around 75% of the population, with the remaining 10% mostly consisting of descendants of other European nations.

Mexicans' Latin character traits make them generally warm, hospitable people. Proud of their folklore, they enjoy life and need no reason to celebrate.

Architecture

Pre-Columbian Mexican pyramids, built by extremely advanced civilizations, never cease to amaze visitors, who come from the four corners of the world to see them. These colossal, geometric structures with monumental stairs are greater in number in the middle and southern parts of the country. The region of Guadalajara features the El Iztépete ceremonial centre, which is a modest example of this splendid tradition, characteristic of ancient Mexicans.

Lost images from the Renaissance, the cities of New Spain were built around a *plaza mayor* (main square), with the cathedral next to the governor's palace. Streets were laid out like a chessboard. The landscape of the new colony included several baroque monasteries, displaying gothic and Moorish influence.

In earlier centuries, the riches of gold and silver mines were reflected in the architecture. The baroque style shifted to Rococo, which reigned in New Spain. The decor of buildings became increasingly elaborate. The Santa Monica church in Guadalajara, with its angels and grape vines sculpted in relief on its facade is, along with the Palacio de Gobierno, one of the most beautiful works in this style.

In Europe, at the end of the 18th century, illustration created a new vision of life that quickly made its way across the Atlantic. Exuberant decor did not correspond with modern ideas. Thus, a new style, neoclassicism, brought about radical change, in which reason and simplicity triumphed. Architects were inspired by Antiquity. Angels and flowers disappeared from facades overnight. Greco-Roman columns and pediments embellished constructions at the time. Sent by the king of Spain, architect Manuel Tolsá built the Palacio de Minería in Mexico City, America's most beautiful neoclassical building. Following this feat, he built the renowned Hospicio

The Old *Haciendas*

The *haciendas* of wealthy landowners once peppered the State of Jalisco. With Mexico's independence in 1810, the *haciendados* began to lose their power and their lands were redistributed. Today, a number of these *haciendas*, over 300 years old, have been preserved in good condition and are open to the public. On the road to Tequila, the village of Amatitán retains a fine example of an old *hacienda*: the **Hacienda de San José del Refugio**, which has been home to an old-style distillery since 1870. In Tequila, the magnificent **Hacienda de San Martín** *(take Hwy. 15 north of Tequila and, exactly 2km or 1.2mi later, take the detour toward the La Toma water park, then turn left on the third road, which leads to the Hacienda)*, which dates from the 17th century, is one of the most beautiful of its kind in Jalisco.

Portrait

Cabañas in Guadalajara. Often compared to the Escorial, this elegant building became one of the city's symbols.

After independence (1821), the country's instability hindered the construction of prestigious buildings and a number of baroque buildings were demolished or modified. Tasteless works were built in the name of a misunderstood modernity. But a magnificent late neoclassical creation inspired by Milan's famous La Scala theatre, the Teatro Degollado in Guadalajara, is a remarkable exception. Edwardian style, which made its way over from Europe, was preferred by the bourgeoisie at the end of the 19th century, as illustrated by the residences built at the time. The Rectoría of the university of Guadalajara, inspired by the Palacio de Bellas Artes in Mexico City, is a marvellous example of a public building built in this style.

The 20th century was characterized by a variety of styles, none of which would dominate. New trends such as Art Deco, neogothicism, and neocolonialism, as well as ultramodern shapes, illustrate the search for a unique style in contemporary Mexico.

Luis Barragán, one of Mexico's most important architects, was born in Guadalajara in 1902. Influenced by the revolutionary Bauhaus (German modernist movement) style, he built several residences in the city. His work reflects the elements of architecture popular in the region of Jalisco, which were incorporated in the simple and functional lines of the style popular in the 1930s. He became a national celebrity when he created the Jardines del Pedregal, an elegant and ultramodern residential district built on a layer of lava south of Mexico City. This urban concept, harmonizing the volcanic surroundings with construction, remains unique in the world.

Arts

Painting

Magnificent, brightly coloured frescoes adorned the temples and palaces of Mexico as early as the pre-Columbian era. Visitors can still admire them at Teotohuacán, Cacaxtla and Bonampak, among other archaeological sites. This tradition remained so strong in the 16th century that evangelized native craftspeople traditional designs on the walls of monasteries built at that time. The two centuries that followed reflected trends popular in the motherland. Soon, the baroque arrived in New Spain. Paintings full of movement and fantasy adorned the walls of churches and cloisters. Miguel Cabrera (1695-1768) is among the most renowned masters of *novo* Spanish baroque.

Following independence in 1821, the New World dis-

tanced itself from Europe. Mexico withdrew into itself and began discovering its own riches. For the first time, Mexican themes were featured in paintings. But still, European influence, this time Romanticism, dominated art in the 19th century. It is only with the Revolution (1910-1917) that a purely Mexican movement was born: muralism.

Rejecting all European influence, artists deeply marked

Portrait

A Few Painters from the Guadalajara Region

José María Estrada (1810-1862) is representative of 19th-century painters who are relatively unacademic; conversely, the spontaneity in their portraits reveals a certain naiveness.

Dr. Atl, born Gerardo Murillo (1876-1964), a lover of volcanoes, was the first person to conceive a modern vision of the Mexican landscape. By simplifying the forms of nature and by illustrating

perspective with curved lines, he created Synthetism.

José Clemente Orozco (1883-1949), the first of the great muralists, blended colourful movement with shapes and forms that intensify human suffering. The impressive frescoes at the Instituto Cultural Cabañas (see p 81) in Guadalajara are among the works Orozco painted in Mexico.

by the Revolution illustrated the history of the Mexican nation by synthesizing the pre-Columbian, colonial and modern periods. The vigour of strokes, abundance of symbols and compositions loaded with political connotations characterize the superb frescoes of the three great artists of the muralist movement: José Clemente Orozco (1883-1949), Diego Rivera (1886-1957) and David Alfaro Siqueiros (1896-1974). Their brightly coloured works adorn several public buildings in Mexico, South America and the United States.

Rufino Tamayo (1899-1991), a painter of indigenous origin, is considered the master of Mexican modern art. Far from the political connotations of the muralists, he incorporated elements of Mexican pop art in contemporary shapes, notably cubism. His *Prometheus*, painted on a wall of the UNESCO building in Paris, is a magnificent example of the work of this universal artist.

Music

Despite the proximity of the United States and the growing Americanization of Mexican society, Mexico continues to create and renew its own music. In fact, Mexican radio plays less American music than do Canada and many European countries.

Mariachi bands, those charming musicians dressed in traditional costumes and sporting enormous Mexican sombreros, are known throughout the world. They are part of Mexico's living folklore and perform at family celebrations as well as in nightclubs. They make up the heart of the *canción ranchera*, a type of music performed by all kinds of singers who are very popular with Mexicans. The rich Mexican folklore was even a source of inspiration for a number of contemporary classical composers. *Sones de mariachi*, a symphonic poem by Blas Galindo, and *Huapango* by Pablo Moncayo, both feature tunes recognizable from popular tradition.

Here is a description of musical styles that you may hear during your visit to Guadalajara:

Ranchera

A song accompanied by mariachis and passionate *aye, aye, aye* cries, this melancholic and fatalist style is the most popular expression of the Mexican people. Vincente Fernández is currently the most popular singer of *música ranchera*.

A Few Composers from the Guadalajara Region

José Rolón (1883-1945) was a student of Paul Dukas and Nadia Boulanger and composed symphonic poems and piano concertos.

Prolific composer **Blas Galindo** (1910-) composed seven ballets, several symphonies, piano concertos and a vast repertoire of chamber music.

José Pablo Moncayo (1912-1958), one of the greatest Mexican composers, is admired for his popularly inspired works, as well as his opera, *La Mulata de Córdoba*.

Hermilo Hernández (1931-) composed many works, including symphonies and piano pieces. He is especially known for his sonata for violin and piano.

Portrait

Salsa

The rhythm par excellence of Latin-American music that gets the whole world on its feet.

Latin Rock

Carlos Santana, born in a village near Guadalajara, was the first Mexican rocker on the international scene. The Guadalajaran group Maná is currently popular with the young Mexican and Latin-American public. Maná won the Grammy for Best Non-English group in 1999.

Romántica

Especially popular among Mexicans and Latin Americans, *música romántica* is full of love and suffering. Introduced in the 1950s, this kind of music has become a pillar of Mexican song. *Música romántica* is especially performed by trios, including the legendary Trio los Panchos, and balladeers such as José-

José, Luis Miguel and Peru's Tania Libertad.

Autóctona

Drums, flutes, trumpets made from whelks and other pre-Columbian instruments resonate the rhythms of Mexican ancestors. This original music often accompanies groups of dancers during popular traditional fiestas.

Norteña

This style was born in the northern part of the country. Characterized by the accordeon and nasal-sounding singing voices, *música norteña* is popular throughout the country. Tigres del Norte and Los Tucanes de Tijuana perform this kind of music.

Banda

Banda ensembles are mainly made up by strident brass bands. This music phenomenon has practically invaded popular Mexican music in the last 10 years. This style is extremely influenced by *norteña* music and salsa rhythms. Banda Machos (from a village near Guadalajara) is perhaps the most popular band performing this kind of music.

Classical

Horacio Franco, a baroque-flute virtuoso, is the best performer of colonial classical music. Carlos Chávez and Manuel M. Ponce are important Mexican classical music composers.

Folklórica

This music is performed with typical folkloric instruments in a style specific to each region: the harp in Veracruz, the marimba in Chiapas and Oaxaca and the accordion in the Northeast.

Literature

Mexican literature dates from before the arrival of the Spanish. The country's early inhabitants developed a system of pictograms and ideograms that they drew on *ámatl* (tree bark treated like paper) and sometimes on animal skins. Of their vast literature, two works, among others, were spared from destruction: Popol Vuh, the Mayan Genesis, and the poetry of the Aztec king Netzahualcóyotl. This noble monarch and poet was amazed by the fleetingness of life. His poems, which were translated into Spanish in the 16th century, are still studied by Mexican school children.

Important literature describing the Conquest developed with the arrival of the Spanish. The life of indigenous peoples, completely unknown to Europeans, fascinated chroniclers of that time. The *Historia Verdadera de la Conquista de México* by Bernal Díaz des Castillo, one of Cortés's captains, is a precious example.

The literature of New Spain developed as a reflection of that of the motherland. Theatre is marked by the Creole playwright Juan Ruiz de Alarcón, author of 26 comedies, which, according to some critics, influenced the French playwright Corneille. Baroque poetry flourished in the 17th century under the pen of Sor Juana Inés de la Cruz, a nun considered the best poet of the colonial period.

At the start of the 19th century, the stirrings of independence were at the heart of Mexican works. Nevertheless, Romanticism, a new spirit from Europe, dominated art and literature.

A Few Writers from the Guadalajara Region

Among its attributes, Guadalajara is known as the birthplace of several men of letters who strongly marked Mexican literature.

Agustín Yáñez (1904-1979) searched for the causes of change in Mexico by writing about the austere and routine life of isolated, marginalized villages. Through an interior monologue, he reveals the wishes and worries of a people torn between religiosity and sin.

Juan Rulfo (1918-1986) created magical realism. His characters, set in a rural setting, are exhausted by their indecision between life and death.

Juan José Arreola (1918-) evokes his childhood and the small world of his village in an ironic and erudite style that surpasses novels of manners.

Among the Romantics, Ignacio Manuel Altamirano is considered the most eloquent. The colours, essences and scenery of Mexico were finally expressed during this period. The taste for all things Mexican developed and even became a necessity. An independent Mexico created its own style, *el costumbrismo* (novel of morals) in its search for its identity. In his picturesque descriptions, Manuel Payno presents imposing scenery animated by Mexican people, portrayed as being somewhat insignificant, unveiled throughout his masterpiece *Los Bandidos de Río Frío*. Another novelist, Angel De Campo sets his characters in a suburb of Mexico City. While prose flourished, a group of poets, including Amado N. and Manuel Gutiérrez Nájera, also wrote for the pleasure of an awakening people. Hellenist Alfonso Reyes cultivated poetry, theatre and essay in a universalist perspective.

In 1910, the Revolution ripped through the country and entered intellectual life. The *novela de la revolución* (novel of the revolution) marked the beginning of contemporary Mexican literature. The first great writer of this style, Mariano Azuela, published *Los de abajo* (Those Below), the gripping story of a dispossessed family full of hope that is swept into the violence of this armed conflict. Martín Luis Guzmán depicted the fight for power by ancestral revolutionary chiefs, who entered government following this rebellion.

A new trend appeared shortly before the Second World War. A whole generation of diplomat writers sought to understand the paradoxes of modern Mexico. Octavio Paz, born in 1914 and ambassador to India in 1968, wrote poems and essays that would strongly influence generations to come. He won the Nobel Prize for Literature in 1990. Carlos Fuentes (ambassador to France from 1975 to 1978), heir to Paz's preoccupations, is the most translated Mexican writer. Considered one of the most important Latin-American men of letters, he deeply shook literary circles by publishing *La región más transparente* (The Limpidest Region) in 1958, a novel showing contempt for the neocapitalist civilization. More recently, Fernando Del Paso (cultural advisor, and, in the 1980s consul of the Mexican embassy in Paris) illustrates the complexity of Mexico today.

Film

In 1896, barely a year after the Parisian premiere of movies such as *L'arroseur arrosé* (The Watered Waterer) and *L'arrivée d'un train* (Arrival of a Train), these legendary works made their Mexican debuts, first in Mexico City and then in Guadalajara. On this occasion, Bernard and Vayre, two Frenchmen sent by the Lumière brothers for the Mexican premiere, filmed General Porfirio Díaz in his presidential duties, as well as a few scenes of Guadalajara—the first shots of the country. A year later, Salvador Toscano purchased a Lumière apparatus and took on the mission of filming the life and history of the country in 50,000m (15,240ft) of passionate footage. This precious material was re-edited in a montage presented to the general public in 1954 under the title *Memorias de un Mexicano* (Memories of a Mexican). At the same time, Frenchman Charles Montgrand settled in Guadalajara, where he organized film seasons at the Degollado theatre. The city's first movie theatre opened its doors in 1906.

The Revolution (1910-1917), an inexhaustible source of inspiration, was the first such event to be immortalized on film. The American Mutual Film Corporation offered to buy the exclusive rights from revolutionary leader Pancho Villa to film his armed movement in order to produce a sensationalist movie. Villa signed a $25,000 contract, which would enable him to finance his campaigns. He then had to carry out his battles in broad daylight, reshoot scenes that were of poor quality, wear a uniform given to him by the company, and, of course, respect the property of U.S. citizens in Mexico. Thus, in 1914 in New York, *The Life of the General* presented the image of a generous hero who stole from the rich and gave to the poor. At the end of the movie, he became president of Mexico. Unfortunately though, this happy ending would not become reality. Americans, who worried about their interests south of the border, doubted the integrity of their new ally. They decided that, despite the agreement, Pancho Villa was extremely dangerous. In their eyes, this noble Latino Robinhood was nothing but a vile, bloodthirsty assassin, who mercilessly murdered his victims. A second movie was thus produced and our hero was given a bad name. In short, the Americans got rid of him. Following an incident on the border, Pancho Villa was chased in vain by the U.S. Army through the Chihuahua Mountains.

From 1916 to 1925, Mexican cinema enjoyed its first boom. Strongly influenced by Italian dramas, Azteca Films produced commercial, tear-jerker movies. Nevertheless, *El automóvil gris* (The Grey Automobile) by Enrique Rosas and Joaquín Coss (1919) did not follow popular trends. By retelling the crimes of a band of thieves from Mexico City, they unveiled the seediest parts of the capital, which were undreamed of at the time, in a precious sociological reflection.

Santa (Saint) by Antonio Moreno (1931) marked the arrival of cinema with sound and the debut of melodramas of another kind: the good girl who is seduced by a smooth talker and thrown on the wrong path. At his time, the famous Soviet cinematographer Sergei Eisenstein arrived in the country for the filming of *¡Qué viva México!*, a Marxist vision of life in the country before the Revolution. In a touching style with a certain authenticity, Fernando De Fuentes returned to the revolutionary inspiration to produce *El Compadre Mendoza* (Comrade mendoza) and *Vámonos con Pancho Villa* (Follow Pancho Villa). In

1936, he threw himself into another genre. His movie *Allá en el rancho Grando* (Over There on Rancho Grande) was a *comedia ranchera* (musical comedy set in an idealized rural setting where everybody sings and where there are plenty of mariachi bands and pretty Mexican girls dressed in traditional costumes). The movie was an instant hit throughout the country. He then became a celebrity among the Hispanic public in the United States and attracted the attention of the Venice Film Festival.

Mexican cinema reached its golden age in the 1940s. Production increased from 27 movies in 1940 to 121 in 1950. Mexico became the main Spanish-language movie producer. In 1947, *María Candelaria* won the Palme d'Or at Cannes. This movie, whose story is set among the indigenous peoples of Xochimilco Lake, is the masterpiece of the classic team of Fernández, Figueroa and Magdaleno. Actors Dolores Del Río and Pedro Armendáriz are among the international stars in this movie, as well as María Félix, an artist known to the French for her role in Jean Renoir's *French Can-Can*.

Loyal to the type of humour characteristic of Mexicans,

comedic actors are particularly popular. Mario Moreno "Cantiflas" probably has the greatest impact. This popular artist, who rose to fame with travelling comedic theatre trends, incarnates the image of an eccentric from Mexico City. Mastering an ambiguous jargon peppered with words with double-meanings, he attacks the bigwigs of the venerable language of Cervantes. Since his first big hit, *Ahí está el detaille* (Here's a Nuance) by Juan Bustillo Oro (1949), this Mexican Charlie Chaplin has fascinated the public. Several expressions that have become popular in Mexican Spanish originated in his spontaneous talk. In 1957, he played the role of Passe-Partout in the U.S. production of *Around the World in 80 Days*.

In 1951, the jury of the Cannes Film Festival awarded the Critic's prize to *Los olvidados* (The Forgotten) by Luis Buñuel, a Spaniard who immigrated to Mexico. But the golden age was short-lived. Successful movies killed the market and production fell to 46 productions per year in 1961. Despite this difficult situation, young film-makers tried to relaunch a more interesting movie industry. *En este pueblo no hay ladrones* (There are No Thieves In this Village) by Alberto Isaac and *La fórmula secreta* (The Secret Formula) by Rubén Gámez are two exceptions to the crisis. Since then, and after a few strong productions, Mexican cinema has renewed itself. In 1985, the first annual Mexican film festival was organized in Guadalajara. Towards the 1990s, a trend toward the representation of the reality of a country in transition attracted a Mexican public that is increasingly eager to see its true story on the screen.

Table of Distances (km/mi)

Via the shortest route

1 mile = 1.62 kilometre
1 kilometre = 0.62 mile

	Acapulco	Cancún	Chapala	Ciudad Guzmán	Guadalajara	Guanajuato	Manzanillo-Colima	Mexico City	Monterrey	Oaxaca	Puerto Vallarta
Cancún	2056/1269										
Chapala	697/430	2378/1468									
Ciudad Guzmán	535/330	2281/1408	162/100								
Guadalajara	934/579	2197/1362	50/31	132/82							
Guanajuato	761/470	2059/1271	319/197	416/257	230/143						
Manzanillo-Colima	497/307	2304/1422	326/201	164/101	230/143	580/358					
Mexico City	695/429	1691/1044	590/364	687/424	546/339	368/227	580/378				
Monterrey	1228/758	2472/1526	596/368	693/428	786/487	578/357	857/529	854/527			
Oaxaca	661/408	1547/955	1082/668	1179/728	1000/620	860/531	1158/715	492/304	1346/831		
Puerto Vallarta	753/465	2594/1601	377/233	420/259	352/218	632/390	256/158	902/557	909/561	1395/861	
Tequila	724/447	2309/1425	92/57	190/117	62/38	347/214	353/218	617/381	624/385	1110/685	285/176

Example: the distance between Guadalajara and Mexico City is 546km or 339mi.

© ULYSSES

Practical Information

This chapter is intended to help you plan your trip to Guadalajara.

It also includes general information and practical advice designed to familiarize you with local customs.

Entrance Formalities

Passport

To enter Mexico, you must have a valid passport. This is by far the most widely accepted piece of identification, and therefore the safest. If your passport will expire within six months of your date of arrival in Mexico, check with your country's embassy or consulate as to the rules and restrictions applicable.

As a general rule, the expiration date of your passport should not fall less than six months after your arrival date. If you have a return ticket, however, your passport need only be valid for the duration of your stay.

Otherwise, proof of sufficient funds may be required. For travellers from most Western countries (Canada, United States, Australia, New Zealand, Western European countries) a simple passport is enough; no visa is necessary. Other citizens are advised to contact the nearest consulate to see whether a visa is required to enter Mexico. Since requirements for entering the country can change quickly, it is wise to double-check them before leaving.

Travellers are advised to keep a photocopy of the most important pages of their passport, as well as to write down its number and date of issue. Keep these copies separate from the originals during your trip and also leave copies with friends or family in your own country. If ever your passport is lost or stolen, this will facilitate the replacement process (the same is true for citizenship cards and birth certificates). In the event that your passport is lost or stolen, contact the local police and your country's embassy or consulate (see addresses further below), in order to be reissued an equivalent document as soon as possible. You will have to fill out a new application form, provide proof of citizenship and new photographs, and pay the full fee for a replacement passport.

Minors Entering the Country

In Mexico, all individuals under 18 years of age are legally considered minors. Each traveller under the age of 18 is therefore required to present written proof of his or her status upon entering the country, namely, a letter of consent signed by his or her parents or legal guardians and notarized or certified by a representative of the court (a justice of the peace or a commissioner for oaths).

A minor accompanied by only one parent must carry a signed letter of consent from the other parent, which also must be notarized or certified by a representative of the court.

If the minor has only one legally recognized parent, he or she must have a paper attesting to that fact. Again, this document must be notarized or certified by a justice of the peace of a commissioner for oaths.

Airline companies require adults who are meeting minors unaccompanied by their parents or an official guardian to provide their address and telephone number.

Customs Declaration Forms and Tourist Cards

Upon your arrival in Mexico, after your proof of citizenship and customs declaration form have been checked, the customs officer will give you a blue tourist card. This card is free and authorizes its holder to visit the country for 60 days. Do not lose it, as **you must return it to Mexican immigration when you leave the country**. Take the same precautions as you did with your passport, by recording the tourist card number somewhere else – on your airline ticket, for example.

Airport Departure Tax

Except for children under two years of age, all passengers taking international flights out of Mexico are required to pay a tax of about $14 US. The major airlines often include this tax in the ticket price; ask your travel agent.

Customs

Visitors are allowed to enter the country with 3L of alcohol, 400 cigarettes and a reasonable quantity of perfume for personal use. Of course, it is strictly forbidden to bring any drugs or firearms into the country. Any personal medication, especially psychotropic drugs, must have a prescription label.

Getting There

Airports

Aeropuerto Internacional Miguel Hidalgo *(departure and arrival information, 24hrs a day ☎688-5894)* is located in the southeast section of Guadalajara's centre, 20min away from the downtown area. You'll find the usual services, including ATMs accepting major credit cards, on the main floor of the terminal, and shops, restaurants and snack-bars on the second.

As in all of Mexico's international airports, travellers going through customs are asked to press a button that activates a green light, which means that they can enter the country with no further ado, or a red light, which means that they will have to be searched first.

If you're feeling peckish before your departure, head upstairs to the small **Los Patos** snack bar. At this inexpensive eatery, you can enjoy a last *comida corrida* for the modest sum of $3.

For last-minute gifts, the Beach shop, located upstairs, offers a good selection of T-shirts in appealing colours. This being the

Practical
Information

airport, however, you'll have to pay the tidy sum of $12 per T-shirt. To pick up a bottle of Mexico's "liquid gold," tequila, head to the shop located right across from Beach, which carries a wide variety of every colour and flavour. For those who want to stock up on the fiery liquor, the duty-free shops are located on the main floor—past customs, of course.

Several **car-rental agencies** are also on site, including **Avis** (☎688-5656), **Hertz** (☎614-6197), **Budget** (☎688-5531), **Optima Rent a Car** (☎688-5360) and **Dollar Rent a Car** (☎688-5659) for cars and limousines. However, prices at the airport are usually higher than downtown, except for travellers who have made reservations ahead of time, which generally results in lower rates. If you plan on touring Guadalajara by car, it's therefore best to rent one downtown, as many car-rental agencies there offer better rates.

To get downtown *by car*, join the link road to the Centro-bound Carretera a Chapala, which is actually Highway 44. You'll have no trouble getting out of the airport since it's relatively set back from the road. After driving a few kilometres without taking your eyes off the signposts for

downtown, take Calzada González Gallo, at the end of which you'll end up at a roundabout located just past Parque Agua Azul. From there, take Calle Constituyentes for a few seconds, then immediately turn right on Avenida 16 de Septiembre, which leads downtown, at the foot of the cathedral.

To get downtown **by bus**, those in a hurry can take the **Atasa** airport-company bus, which runs downtown by way of Calle Enrique Díaz de León and Calzada Independencia. Tickets are sold on board. Another cheaper but longer option is the Chapala-company bus, which also runs downtown. Moreover, many other buses on Carretera Chapala also travel to the city centre, though catching a bus on this road, located at the exit to the airport, entails several minutes of walking.

Like at most international airports, you'll have no trouble finding a **taxi** to take you right downtown. Expect to pay about $8 to get downtown and $9.50 for the Fuente de la Minerva. Taxi vans also offer shared service for $3.50 per person.

By Car

If you're already in Mexico, continuing on to Guadalajara will spare you from renting on site. But you must still account for tolls and gas (about $0.50/L or $1.89/gal) as well as the wear and tear on your car.

From Mexico City, the most direct route is obviously the highway that runs to Guadalajara by way of Toluca, a 7hr drive. From Puerto Vallarta, take the Ruta Nacional 200 to Mozatan, then the highway to Guadalajara, which takes about 4hrs. Moreover, two direct highways link Colima, Aguascalientes and León to Guadalajara.

The Road Network

Driving is the best way to visit all the small towns and *haciendas* in Jalisco, so characteristic of authentic Mexico. Though Mexico City and Guadalajara are both attractive short-term destinations, you can also get to know the country by exploring its countryside, which can only be done by car.

Although a lot of progress remains to be made, Mexico's road network is relatively well developed. Until the 1950s, no highway system covered the country's undulating terrain. But the government has since fully remedied the situation by launching major make-work road projects, thus promoting the integration of remote regions into the national economy.

A large percentage of Mexico's new highways is a product of the private sector. Modern, safe, and linking the country's major cities, the new two-lane highways represent enormous progress when compared to the old roads that were often congested with badly maintained heavy vehicles.

Travelling on secondary roads can be dangerous as they're often strewn with stray rocks and potholes. Some are paved, but most are pitted with holes and must therefore be navigated more slowly. These roads also run through small villages where it's especially important to drive slowly as pedestrians sometimes appear out of nowhere. Moreover, many speed bumps *(topes)* have been set up on roads in order to reduce speeding in urban areas.

Road signs (speed limits, stops and traffic lights) are few and far between in the Mexican countryside. Signs are sometimes even simply scrawled on a piece of cardboard nailed to a tree. Driving at night is highly inadvisable. The risk of robbery increases come nightfall and visibility is often very poor. The speed limit on highways is generally 100km/h (62mph) and 90km/h (56mph) on secondary roads.

A Few Tips

Your national (European or North American) driver's license is valid in Mexico.

In case of accident or mechanical problems, pull over on the shoulder and lift the hood of the car. Other drivers will soon stop to lend you assistance.

Police officers on motorcycles are posted along highways and have the authority to stop drivers who contravene the highway code or to simply make a routine check. Remember that it is police officers' duty to come to your aid if you encounter problems on the road. To reach them in Guadalajara, call ☎617-6060. You can also contact the *policía turística* (tourist police) at ☎01-800-903-92.

Gas is sold by the litre and available in Premium (red pumps), a higher-octane unleaded gasoline, and Magna Sin (green pumps), also unleaded and found at all PEMEX (Petróleos

Mexicanos, the monopolistic State-owned oil company) gas stations. It's customary to tip the pump attendant a few pesos. Gas prices are on a par with Canada's and lower than in Europe. A word of advice: fill up whenever you get the chance as there are relatively few service stations.

Car Rental

All major car-rental companies operate in Guadalajara. In fact, most have offices at the airport and around main bus stations. Rental rates at the airport are generally higher, however.

A valid driver's license is sufficient to drive and rent a car in Mexico.

Budget
Avenida Niños Héroes no. 934
at Avenida 16 de Septiembre
☎*613-0027*

Quick
Avenida Niños Héroes no. 954
☎*614-6052*

Avis
Miguel Hidalgo Airport
☎*688-5656*

Arrasa
Avenida López Mateos Nte. no. 62
☎*615-0522*

By Bus

Plentiful and running just about everywhere, buses are an inexpensive and original way of getting around. There are several bus companies in Mexico and the quality of the service varies greatly in accordance with the price. Given the sometimes considerable distances to cover, it is strongly advised to take a first-class bus. They are generally newer vehicles with bathrooms and a television, and sometimes even offer refreshments and sandwiches. Listed below are the main bus companies that provide service to Mexico's major cities.

Bus Stations

Nueva Central Camionera
at Carretera Libre a Zapotlanejo and Carretera Entroque a Tonalá
☎ *600-0007 or 600-0331*

Bus Companies

Elite Futura
☎ *679-0404*

Primera Plus
☎ *600-0398*

ETN (deluxe)
☎ *600-0571*

Omnibus de México
☎ *600-0718*

Transportes del Pacífico
☎ *600-0339*

Hitchhiking

For safety reasons, hitchhiking in Mexico is highly inadvisable.

Embassies and Consulates

Mexican Embassies and Consulates Abroad

AUSTRALIA
14 Perth Avenue Yarralumla
ACT 2600
☎ *(02-6) 273-3963*
☎ *(02-6) 273-3905*
☎ *(02-6) 273-3947*
⇄ *(02-6) 273-1190*
embmex@enternet.com.au

BELGIUM
Franklin Roosevelt 94
1050 Bruxelles
☎ *(32-2) 629-0777*
⇄ *(32-2) 646-8768*

CANADA
45 O'Connor Street, Office 1500
Ottawa, Ontario, K1P 1A4
☎ *(613) 233-8988*
☎ *(613) 233-9572*
⇄ *(613) 235-9123*
info@embamexcan.com
www.embamexcan.com

Practical Information

Consulate
2000 rue Mansfield, Bureau 1015
10th floor, Montréal, Québec, H3A 2Z7
☎ *(514) 288-2502*
≈ *(514) 288-8287*
info.general@consulmex.qc.ca
www.consulmex.qc.ca

Consulate
Commerce Court West, 99 Bay Street
Suite 4440, Toronto, Ontario M5L 1E9
☎ *(416) 368-2875/1847/8184*
≈ *(416) 368-8342/9348*
consulad@interlog.com

DENMARK
Strandvejen 64E, 2900 Hellerup
Copenhagen
☎ *(39) 61-05-00*
≈ *(39) 61-05-12*
embmxdin@inet.uni2.dk

GERMANY
Adenaueralle 100, 53113 Bonn
☎ *(228) 91-48-60*
≈ *(228) 91-48-217*
≈ *(228) 21-11-13*
rfaemb@edina.xnc.com

GREAT BRITAIN
8 Halkin Street, London SWIX 7DW
☎ *(0171) 235-6393*
≈ *(0171) 235-5480*
consullondon@easynet.co.uk

ITALY
Via Lazzaro Spallanzani 16, 00161
Rome
☎ *(6) 441-151*
≈ *(6) 440-3876*
www.target.it/messico/

Consulate
Via Cappuccini, 4
20122 Milan
☎ *(2) 7602-0541*
☎ *(2) 760-02310*
≈ *(2) 7602-1949*
www.mexico.it

NEW ZEALAND
111-115 Customhouse Quay, 8th
floor, Wellington
☎ *(644) 472-5555*

SPAIN
Carrera de San Jerónimo, 46, 28014
Madrid
☎ *(91) 420-2017*
≈ *(91) 420-2736*
bmadrid@bancomext-esp.com
www.embamex.es/

Consulate
Av. Díagonal 626, 4 Planta
08021 Barcelona
☎ *(93) 201-1822*
≈ *(93) 200-9206*

Switzerland
Embassy and Consulate
Bernastrasse, no. 57, 3005 - Berne
☎ *(31) 351-1875*
≈ *(31) 351-3492*

UNITED STATES
1911 Pennsylvania Avenue, N.W.,
20006 - Washington D.C.
☎ *(202) 728-1633*
☎ *(202) 736-1012*
≈ *(202) 728-1698*

Consulate
27 East 39th Street, New York
N.Y. 10016
☎ *(212) 217-6400*
≈ *(212) 217-6493*

Consulate
2401 W. 6th St.
Los Angeles, CA, 90057
☎*(213) 351-6800*
☎*(213) 651-6825*
⇋*(213) 351-6844*
⇋*(213) 383-4927*

Consulate
300 North Michigan Ave., 2nd floor,
Chicago, IL, 60601
☎*(312) 855-0056*
☎*(312) 855-0066*
⇋*(312) 855-9257*

Foreign Embassies and Consulates in Mexico

Embassies and consulates can provide precious information to visitors who find themselves in a difficult situation (for example, loss of passport or in the event of an accident or death, they can provide names of doctors, lawyers, etc.). They deal only with urgent cases, however. It should be noted that costs arising from such services are not paid by these consular missions.

DENMARK
Calle 3 Picos no. 43
Col. Polanco Chapultepec
Mexico, D.F. 11580
☎*(5) 255-339*
☎*(5) 255-8403*
⇋*(5) 245-5797*

GREAT BRITAIN
Lerma 71, Col. Cuauhtémoc, 06500
Mexico D.F.
☎*(5) 207-2089*
⇋*(5) 207-7672*

HOLLAND
Mentes Urales Sur no. 635
2nd floor, Col. Lomas de Chapultepec
Mexico, D.F., 11000
☎*(5) 202-8267*
☎*(5) 202-8346*

NEW ZEALAND
Jose Luis Lagrange 103, 10th floor,
Colonia Los Morales, Polanco, 11510
Mexico D.F.
☎*(5) 281-5486*
⇋*(5) 281-5212*

NORWAY
Virreyes no. 1460
Col. Lomas Virreyes
Mexico, D.F., 11000
☎*(5) 540-3486*
☎*(5) 540-5220*
⇋*(5) 202-3019*

SWEDEN
Avenida Insurgentes, no. 2-4, Fracc.
Homos Insurgentes
☎*85-29-35*
⇋*85-29-36*

Foreign Consulates in Guadalajara

BELGIUM
Consulate
Metalurgia no. 2818
Parque Industrial El Alamo
☎*670-4825*
☎*670-0346*

CANADA
Consulate
Hotel Fiesta Americana, Local 30
☎*615-6270*
☎*615-8665*

ITALY
Consulate
Avenida López Mateos Nte. no. 790-1
☎*616-1700*
≈*616-2092*

SPAIN
Consulate
Avenida Vallarta no.2185 S.J.
☎*630-0450*
☎*616-0396*

SWITZERLAND
Consulate
Avenida Revolución no. 707, Sector Reforma
☎*616-5900*
☎*617-3208*

UNITED STATES
Consulate
Progreso 175
44100 Guadalajara
☎*(3) 825-2998 or 825-2700*
≈*(3) 826-6549*

Tourist Information

Tourist Information Offices Abroad

NORTH AMERICA
Mexico Hotline
☎*800-44-MEXICO*
☎*800-446-3942*

CANADA
1, Place Ville-Marie, Bureau 1526
Montréal, Québec, H3B 2C3
☎*(514) 871-1052*
≈*(514) 871-3825*

2 Bloor Street West, Office 1801
Toronto, Ontario, M4W 3E2
☎*(416) 925-2753*
☎*(416) 925-1876*
≈*(416) 925-6061*

999 West Hastings, Suite 1610
Vancouver, BC, V6C 2W2
☎*(604) 669-2845*
≈*(604) 669-3498*
mgto@bc.sympatico.ca

GERMANY
Wiesenhüttenplatz 26, d-60329 Frankfurt am Main 1 Germany
☎*(496) 925-3509*
☎*(496) 925-3755*
106132.3031@compuserve.com

GREAT BRITAIN
60-61 Trafalgar Sq., London
WC2 N5DS, United Kingdom
☎*(171) 734-1058*
≈*(171) 930-9202*
mexicanministry@easynet.co.uk

ITALY
Via Barberini no. 23
00187 - Rome
☎*(6) 25-3413 or 25-3541*
≈*(6) 25-3755*

SPAIN
Calle Velazquez, no. 126
28006 - Madrid
☎*(91) 561-3520*
≈*(91) 411-0759*
mexico@lander.es

UNITED STATES
21 East 63rd Street, 3rd floor
New York, NY 10021
☎*(212) 821-0313*
⇌*(212) 821-0367*
jcrmgto@interport.net

2401 West 6th Street, 5th floor
Los Angeles, CA 90057
☎*(213) 351-2069/2057/2076*
⇌*(213) 351-2074*
ghuerta@compuserve.com

300 N. Michigan Avenue, 4th floor
Chicago, IL 60601
☎*(312) 606-9252*
⇌*(312) 606-9012*

Belgium and **Switzerland**
Please see "Embassies and
Consulates."

Tourist Information Offices in Guadalajara

Miguel Hidalgo Airport

The tourist information
office is located near the
exit of the airport.

Downtown Area

**Secretaría de Turismo del
Estado de Jalisco (SETULAL)**
Mon to Fri 9am to 8pm
Sat and Sun 9am to 7pm
Calle Morelos no. 102
Plaza Tapatía
☎*613-0306*
☎*658-2222 or 91-800-363-22*
Here you'll find maps bro-
chures and guide books,
and the multi-lingual staff

will be happy to give you
travel tips.

Tourist Information Offices in the Surrounding Area

Tlaquepaque

Tourist Office
Pila Seca local 15
☎*637-5756*

Tonalá

Tourist Office
Avenida Tonaltecas no. 140 Sur

Chapala

Tourist Office
Avenida Madero no. 407 (Planta alta)
☎*765-3141*

Tequila

Tourist Office
José Cuevo no. 33 (Plaza de Armas)
☎*742-1819*

Tapalpa

Morelos (in front of the stand)

Excursions and Guided Tours

Many options are open to
visitors looking to explore
the city by means of a
guided tour, including a
few mentioned below.

Practical
Information

Given frequent changes, we encourage you to communicate with each of the following organizations for detailed information about their programmes and rates.

On Foot

Every Saturday morning, the **Dirección General de Turismo y de la Promoción Económica de la Ciudad de Guadalajara** (☎616-3332) offers visitors a Spanish-language guided tour of the historic centre's 10 leading monuments, including the cathedral, the Palacio de Gobierno and Plaza Fundadores. Departures are at 10am from the Presidencia Municipal (Hidalgo no. 400). The 3hr tours are free.

During the months of July and August, as well as Semana Santa (Holy Week) and year-end holidays, the **Secretaría de Turismo del Estado de Jalisco** also offers a guided tour, in both Spanish and English, of the main attractions in the historic centre of Guadalajara, Tlaquepaque and Tonalá. Departures are on predetermined dates (information and registration: ☎614-8686 ext. 111 or 133) at 9:30am from Plaza de Armas. The walking tours last 3hrs.

By Horse-Drawn Carriage

For hopeless romantics, many coach drivers offer English- or Spanish-narrated rides year-round aboard charming horse-drawn carriages. Departures are in front of the Museo Regional (near the Rotonda), the Templo San Francisco and the Mercado Libertad at all hours of the day and night. Tickets are purchased from the driver and cost 120 pesos, with a maximum capacity of five passengers. The 1hr tour winds through the historic centre, the Exconvento del Carmen, Parque Revolución, the residential district and the university.

By Bus

Panoramex Tours (Federalismo no. 944, España, ☎810-5109 or 810-5005) offers visitors English- and Spanish-narrated tours aboard air-conditioned buses year-round. You can therefore enjoy various guided tours of Guadalajara and Tlaquepaque, Tequila, Lake Chapala and Ajijic from the comfort of its cushy seats. Each tour lasts 6hrs and departs from the Jardín de San Francisco at 9:30am and from Los Arcos (Calle Fernando Celada) at

9:45am. Tickets are purchased on board and cost $9 for the tour of Guadalajara and Tlaquepaque *(Mon to Sat)*, $12 for Tequila *(Mon, Wed and Fri)* and $11 for Lake Chapala and Ajijic *(Tue, Thu, Sat and Sun)*.

By Train

Every Saturday morning, the **Guadalajara chamber of commerce** *(☎122-7920)* offers both out-of-towners and locals a one-day train excursion to Tequila, the capital of Mexico's national drink. Passengers crisscross the region aboard the **Tequila Express**, patterned with the colours of the blue agave (the plant from which tequila is made) and specially designed with that in mind. The trip is made with a bilingual (Spanish-English) guide and genuine mariachis who add to the atmosphere. Once in Tequila, the whole town comes to life to receive train passengers in the town centre, where a variety show is presented. Then, a tour of the José Cuervo distillery enlightens visitors about the tequila-making process. The trip ends with a buffet served beneath a canopy tent where the show continues for those who are not too inebriated. Inebriated, because passengers are lavished with te-

quila prepared in every way imaginable from the moment the train pulls out of the Guadalajara station until its return. Departures are from the train station every Saturday at 10am, and tickets are purchased on site or in advance by telephone *(☎122-7920)*. The return fare is $45 (everything included).

Train Station
Ferrocarril Mexicano Estación Central de Pasajeros
at Avenida 16 de Septiembre and Avenida Washington
☎650-0826 or 650-0444

Getting Around Guadalajara

By Car

As a general rule, getting around in Guadalajara is fairly uncomplicated as the city is laid out in a checkerboard pattern and around functional roundabouts. It's safe to say that the car reigns supreme in Guadalajara, having priority over pedestrians and access to all areas of the city, with the exception of a few small downtown streets. The problem rather lies in finding parking downtown. It's easier to do so at night, however, as many people (students or the unemployed) stand by the side of the road pointing out free parking spaces. It is customary to tip that person a few pesos. Many restaurants and bars also offer convenient valet parking. Moreover, rush-hour traffic is a real headache. We therefore advise you to explore the city by other means, such as public transportation, taxi or even on foot.

Public Transportation

Buses

Though rather uncomfortable, Guadalajara's transport system is plentiful and efficient. Public buses, known as *camiónes* in Mexico, cover the city's entire metropolitan area (including Tlaquepaque, Zapopan, Tonalá and the airport). You'll never have to wait more than 3min for the bus, which stops to pick you up when you raise your arm. Standard-bus fare is $0.30 per trip (without a transfer) and six pesos for more comfortable buses or long distances. Bus stops are generally set up on the road. Bus service is offered from 5:30am to 10:30pm, with a few one-way buses at midnight. Destinations are usually displayed on the windshield, but be sure to always check the letter of the bus (A, B, C or D): as a general rule, C and D buses serve the suburbs.

Climbing aboard one of these buses is a real adventure. Buses slow down to allow passengers to board or disembark, of course, but barely even stop to do so. A word of advice: hold on tight to whatever you can! Always have your money ready before boarding. You don't need to have the exact fare as drivers provide change.

A Sampling of Bus Routes:

Downtown–Cubos	**629**
Minerva–Zapopan town centre	**635A**
Downtown–Zapopan town centre	**275A**
Downtown–Niñoes Héroes–Plaza del Sol	**101**
Downtown–Arcos *Par Vial*	**400**
Centro–Plaza del Sol	**251**
Niños Héroes–Plaza Patria	**622**
Americas–Downtown–Niños Héroes	**604**
Guadalupe	**51A**
Cubos–Lazaro Carderas–Downtown	**626**
Calzada Independencia	**60** and **62**

The *Par Vial* Bus

An electric bus known as the *Par Vial* travels west along Independencia, then Hidalgo, before heading to Vallarta, right near López Mateos, at Los Arcos. On the way back, it travels east along Hidalgo, three blocks north of Juárez (route 400). More comfortable but a little slower, this bus has the advantage of being quieter and non-polluting.

The Metro

Despite its speed and efficiency, the metro only covers a limited part of the city. It is especially useful for travelling quickly over long distances. The only two lines serve the north, south and east districts of the city, where the population is smaller and the demand for public transportation is high. Each station is equipped with a ticket-token dispenser; the fare is $0.30.

By Taxi

Taxis are probably the most efficient way of getting around in the city. And you'll have no trouble finding a taxi (easily identified by their yellow colour), as they literally seek you out. Most have meters, with a fixed rate per kilometre.

As a general rule, taxis parked in front of hotels and restaurants give these establishments a commission and therefore cost slightly more than those hailed on the street. The situation is similar when someone calls you a taxi. Unless you have luggage, tipping isn't required.

On Foot

The fascinating city of Guadalajara and its surroundings are multifaceted and, though accessible by several means, exploring them on foot is the best way to discover their hidden treasures. Some districts are rather inaccessible to pedestrians due to traffic and long distances. Moreover, pedestrians must always beware of motorists. Crossing the street, even at an intersection, is a real ordeal, especially since pedestrian-safety infrastructures are virtually nonexistent. Vigilance is therefore the watchword.

While exploring Guadalajara on foot, it's important to remember that the city is very extensive and that distances to cover can be greater that you think. So take a little breather every once in a while and drink a lot of water. The combined effect

Practical Information

of the sun, heat and walking can cause dehydration. Also, a pair of comfortable walking shoes and a sunhat will be welcome. Lastly, because of its configuration, repeated street names and badly indicated streets, it's easy to get lost without a map.

City Maps

Unfortunately, despite the many maps available (including the free one issued by the tourist office), few offer a precise overview of the metropolitan area. If you can afford it or are planning on an extended stay in the metropolis, be sure to pick up a copy of the *Guia Roji—Ciudad de Guadalajara ($7, available in all fine bookshops)*, the most detailed atlas of the city, with a particularly comprehensive street directory.

Getting Around Guadalajara's Surrounding Area

By Car from Guadalajara

The fastest way of reaching **Tequila** and **Magdalena** is to head to La Minerva to take Avenida Vallarta, which turns into Carretera a Nogales, which in turn leads straight to Highway 15 toward Tequila and Tepic. Take the Tequila- or Magdalena-bound exit.

To get to **Chapala** and **Ajijic**, take southbound Calzada Independencia, then Avenida Dr. R. Michel toward the airport, which leads to Highway 44 toward Chapala and Ajijic.

To reach **Tlaquepaque**, once on southbound Calzada Independencia, take Calzada Revolución toward Tlaquepaque. A few kilometres farther, turn right on Avenida San Rafael, which you can't miss. Once there, look out for directions to the Centro, immediately on your left. To reach **Tonalá**, head south along Calzada Independencia, then take Calzada Revolución toward Tonalá. Farther on, turn left on Carretera a Tonalá, which leads to the heart of the village. To get there from Tlaquepaque, take westbound Calzada Revolución toward Tonalá, then turn left on Carretera a Tonalá, which leads straight to the village.

To get to **Tapalpa**, head to La Minerva to reach Avenida López Mateos Sur, which turns into Carretera Manzanillo, which in turn leads straight to Highway 15 toward Ciudad Guzmán and Colima. Take the

Tapalpa-bound exit and follow directions up the Sierra Madre.

By Bus from Guadalajara

Departures for **Tequila** and **Magdalena** are made daily every 15min between 5:30am and 9:15pm from Antigua Central Camionera with the Rojo de Los Altos company (☎619-2309). Travel time: about 90min. Fare: $2.20.

There are several departures a day for **Chapala** and **Ajijic**, made from Antigua Central Camionera every 30min between 6am and 9pm with the Autotransporte Guadalajara-Chapala company (☎619-5675). Travel time: 45min. Fare: $2.

To get to **Tlaquepaque** and **Tonalá**, take bus no. 275 A or B ($0.30 per ticket) or bus no. 706 of the TUR company ($0.60 per ticket), which is more comfortable. Both run along Avenida 16 de Septiembre and first lead to Tlaquepaque, then Tonalá. To reach Tlaquepaque from La Minerva, take the Cardinal company's bus no. 710 for the modest sum of $0.60. The return trip from Tlaquepaque to downtown Guadalajara is made on bus

no. 275, or a TUR bus from the corner of Niñoes Héroes and Constitutión, that is some 100m (328ft) north of Independencia.

Departures for **Tapalpa** are made daily from 6:30am to 6:30pm from Antigua Central Camionera with the Sur de Jalisco company. Travel time: about 3hrs. Fare: $4.20.

Antigua Central Camionera
Los Angeles no. 218
Zona Olímpica, Sector Reforma
☎650-0479

Health

Mexico is a wonderful country to visit. Unfortunately, travellers do run the risk of contracting certain diseases there, such as malaria, typhoid, diphtheria, tetanus, polio and hepatitis A and B. Though such cases are rare they do occur. When planning your trip, therefore, consult your doctor (or a clinic for travellers) about what precautions to take. Don't forget that preventing these illnesses is easier than curing them. It is therefore practical to take medications, vaccines and necessary precautions in order to avoid medical problems likely to become serious. If, however, you do have to see a doctor, keep in mind that most large hotels have in-house medical clinics. If not, hotel staff or on-site travel agents will be able to help you find a doctor.

Here is a list of **private hospitals** offering excellent medical care:

Hospital del Carmen
Tarasco no. 3435, Fracc. Monraz
☎ *813-0025*

Hospital San Javier
Avenida Pablo Casals no. 640
Col. Providencia
☎ *669-0222*

Illnesses

Cases of hepatitis A and B, AIDS and certain venereal diseases have been reported in Mexico, so it is wise to take necessary precautions. Hepatitis A and B shots are available in your home country.

Bodies of fresh water are often contaminated with the bacteria that causes schistosomiasis. This illness results when a parasite invades the body and attacks the liver and nervous system, and it is difficult to treat. Swimming in fresh water should therefore be avoided.

Remember that excessive alcohol intake can cause dehydration and illness, especially when accompanied by lengthy exposure to the sun.

The tap water in Guadalajara isn't potable for foreign visitors. It is therefore strongly advised to drink purified water only.

The medical problems travellers are most likely to encounter are usually a result of poorly treated water containing bacteria that cause upset stomach, diarrhea or fever (the same symptoms can also be caused by altitude). To avoid this risk, drink only bottled water, which is available just about everywhere. When buying a bottle, whether in a restaurant or a store, always make sure that it is well sealed. Only a few hotels in Guadalajara are equipped with water purifying systems, so visitors should avoid drinking hotel tap water. Fruit and vegetables rinsed in tap water (those not peeled before eating) can cause the same problems. Visitors should be doubly careful in low budget restaurants, which do not always have the equipment necessary to ensure proper hygiene. The same goes for the small vendors on the street and the beach. On the other hand, dairy products in Guadalajara and the surrounding area shouldn't pose any threat to visitors' health.

If you do get diarrhea, there are several methods of

treating it. Try to soothe your digestive system by avoiding solid food, and dairy products. Drink a lot of liquids to avoid dehydration, which can be dangerous. To remedy severe dehydration, drink a solution made up of one litre (4 cups) of water, three teaspoons of salt and one teaspoon of sugar. You can also find ready-made preparations in most pharmacies. Next, gradually start reintroducing solids to your diet by eating foods that are easy to digest. Medications can help control an upset stomach. If your symptoms persist and are severe (high fever, violent diarrhea), you may need antibiotics, in which case it is best to consult a doctor.

Food and climate can also cause various health problems. Make sure that food is fresh (especially fish and meat) and that the area where it is prepared is clean. Proper hygiene, such as washing hands frequently, will also help prevent you from getting sick. Furthermore, some people experience health problems caused by pollution. Traffic jams create serious air pollution, especially during the week. Travellers with respiratory problems should therefore be particularly careful and take the necessary precautions.

Insects, Scorpions and Snakes

Insects are not so numerous in the Guadalajara urban area, and the worst you will encounter is a couple of mosquito bites. Nevertheless, in order to avoid being bitten, cover up well in the evening (when insects are most active), avoid perfume and brightly coloured clothing and arm yourself with a good insect repellant. It is also advisable to bring along ointment to relieve the irritation in case you do get bitten.

Scorpions can be a problem, especially during the dry season. Scorpion stings can cause high fever and can even be fatal if the victim is in poor health. If you are travelling outside Guadalajara you should be vigilant, as scorpions have the annoying habit of creeping into houses and other buildings on the ground floor. It is therefore necessary to take a few precautions against them. Avoid leaving your shoes on the ground. When hiking in mountainous or wooded areas, remember to wear adequate shoes and socks, and avoid walking in ditches and tall grass. Anyone who gets stung by a scorpion or bitten by a snake should be taken to a

Practical Information

doctor or a hospital imme-diately.

The Sun

Despite its benefits, the sun also causes numerous prob-lems. It is needless to say that the rising occurrence of skin cancer is due to overexposure to the sun's harmful rays. It is important to keep well protected and avoid prolonged exposure, especially during the first few days of your trip, as it takes a while to get used to the sun's strength. Overexposure to the sun can also cause sunstroke, symptoms of which include dizziness, vomiting and fever. Always use sunblock to protect yourself from the sun's harmful rays. Many of the sunscreens on the mar-ket do not provide ade-quate protection. Before setting off on your trip, ask your pharmacist which ones are truly effective against the UVA and UVB rays. For the best results, apply the cream at least 20 minutes before going out in the sun. Even after a few days, moderate exposure is best. A hat and pair of sunglasses are indispensable accesso-ries in this part of the world.

First-Aid Kit

A small first-aid kit can be useful in many situations. Prepare one carefully be-fore your departure. Be sure to include a sufficient quantity of every medica-tion that you take regularly, in its original container, as well as a valid prescription for each in case you lose or run out of it. Non-prescrip-tion drugs and first-aid supplies can easily be pur-chased in the city's many first-rate pharmacies, as well as in some smaller villages.

Safety and Security

Guadalajarans will generally tell you that their city is pretty safe, but here as else-where, robbery remains a risk. Fortunately, some ba-sic safety precautions, a few of which are mentioned below, will help you avoid needless mishaps.

Avoid walking or driving on side streets and roads be-tween 7pm and 6am, espe-cially in the neighbour-hoods near Antigua Central Camionera and in the sub-urbs *(colonias)*, which can prove dangerous at any time of day or night. Even though you'll notice a few police cars driving around with flashing lights to make their presence known, they're not in sufficient number to ensure adequate protection at night. It's also best to stick to well-lit streets, and take a taxi after 10pm.

If you're unlucky enough to be mugged, don't attempt to flee or resist, but simply hand over your money, jewellery and camera without a fuss. Then, be sure to report the crime to the local police and remember to ask for a copy of the police report for insurance purposes.

Conceal your travellers' cheques, passport and some cash in a money belt under your clothes. Remember that the less attention you attract, the less chance you have of being robbed. Finally, be sure to keep a photocopy of your passport and a record of your traveller's-cheque serial numbers in a separate place so that if these papers are stolen, they'll be easier to replace.

An invaluable tip when making cash transactions of any nature: always count your change. Take the time to calculate the amount that should be returned to you, as some merchants will try to pocket a few extra pesos when doing business with tourists. This is even more crucial when you pay with large denominations or in a

dimly lit bar, where it's easier to swindle unsuspecting visitors.

Police and Emergency Numbers

In case of emergency, dial ☎080; an official will explain the procedures to follow. To reach the police, dial ☎617-6060; for the tourist police, call ☎01-800-9-0392.

Theft in Cars

In Mexico, car break-ins occur just as often as any where else. Never leave your luggage in an unsupervised car. Thieves need only 5min to take what they want without leaving any trace, even in the most remote places. Car door locks are no obstacle to these professional pilferers.

Most vehicles are equipped with alarm systems. Make sure that your car's is activated at all times.

Above all, do not leave anything visible that might have any value: bags, jackets. The lock might be picked in hopes that the jacket contains a wallet.

If you must keep your luggage in your car be careful when stopping for gas or for a quick bite. Place the car where you can see it constantly. In the city, pay for a parking lot, and choose a spot near the attendant.

Always leave the glove compartment wide open, to avoid the supposition that your camera might be inside.

In general, leave your bags at the hotel while you are sightseeing, even if you have checked out. The reception desk will usually keep them for you. Finally, always remember that whatever precautions you've taken, you could still be robbed and avoid carrying valuables with you.

If despite all these precautions, you are unlucky enough to be robbed, be sure to file a police report. You will need it to be reimbursed by your insurance company. You will, however, have to deal with the inefficient bureaucracy.

Women Travellers

Women travelling alone in this city should not have any problems. In general, locals are friendly and not too aggressive. Although men treat women with respect and harassment is relatively rare, Mexicans will undoubtedly flirt with female travellers—politely, though. Just ignore it and walk away, or give a firm negative reply if this continues. Of course, a minimum amount of caution is required; for example, women should avoid walking alone through poorly lit areas at night. Furthermore, wearing clothes that are not too revealing and not making certain movements will probably spare you some aggravation in this primarily Catholic country.

Unescorted women should also avoid Calzada Independencia after 10pm. Indeed, this street unfortunately attracts drunk and disorderly men, and prostitution flourishes here day and night. Moreover, the farther west you go along Calzada Independencia, the worse it gets. Remember that common sense is your best ally when walking around the city.

Climate

In such a mountainous country as Mexico, the temperature obviously varies from place to place. The state of Jalisco alone encompasses four climatic areas, which vary according to altitude and geographic location.

As far back as the dawn of colonization, the Spanish noticed that high-altitude regions enjoyed a very temperate climate and readily

Temperature

Month	High	Low	Precipitation
	Daily average (in celcius)	Night-time average (in celcius)	(in mm)
January	22.5	7.3	12.4
February	24.3	8	5.2
March	30.3	7.4	4.3
April	32	7.1	6.4
May	33.3	10.6	25
June	31.2	14.2	168.1
July	28.3	13	269.4
August	28.3	13.1	216.4
September	28.4	11.2	144.4
October	27.9	8.8	59.5
November	27.1	6.3	15.7
December	27.3	4.8	12

Source: *Datos climatológicos de Guadalajara 1991, Instituto de Astronomía y meteorología, Universidad de Guadalajara.*

settled in these areas. This was no secret to the Aztecs who built the imperial city of Tenochtitlán (now Mexico City) at more than 2,000m (6,562ft) above sea level, which protected the inhabitants from the scorching heat encountered in other Mexican regions. It is, among other things, in this spirit that the site of the city of Guadalajara, located 1,592m (5,223ft) above sea level, was chosen. Indeed, the city of eternal spring boasts one of the best climates in the world: dry and sunny from October to May, hot and sprinkled with tropical rain throughout the rest of the year. The many expats who live on the shores of the Laguna de Chapala could speak to you at great length about the region's perfect climate. If nothing else, a glance at the following statistics on the average temperatures will undoubtedly convince you.

Packing

The type of clothing visitors should bring varies little from one season to the next. For walking in the city, it is better to wear shoes that cover the entire foot, since these provide the best protection against cuts that can become infected. In fact, what with uneven sidewalks and numerous obstacles (holes, poorly installed sewer grills, metal poles sticking out of the ground), shoes protect you from every possible injury. For cool evenings, a long-sleeved shirt or sweater may be necessary. Remember to wear rubber sandals on the beach. During the rainy season, bring a small umbrella to keep dry during the showers. When visiting certain sights (churches for example), a skirt that hangs below the knees or a pair of pants should be worn, so don't forget to include the appropriate article of clothing in your suitcase. If you intend to go on an excursion in the mountains, take along a good pair of shoes and a sweater. Finally, don't for-

get to bring a sunhat and sunglasses.

Telecommunications

Mail

Stamps are available at post offices, of course, but also in the major hotels. The mail is collected on a daily basis. Mail delivery to foreign parts generally takes two weeks.

In addition to many neighbourhood *correos*, there are two main **post offices** downtown:

Servicio Postal Mexicano
Administracion no. 1
Venustiano Carranza, Esq.
Independencia S.H.
☎614-2482

Servicio Postal Mexicano
Administracion no. 2
Alcade, Esq. Hospital S.H.
Palacio Federal
☎614-9418

Telephone

The area code for Guadalajara is **3**.

In case of an emergency, dial **080**.

For operator assistance for international calls, dial **090**; for long-distance calls in

Mexico, 020 and finally for information, dial 040.

Calling Mexico from Abroad

From North America:
Dial *011* (for the international operator) + *52* (the country code for Mexico) + the area code + local number.

From Great Britain, New Zealand and Gemrany:
Dial *00* (for the international operator) + *52* (the country code for Mexico) + the area code + local number.

From Australia:
Dial *0011* (for the international operator) + *52* (the country code for Mexico) + the area code + local number.

You can save a lot of money by calling at certain hours of the day. Furthermore, sending a fax takes only a minute and costs much less than a phone call.

Calling Abroad from Mexico

Guadalajara has many phone booths that accept calling cards and *tarjetas de telefono* (calling cards) can easily be purchased in stores and grocery stores of all sizes, as well as in res-

taurants all over town ($3, $5, or $10 for 30-, 50- or 100-unit cards).

As Mexico has the highest long-distance rates in North America, it is more economical to call collect; the best option for Canadian, American and British citizens wishing to call someone in their native country is through a direct collect-call service (eg. Canada Direct). It is recommended that you not make calls abroad from hotels as these charge guests up to $4, even for collect and toll-free calls. Making a local call from a hotel room can cost up to $0.30 per call, while the same call placed from a phone booth costs only $0.05.

Direct Access Numbers

Canada Direct
☎*95-800-010-1990*

AT&T (CAN)
☎*95-800-010-1991*

AT&T (US)
☎*95-800-462-4240*

Sprint (US)
☎*95-800-877-8000*

MCI (US)
☎*95-800-674-7000*

BT (GB)
☎*98 800 4400*

Dialling Direct

To call North America:
Dial **00-1** + the area code + the local number.

For other international calls:
Dial **00** + country code + area code + local number.

For long-distance calls within Mexico: dial **0** + regional code + local number.

Internet Sites

Tourism related

www.jalisco.gob.mx

www.vivegdl.com.mx

www.guadalajara.net

www.viva-mexico.com.mx

Information on Mexico

www.yahoo.com.mx

www.espanol.yahoo.com

www.yupi.com.mx

www.adnet.com.mx

www.iguana.com.mx

www.mexplaza.com.mx

Yellow Pages

www.seccionamarilla.com.mx

www.yellow.com/mx

Country Codes

Australia	*61*
Belgium	*32*
Germany	*49*
Great Britain	*44*
Holland	*31*
Italy	*39*
New Zealand	*64*
Spain	*34*
Switzerland	*41*

Internet

Telmex, the formerly state-owned telecommunications company, offers Internet service throughout Mexico. Unlimited Internet access is offered for $20 a month, though this rate only applies to those with a preexisting phone line. To sign up with Telmex, call the business department at ☎800-701-0000.

Of course, you can also send, and sometimes even receive, e-mail from various cybercafés listed in the "Restaurants" section of this guide or encountered while roaming the city.

Financial Services

Currency

The country's currency is the nuevo peso, usually simply called "peso." The peso sign is $MEX. There are 20, 50, 100, 200 and 500 peso bills and 1, 2, 5 and 10 peso coins, as well as 5, 10, 20 and 50 centavo pieces.

Mexican currency is subject to major fluctuations, and has been devalued numerous times in recent years. The exchange rates for various foreign currencies are listed on the next page. These were in effect at press time, and are only intended to give you a general idea.

Banks

Banks generally offer the best exchange rates on foreign currency. Most banks are open Monday to Friday from 9am to 5pm. All have ATMs (automated teller machines) for cash withdrawals with bank cards or credit cards.

Credit Cards and Traveller's Cheques

Visa, MasterCard and American Express are the most widely accepted credit cards, but it's best to take nothing for granted and make inquiries.

There are foreign-exchange offices *(casas de cambio)* all over the city, including many on the stretch of Avenida López Cotilla between Calle Molina and

Practical Information

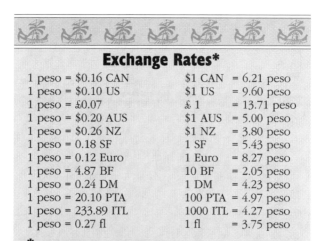

Exchange Rates*

1 peso = $0.16 CAN	$1 CAN = 6.21 peso
1 peso = $0.10 US	$1 US = 9.60 peso
1 peso = £0.07	£1 = 13.71 peso
1 peso = $0.20 AUS	$1 AUS = 5.00 peso
1 peso = $0.26 NZ	$1 NZ = 3.80 peso
1 peso = 0.18 SF	1 SF = 5.43 peso
1 peso = 0.12 Euro	1 Euro = 8.27 peso
1 peso = 4.87 BF	10 BF = 2.05 peso
1 peso = 0.24 DM	1 DM = 4.23 peso
1 peso = 20.10 PTA	100 PTA = 4.97 peso
1 peso = 233.89 ITL	1000 ITL = 4.27 peso
1 peso = 0.27 fl	1 fl = 3.75 peso

*Samples Only – Rates Fluctuate

Calle Colón, making it easy to shop around for the best rates. Although these exchange offices convert most major currencies (Canadian and U.S. dollars, European currency and the yen), U.S. dollars are always exchanged at more worthwhile rates. For those with Canadian, and particularly European money, it's far better to use a credit card (see below) or change your money into U.S. dollars prior to departure. Be sure to bring along your passport as it's required for transactions. Lastly, if at all possible, avoid changing money in hotels as they offer very unfavourable exchange rates.

It's always wise to keep part of your money in traveller's cheques, which are sometimes accepted in restaurants, hotels and some shops, although at less favourable rates. They're also easy to exchange in Mexican banks and foreign-exchange offices (when in U.S. or Canadian dollars). Be sure to keep a copy of your traveller's-cheques' serial numbers in a separate place so that if ever they're lost or stolen, the issuing bank can replace them more easily and quickly. Nevertheless, always keep some cash on hand.

Also, most ATMs accept Visa, MasterCard and the

Plus debit card; such transactions entail nominal fees (2% in Canada), but generally a better exchange rate than at banks and exchange bureaus. Moreover, you won't have to wait in line, and ATMs operate everywhere, 24hrs a day.

When withdrawing or changing money, if you have the choice, opt for small denominations as the shortage of small bills is a real bane in Mexico. Indeed, you'll have trouble getting change for your 200-peso bills without incurring grumbles from store cashiers or leaving with pocketfuls of coins.

Public Holidays and Calendar of Events

All banks and many businesses are closed on holidays, and the country seems to slow down. Be sure to do your banking ahead of time.

January 1
Año Nuevo
(New Year's Day)

January 6
Día de los Reyes Magos
(Epiphany)

February 5
Día de la Constitución
(Constitution Day)

February 24
Día de la Bandera
(Flag Day)

March 21
Día de Nacimiento de Benito Juárez (Benito Juárez's Birthday)

May 1
Día del Trabajo (May Day)

May 5
Cinco de Mayo
(anniversary of the Battle of Puebla)

September 16
Día de la Independencia
(Independence Day)

October 12
Día de la Raza
(Colombus Day)

November 1
Día de Todos Santos
(All Saints Day)
Informe Presidencial
(president's address to the nation)

November 2
Día de los Muertos
(Day of the Dead)

November 20
Día de la Revolución
(Revolution Day)

December 12
Día de Nuestra Señora de Guadeloupe (festival of the Virgin of Guadeloupe)

Practical Information

December 25
Día de Navidad
(Christmas Day)

Banks and government offices are also closed during Holy Week, particularly on the Thursday and the Friday preceding Easter (Holy Week begins Palm Sunday). Many offices and businesses are closed during Christmas Week, between December 25 and January 2.

Miscellaneous

Gay Life

Guadalajara is a boom town that has retained a very provincial mentality. The values that govern this society remain those of a puritanical Catholicism that leaves no room for the gay community. One need only recall the events of 1989 to realize that it's not always easy being gay here: the PRI government in power at the time decided to close virtually all gay bars in the city for reasons of so-called immorality. These days, despite the nonacceptance of homosexuality on principle, members of the gay community are fortunately treated with greater respect and physical assault is thus no longer a part of their daily lives.

Guadalajara hardly boasts a lively gay community life. Apart from AIDS support networks and a tiny gay-pride parade, there are no organizations that fight against discrimination and intolerance toward the gay community. Communication and organizational difficulties may explain this deficiency, but it can primarily be attributed to cultural differences with Europe and the rest of North America. Mexicans are traditionally more apt to seek support and comfort from their families rather than outside help. Although this attitude has as yet done nothing for the recognition of gay rights in society, it seems to work to a certain extent nonetheless. Indeed, as everywhere else in the western world, it's now easier for gay youth here to accept their sexuality and celebrate their difference.

Over the last few years, gay life has flourished in Guadalajara. More than 25 openly gay bars and nightclubs pack them in every weekend and a handful of gay cultural events enrich the city's cultural life. In fact, gay plays, exhibitions and films presented to the general public are not uncommon. Slowly but surely, these events are increasing public awareness and helping to carve out a place for the gay community in a nondiscriminatory society.

Time Difference

Mexico is divided into three time zones. The country switches to daylight-saving time between the first Sunday in April and the last Sunday in October (clocks are put ahead one hour). Guadalajara is one hour behind Eastern Standard Time and six hours behind Greenwich Mean Time.

Electricity

Local electricity operates at 110 volts AC, as in North America. Plugs have two flat pins, so Europeans will need both a converter and a wall socket adapter.

Language

Having the same Latin roots as Italian, Portuguese and French, Spanish may seem somewhat incomprehensible at first. But you need only know a few key words and phrases to be understood; moreover, your efforts will be greatly appreciated. As in all countries, knowing a few basics of the mother tongue when travelling enhances the experience. As well, language definitely reveals a lot about a people's character and cultural heritage.

The Spanish spoken in North, South and Central America is known as "Latin-American Spanish," which is different from the "Castilian Spanish" spoken in Spain. Like all languages, Spanish has a whole set of nuances and subtleties that can easily be mastered by paying attention when you're spoken to.

The better your command of the language, the more you'll notice the great variations in intonation of "Mexican Spanish" and expressions unique to the country (including *camión*, *refresco* and *chamba*). Another peculiarity of the language here is that it's enriched with many Nahuatl words (such as *chocolate*, *cacahuate* and *tlapalería*), an Aztec language still spoken by one million Mexicans. Moreover, many archaisms of old Spanish are still in use today, which demonstrates the different tangent the language took in the days following independence in 1821.

Getting acquainted with this language is a wonderful adventure and easier than you might think. We've included tips on Spanish pronunciation and a short glossary at the end of this guide to help you start

Practical Information

Weights and Measures

Mexico uses the metric system.

Weights
1 pound (lb) = 454 grams (g)
1 kilogram (kg) = 2.2 pounds (lbs)

Linear Measure
1 inch = 2.54 centimetres (cm)
1 foot (ft) = 30 centimetres (cm)
1 mile = 1.6 kilometres (km)
1 kilometres (km) = 0.63 miles (mi)
1 metre (m) = 39.37 inches (in)

Land Measure
1 acre = 0.4 hectare (ha)
1 hectare (ha) = 2.471 acres

Volume Measure
1 U.S. gallon (gal) = 3.79 litres
1 U.S. gallon (gal) = 0.8 imperial gallons

Temperature
To convert °F into °C: subtract 32, divide by 9, multiply by 5.
To convert °C into °F: multiply by 9, divide by 5, add 32.

conversing with the Mexican people.

Short- and long-term Spanish classes are available at:

Centro de Estudios Para Extranjeros (CEPE)
Universidad de Guadalajara
Tomás V. Gómez no. 125
Col. Ladrón de Guevara
☎*616-4399*
⇌*616-4013*

Exploring

L ocated in western
Mexico, the city of Guadalajara, the
Perla del Occidente, lies in the Atemajac
Valley, 1,561m
(5,118ft) above sea
level.

I ts historic district is located at the heart of the
former capital of New
Galicia, surrounded by the
antiguos barrios of Belém,
Analco and Nueve
Esquinas. The city is di-
vided into seven administrative *zonas*, each named after
one of its attractions, such
as Centro, Huentitán and
Minerva.

B elow we propose eight
tours. But first of all we
offer a "Flash Tour," which
highlights not-to-be-missed
attractions according to
interest and the length of
time available.

Flash Tour

The **Cerro de la Reina** (see
p 119) and the **Parque
Mirador Independencia**, better

known as the **Barranca de
Huentitán** (see p 111).

If you have two to three
days:

Church lovers should not
miss the **Catedral de
Guadalajara** (see p 77) and
the **Iglesia de Santa Mónica**
(see p 86).

Museum fans should visit the **Museo Regional** (see p 78).

Outdoor enthusiasts must go to the **Parque Los Colomos** (see p 111).

Castle lovers will enjoy the **Palacio de Gobierno** (see p 76).

Those interested in pre-Columbian archaeology should not miss the **El Iztépete** (see p 104).

Fresco lovers should visit the **Instituto Cultural Cabañas** (see p 81).

If you have three to five days:

Church lovers should not miss the **Catedral de Guadalajara** (see p 77), the **Iglesia de Santa Mónica** (see p 86), the **Iglesia San Francisco de Asís** (see p 94) and the **Basílica de la Virgen de Zapopan** (see p 108).

Museum fans should visit the **Museo Regional** (see p 78), the **Museo de Arqueología del Occidente de México** (see p 96), the **Casa Museo José López Portillo y Rojas** (see p 84), the **Museo de la Ciudad** (see

p 86) and the **Museo del Ferrocarril** (see p 102).

Outdoor enthusiasts must go to the **Parque Los Colomos** (see p 111) and the **Plaza de la Liberación** (see p 79)

Castle lovers will enjoy the **Palacio de Gobierno** (see p 76) and the **Palacio Legislativo** (see p 80).

Those interested in pre-Columbian archaeology should not miss the **El Iztépete** (see p 104).

Fresco lovers should visit the **Instituto Cultural Cabañas** (see p 81).

Tour A: The Cradle of Guadalajara

Your visit to Guadalajara begins in the centre of town at the **Plaza de Armas** ★★★, which was the city's recreation and meeting place up until the 1950s. It featured a fountain and a bull-fighting arena during the colonial period. In 1851, 30 years after the coun-

Bandstand in the Plaza de Armas

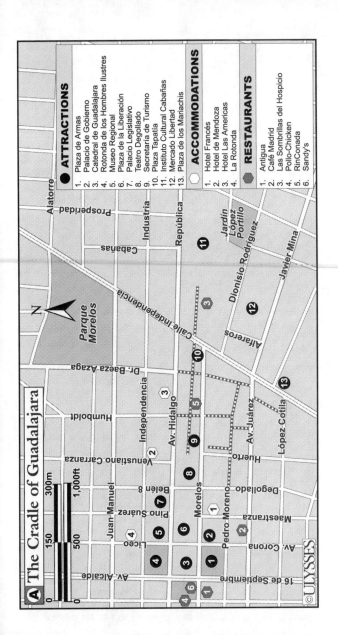

A The Cradle of Guadalajara

● ATTRACTIONS

1. Plaza de Armas
2. Palacio de Gobierno
3. Catedral de Guadalajara
4. Rotonda de los Hombres Ilustres
5. Museo Regional
6. Plaza de la Liberación
7. Palacio Legislativo
8. Teatro Degollado
9. Secretaría de Turismo
10. Plaza Tapatía
11. Instituto Cultural Cabañas
12. Mercado Libertad
13. Plaza de los Mariachis

⬡ ACCOMMODATIONS

1. Hotel Francés
2. Hotel de Mendoza
3. Hotel Las Americas
4. La Rotonda

⬢ RESTAURANTS

1. Antigua
2. Café Madrid
3. Las Sombrillas del Hospicio
4. Pollo-Chicken
5. RinConada
6. Sandy's

© ULYSSES

José Clemente Orozco

Orozco (Ciudad Guzmán 1883 – Mexico City 1949), a painter and fresco specialist native to the region, is the representative and the co-founder of muralism. His portraits, and especially his large murals, express the terror and suffering of the poor in the face of violence and war. His major works date from the late 1930s and include the fresco at the University of Guadalajara (*Triumph of liberated creativity*, 1936), the fresco at the Palacio de Gobierno (1937) and the fresco at the Institutio Cultural Cabañas, which is home to his masterpiece, *Hombre de fuego* (1938-1939). Its fluid and moving forms and its rigorous composition illustrate his perfect mastery of technique. Created in the context of renewing Mexican art—an attempt to revive pre-Columbian tradition—Orozco's work also features European influence, notably those of Greco, Picasso and the Expressionists.

try's independence, a stand was set up in the middle of the square, where musicians performed on Sunday evenings and holidays. Come listen to Guadalajara's municipal brass band, which serenades the crowd on Tuesdays, Thursdays and Sundays at 6:30pm. The current Art Nouveau **bandstand ★★★**, considered Mexico's most beautiful, as made in Paris in 1909. Take the time to visit and admire its eight wrought-iron caryatids, which hold a veil in one hand and a musical instrument in the other. A winged lion with a female body keeps watch above their heads. Four sculptures mounted on a bronze pedestal stand around the square and indicate the four cardinal points. These sculptures, which were built in New York in the 1930s, represent the four seasons.

Across the square stands the **Palacio de Gobierno ★★★**, a monument not to be missed. Built in the second half of the 18th century on the site of the previous palace, which was destroyed in an earthquake, it features a lovely baroque stone facade and has two levels. An elaborate arch between two rococo columns adorns the main entrance. On the first floor, wrought-iron balconies run along the facade and canon-shaped gargoyles recall the presence of the Spanish army during the colonial period. The main balcony is crowned with a replica of the bell of Dolores, a symbol of Mexican independence; the clock's cube was added in 1885. After enjoying the harmonious setting of the **central patio**, go up the stairs inside to discover the impressive **fresco ★★★**, entitled *Padre Hidalgo*, father of the homeland, who holds a torch that lights the way to freedom. This work is by José Clemente Orozco, a great Mexican mural painter. His last **fresco ★★★**, *Los tres grandes movimientos revolucionarios de México*, is located on the second floor, where the state legislature once sat.

Trek back towards Avenida Alcalde and walk past the **Sagrario Metropolitano ★**, a strictly neoclassical building, to visit

the **Catedral de Guadalajara ★★★** *(every day, 7am to 9pm)*, one of the seven Mexican cathedrals that date from the 16th century. This magnificent building is one of the city's largest and encompasses four centuries of liturgy and devotion with its altars, reliquaries and holy images. Several elements of different styles have been added to it. Its famous yellow-and-blue-tiled towers, built following an earthquake in 1818, became the city's symbol. Its Renaissance-style facade is adorned with sculptures of the Virgin Mary, St. Peter and St. Paul, which stand in its niches separated from the main entrance by Corinthian columns. The facade is crowned by an austere

Catedral de Guadalajara

pediment depicting the ascension of the Virgin Mary, who is surrounded by apostles sculpted in relief. Inside, an elegant gold ribbed ceiling catches your eye, as does the harmonious neoclassical style.

Unfortunately, nothing remains of the original altar, which was a magnificent silver baroque masterpiece; a general had it melted during the Reform War. A wooden sculpted choir is featured deep in the central nave. The cupola, built in the second half of the 19th century, is dec-

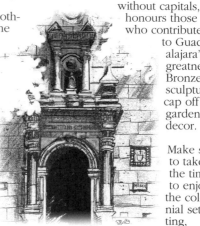

Museo Regional

orated with golden French-style floral designs. The multicoloured stained glass, brought over from Germany at the same time, adds a special touch to the cathedral's interior. Art lovers will particularly enjoy the many baroque paintings from the colonial period. Before exiting the cathedral, raise your eyes above the main entrance, where you will see the imposing French-made organ that managed to escape the vicissitudes of history.

Next to the cathedral, the **Rotonda de los Hombres Ilustres ★** provides a pleasant, shaded green space in the centre of town. This rotunda, located in the middle of the square and clad with 17 striated columns without capitals, honours those who contributed to Guadalajara's greatness. Bronze sculptures cap off the garden's decor.

Make sure to take the time to enjoy the colonial setting, which features pleasant *calandrias* (traditional Guadalajaran horse-drawn carriages), lined up in front of the **Museo Regional ★ ★ ★** (*$20, free admission Tue and Sun; guided tours in Spanish Tue to Fri at noon, in English on request; Tue to Sat 9am to 5:45pm, Sun 9am to 1:45pm; Liceo no. 60, ☎614-5257*). This interesting Spanish hotel, dating from the end of the 17th century, originally housed the St. Joseph seminary. The building was later home to a boys' school and was finally destined to house the fine arts museum in 1918, today the Museo Regional.

Since its complete renovation in 1976, the museum holds 16 exhibition rooms, the former chapel, an auditorium, administrative offices and a shop offering reproductions of archaeological items, silver objects and books published by the Instituto Nacional de Antropología e Historia. The entrance, which consists of an arch supported by two austere columns, is crowned with a baroque niche featuring a sculpture of St. Joseph. Barred windows and a wrought-iron balcony on the first floor complete the elegant facade. The building's four corners are embellished by a monumental column. Inside, behind a polygonal fountain on the left, an impressive plateresque portal, originally from a colonial hotel, is worth a look.

Rooms one and two on the main floor will especially interest those fascinated by paleontology and archaeology. Three rooms on the main floor

house an important ethnographic exhibit on the indigenous peoples of Jalisco. Art lovers will also find five rooms devoted to 17th century arts and crafts from the region and the rest of the country. Among the masterpieces, do not miss the works of Manuel Cabrera, José de Ibarra (called the Mexican Murillo), and José María Estrada. The forecours, adorned by a lovely collection of Spanish, French and Italian works, is worth a look. You will learn some of Mexico's post-independence history with the help of objects, pictures and paintings displayed in the other two rooms. Horse-drawn carriages dating from that time are parked in the hall in front of the rooms. Finally, you can end your tour on the main floor, in the chapel used for concerts, where the acoustics are excellent.

One of the city's most beautiful spots is the **Plaza de la Liberación ★★★**, located behind the cathedral, which is known as one of Mexico's best creations of the 20th century and is worth special attention, both for its liveliness as well as the view of the main monuments at the heart of New

Horse-drawn carriage

Exploring

Galicia. It commemorates the abolition of colonial rule decreed by Padre Hidalgo in Guadalajara in 1810. A statue representing this event shows him holding the broken chains of slavery in his hands. A series of important palaces line Avenida Hidalgo, on the northern side of the square.

Between Calle Pino Suárez and Calle Belén stands the **Palacio Legislativo** ★★★, which dates from the 18th century. Built as the residence of Bishop Juan Gómez de Parada, one of the city's important benefactors, it later became the home of **Real Fábrica de Tabaco** and has housed the local congress since its renovation in 1982. Its neoclassical facade is superb.

A little farther along the same street, past the **Palacio de Justicia** ★, stands the famous **Teatro Degollado** ★★★ *(free admission; Mon to Fri 10:30am to 11am and 12:30pm to 2pm; the Folkloric Ballet of the University of Guadalajara performs here on Sun at 10am; admission is $20 to $100; ☎614-4773)*, which is by far Guadalajara's most stunning theatre and one of the city's most important monuments. Legendary Mexican soprano Angela Peralta played "Lucia di Lammermoor" here for her inauguration in

1866. Inspired by Milan's La Scala opera house, it was built in a strong Italian neoclassical style. Eight Corinthian columns make up its monumental portico. The cornice features the legendary inscription *Qué nunca llegue el rumor de la discordia* (May discord never fall upon us), alluding to Greek mythology. Its pediment displays a remarkable relief representing Apollo surrounded by the nine muses. Five wrought-iron doors lead to an elegant elliptical vestibule. The refined space is adorned with a lovely colonnade and two bronze sculpted busts, one of General Santos Degollada, the designer of the theatre, and the other of Jacobo Gálvez, the architect who carried out the project.

Temporary painting exhibitions are held on the first floor. The stairs lead up to a concert hall. You can enjoy an allegorical fresco, *El tiempo y las horas*, over the arch of the stage's apron, and a wooden eagle grasping the Mexican flag in its claws and holding a chain in its beak on the right voussoir. Legend says the theatre will collapse the day the eagle lets go of the chain. The beautiful ceiling fresco, representing a scene in Act IV of Dante's *Divine Comedy*, will surely grab your attention before you leave the room.

Right behind the theatre lies the **Plaza Fundadores ★**, which features a huge sculpture of the definitive founding of the city in 1542. It is 21m (69ft) long and 3m (10ft) high.

Take the **Paseo Degollado**, which is just a stone's throw away and leads to the **Secretaría de Turismo** *(Paseo Degollado no. 105)*. You can't miss it, with its modern facade. Inside, visitors will discover the former headquarters of the St. Inquisition, one of the city's first large buildings. Do not be shy to go to the information desk where you will find a pleasant reception staff and specific information in Spanish and English.

By crossing the inner courtyard, you can exit by the door leading onto Calle Morelos to admire the building's pretty facade. On the corner of Calle Morelos and Callejón del Diablo, the **Fuente de los niños** livens up the area, called **el Rincón del diablo** (the devil's corner), which is enveloped in a thousand colonial anecdotes and legends. The Edwardian facade of the La Rinconada restuarant on this same street is worth a look. Take the time to wander around this pleasant pedestrian street, on which you will come across a **monumental sculpture of the city of Guadalajara's crest**, granted

by Charles V, the king of Spain, in 1539. A lovely **classical sculpture** of a young woman with a horn of plenty at her feet is just a stone's throw away.

A little farther, in the centre of the **Plaza Tapatía ★★★**, stands an enormous **sculpture** entitled *La inmolación de Quetzalcóatl* in the middle of a cross-shaped fountain. The flame, symbolizing the "new fire," is 23m (75ft) high. Quetzalcóatl is surrounded by four allegorical figures representing Aztlán, the mythical place where the Aztecs originated.

Keep walking straight ahead towards the Instituto Cultural Cabañas, and you will come across a colonnade of fountains on your way. Legend says that the visitor who crosses through these jets of water will return to Guadalajara as many times as the number of drops that soak his or her clothes.

If you can only visit one place in Guadalajara, the **Instituto Cultural Cabañas ★★★** *($8, no fee for guided tours in Spanish or English; Tue to Sat 10am to 5:45pm, Sun 10am to 3pm; movie-club Thu to Tue at 6pm and 8pm, admission $20; folkloric ballet Wed at 8:30pm, admission $25; ☎617-4248)* wins hands down as the place to go. It is

Exploring

Instituto Cultural Cabañas

Guadalajara's most impressive monument, located at the end of the Plaza Tapatía. Built by Bishop Juan Cruz Ruiz de Cabañas y Crespo as a home for the city's poor orphans, this magnificent building was opened in 1810. Since 1983, it has housed one of the country's most important cultural centres and was named a UNESCO World Heritage Site in 1997.

The Hospico Cabañas, work of Valencian architect Manuel Tolsá (creator of the Palace of Mines in Mexico City), was built in an austere neoclassical style: a pediment without relief, elevated by six Doric columns, and a sober facade without any attractive elements, except for a series of wrought-iron barred windows. Inside stands the **Capilla Clementina**, nicknamed the "Sistine Chapel of the Americas," deep in the **Patio de los Naranjos** (orange tree courtyard). Its interior is absolutely stunning. It is completely covered by a mural painting composition by José Clemente Orozco, completed just before the Second World War. On a simple, though original background featuring the grey profile of the city of Guadalajara, Orozco illustrates with brilliant colours Mexican reality since its origins. The **cupola** reflects the painter's thoughts. It depicts human beings in different positions, surrounded by a fire that represents the essence of human existence. Take the time to explore the nooks and crannies of this labyrinth—with its 106 rooms, 72 hallways and 23 patios, it is definitely worth a stop. Many rooms are devoted to art exhibits.

Lovers of Mexican crafts must stop at the **Mercado Libertad ★★★**, better known as the **Mercado de San Juan de Dios** (*every day 9am to 7pm; see p 214*). Shops are well stocked and prices are

Mariachis

Mariachi music is an inescapable fact during Guadalajara's fiestas and is the very symbol of Mexico's cultural vitality. Mariachi bands originated in the 1930s in the state of Jalisco, from Cocula bands established in Mexico City.

Mariachis decided to change the style of *sones* songs by changing a few instruments in the band. In the beginning, the bands consisted of four violins, a harp, a *vihuela* (ancient Spanish guitar) and two guitars (one big and one small). The harp disappeared, the *vihuela* was replaced by a third guitar and a trumpet—an instrument that became indispensable to the bands—was introduced. With the arrival of radio and television (which played their music a great deal), mariachis quickly became popular throughout Mexico.

At first, the repertoire of songs only consisted of *rancheras*. Today, it covers all genres, including classical music. Mariachis are nevertheless most associated with *ranchera* music, which has been given national anthem status. Themes range from relationships between men and women to the relationship between men and animals, their community, their country and their masculinity. Proud Mexicans know at least two or three verses of several mariachi songs by heart.

Whether it be during grand occasions or private serenades, mariachis are today found throughout the entire state. For a few pesos, you can watch them perform at the Plaza de los Mariachis, where a good number of them offer to sing for you.

Exploring

extremely affordable. To get there, go down the stairs south of the entrance to the Hospicio Cabañas.

Finally, fans of mariachi music should visit the **Plaza de los Mariachis**, near the market. Located at the end of a small street that begins at the intersection of Calzada Independencia and Avenida Javier Mina, this place comes alive day and night thanks to these charming musicians sporting traditional costumes, who will serenade restaurant customers for a tip.

Tour B: Residences and Squares of Old Guadalajara

Heading north on Calle Liceo, two streets from the Museo Regional, you will come to a beautiful former residence, the **Casa Museo José López Portillo y Rojas** ★ *(free admission; Mon to Fri 9am to 8pm; Liceo no.177, ☎613-2411)*. Housed in the former residence of the writer after whom the museum is named, the Casa Museo exhibits furniture and art from the 18th and 19th centuries. Some of the work on display includes 18 paintings depicting La Fontaine's fables, china,

Louis XVI furniture and a piano built in 1800.

Keep walking westward on Calle San Felipe, which leads to the **Jardín de la Reforma** ★. This peaceful garden was a battleground in the Reform War of the 19th century. The **Iglesia San José de Gracia** ★ stands on the northern side of the garden and is a great example of neoclassical architecture, featuring only a single tower. The **Museo del Periodismo** ★ (journalism museum) *($6; Tue to Sat 9am to 6pm, Sun 10:30am to 3pm; Avenida Alcalde no. 225, ☎613-9285)* is located across from the garden on Avenida Alcalde. The journalism museum is also known as the **Casa de los Perros** (the dogs' house), for the canine sculptures that adorn its facade. This historic site was where the city's first printing house once stood (1793). The printing house had published the rebels' first newspaper at the beginning of the War of Independence, in 1810. The house features a neoclassical style and dates from the end of the 19th century. It displays interesting exhibitions illustrating the development of the press, radio and television in Guadalajara, as well as temporary exhibits.

Keep walking westward on Calle Reforma to the corner

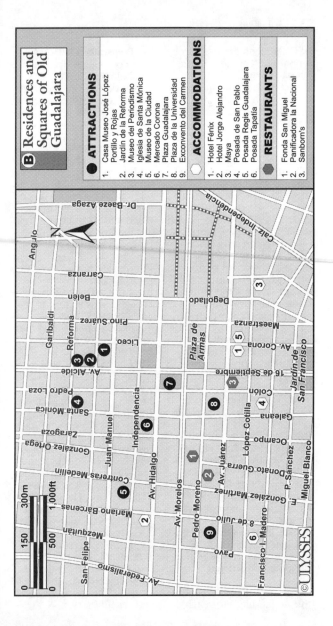

B Residences and Squares of Old Guadalajara

● ATTRACTIONS

1. Casa Museo José López Portillo y Rojas
2. Jardin de la Reforma
3. Museo del Periodismo
4. Iglesia de Santa Mónica
5. Museo de la Ciudad
6. Mercado Corona
7. Plaza Guadalajara
8. Plaza de la Universidad
9. Exconvento del Carmen

⬡ ACCOMMODATIONS

1. Hotel Fénix
2. Hotel Jorge Alejandro
3. Maya
4. Posada de San Pablo
5. Posada Regis Guadalajara
6. Posada Tapatía

⬣ RESTAURANTS

1. Fonda San Miguel
2. Panificadora la Nacional
3. Sanborn's

© ULYSSES

of Calla Santa Monica, from where you can admire the **Iglesia de Santa Mónica ★★★**, the most important baroque monument in western Mexico. This magnificent structure, built in the 18th century, was once part of a convent that was demolished in the Reform War (its arches and capitals were recovered and moved to the Patio de los Angeles, see p 98). Its facade, which is adorned with exuberant Art Nouveau reliefs, features rococo columns and a two-headed eagle, the symbol of Spanish royalty. The upper right corner features the famous **statue of St. Christopher**, who is traditionally venerated by single women searching for a husband, as well as by women whose relationships with their spouse is suffering. There is nothing left of the superb original rococo altar. The current decor features a neoclassical style.

Right behind the church, on the site of the former convent, lies the **XVª Zona Militar ★**, a red-brick and grey-stone building which contrasts with most of the city's ancient monuments. Its facade, featuring four atlases that sustain the central balcony, is worth a look. Access to inside the building is restricted.

Cross the square in front of the Zona Militar to reach the **Preparatoría Jalisco ★** (Jalisco college), formerly the Colegio San Felipe Neri, which dates from the beginning of the 19th century. Having once housed a hospital and later an orphanage, it has been the home of the Preparatoria de Jalisco since 1914. It has undergone many modifications and the building is not without interest, but it's the harmonized setting of the place and its buildings that are the main attractions here.

For a more in-depth visit of Guadalajara, history buffs must not miss the **Museo de la Ciudad ★★★** *($3; Wed to Sat 10am to 5:30pm, Sun 10am to 2:30pm; guided tours in Spanish upon request; Independencia no. 684, ☎658-2531 or 658-2665, ≈658-3706)*. To get there, take Calle González Ortega heading south until Calle Independencia. Turn right and you will view the museum's lovely facade featuring wrought-iron balconies, which is only a block and a half away. The core of this residence dates from the 18th century. Having been modified several times, the building was renovated by the city administration in 1991. Objects, paintings, models and photographs make up an interesting exhibit that retraces the city's history. The museum also houses a library.

The Reform War

Following its war with the United States, Mexico lost half of its territory in 1848. The instability that resulted gave way to internal strife. Trends were polarized due to the new constitution proclaiming the laws of the Reform: the separation of Church and State, the nationalization of Church property and the creation of a register of births, marriages and deaths. Finally, the liberal presidency of Benito Juárez, the first indigenous person to hold this position, seemed to give the country a stable government and the hope that Mexico would ease into a new era of peace. Conservative partisans, however, contested this new order and once again the country was plunged into strife and turmoil. Juárez and his ministers took refuge in Guadalajara, and the city was declared the country's capital on February 18, 1858.

Despite the protection of a makeshift and poorly equipped army, Juárez stayed only a month. He was nearly assassinated and escaped to Manzanillo. (He only returned to Mexico City after detours through Panamá, New Orleans and Veracruz.) Following his departure from Guadalajara, conservative partisans resumed the fight and the city changed hands five times in the next two years. Destruction was heavy; several downtown convents were destroyed and new streets sprang up where they had stood. Liberals occupied the city for good towards the end of 1860 and only gave up power when French troops under General Bazaine entered the city in early 1864. Three years later, at the end of the French intervention, the Liberal Party returned to power in Mexico.

Exploring

As you make your way towards the cathedral, you will pass the **Mercado Corona ★**, an extremely lively market where people stop to munch on something tasty before getting on with their errands. Turn onto Calle Pedro Loza, a pedestrian street, which features the **city hall's lateral archway ★** on the left and the **Iglesia La Merced ★** on the right. The modern **Plaza Guadalajara ★★★**, which offers a **superb view** of the cathedral's main facade, is a stone's throw away. Go down the same street a little farther to see the charming and lively **Plaza de la Universidad ★★★**, where Real Universidad de Guadalajara was founded at the end of the 18th century in the building housing the **Biblioteca Iberoamericana Octavio Paz ★★★** *(Mon to Sat 9am to 8pm)*. Its **monumental neoclassical portico** was added in 1826. Its interior houses important **frescoes** painted by the great muralist painter, David Alfaro Siqueiros. Book lovers who take the time to browse will enjoy books covering every theme,

stacked on wooden shelves. The view from the fountain features the **arcade** of the buildings on Calle Pedro Loza and the **French-style stores** of Avenida Juárez.

Your tour finally comes to an end at the **Ex-Convento del Carmen ★★★** *(free admission to exhibitions; Tue to Sat 9am to 8pm, Sun 9am to 3pm; Avenida Juárez no. 638, ☎613-1544, cultural program: ☎614-7184, see also p 209)*, an important cultural centre located five streets west on Avenida Juárez. The original convent, dating from 1758, was partially demolished in the 19th century. Today, half of the cloister and the small chapel house art galleries, a movie-club, a theatre and a concert hall. A small shop sells books and old postcards.

Right across from the Exconvento lies the **Jardín del Carmen ★**, which provides a green space shaded by trees and features the elegant **Iglesia del Carmen ★★**, once the convent's chapel. Completely modified in 1830, the convent features a superb neoclassical facade and colonial paintings adorned with gold decorations, as well as a pretty fresco on the cupola's ceiling inside. It's worth a visit.

The Legend of the Barcelonnettes

The term "Barcelonnette" brings to mind an unusual event that occurred over a period of 150 years: the emigration of agricultural workers and shepherds from the southeast of France to Mexico. This emigration was not only unique, but daring for its time. "Barcelonnette" had once only referred to residents of the Ubaye Valley, whose main town was Barcelonnette. This small city, located in the southern Alps near the Italian border, was founded in the 13th century by Béranger, count of Provence and Barcelona. For centuries, local men left the region during the long winter months to sell fabric in the region of Lyon, Burgundy, the Rhine and Flemish countries.

When Mexico gained its independence in 1821, it opened its door to foreigners. That same year, the Arnaud brothers left the Lower Alps for America. After a stop in New Orleans, they reached Mexico City in 1823 and opened a retail novelty shop featuring the sign *El cajón de ropa de las siete puertas* (the clothes drawer of the seven doors). Thus, they established the first and main activity of future Barcelonnettes who would emigrate to Mexico: selling clothes, a specialty they would forever claim as their own. Business was excellent, and the brothers soon brought over three of their fellow countrymen from the Alps. In 1845, two of the emigrants returned to France, each with 250,000 gold francs, a fortune that, as the local notary put it, "never ceased to stir the mind's eye" and unleashed the Barcelonnette migration to Mexico. At the start of the 20th century, the French consulate in Mexico counted around 5,000 families in Mexico that were originally from the Alps.

Over the years, they built a true business empire, which even supplanted their English and German

Exploring

competitors. From retail textile trade, the Barcelonnettes moved quickly into wholesale trade, then industrial manufacturing, when they established Latin America's first textile industry.

They also diversified their activities by expanding into pulp and paper, canning, tobacco and beer industries, as well as banking. As of 1880, they began building department stores reminiscent of Paris in the capital and other large cities. The stores featured evocative signs such as *"El Palacio de Hierro," "El Puerto de Liverpool," "La Fábricas de Francia"* and *"El Nuevo Paris."* They founded a series of important cultural and social institutions during that time, notably the Cercle Français, the Société Philharmonique et Dramatique Française, the Société Hippique Française and the Société de Bienfaisance Française, Suisse et Belge.

The Barcelonnette identity remains alive and well in Mexico. There are currently some 50,000 Barcelonnettes among the emigrants and their descendants residing in Mexico. A much smaller number of expatriates, who had made their fortunes in Mexico moved back to the Ubaye Valley and beautiful villas surrounded by large parks in Barcelonnette and Jausiers. Barcelonnette has an honorary Mexican consulate, located at 7 Avenue Porfirio-Díaz, in honour of this remarkable bond between the French region and Mexico.

Tour C: The Panteón de Belén and Surrounding Area

Before exploring the historic district of Belén, it is worth visiting the **Jardín** and the **Iglesia del Santuario de Guadalupe** ★★, a famous site in Guadalajara that is especially known for its traditional fiestas honouring the Virgin of Guadalupe, the patron saint of Mexicans *(To get there, take one of the buses travelling on Avenida Alcalde heading north)*. At the end of the 18th century, the city's remarkable bishop benefactor, Fray Antonio Alcalde, built a church and Las Cuadritas del Santuario, a small public-housing neighbourhood, at his own expense.

As you begin your tour, you will notice **two massive buttresses** next to the facade. The interior, which is adorned with neoclassical gilding, features a painting of the Virgin of Guadalupe, dating from 1779. The main attraction of the Santuario lies in its **patron saint's day** ★★★, which is held December 12. Those who enjoy folklore and traditions shouldn't miss it. Guada-lajaran faithful, dressed in native costumes, make a pilgrimage to Santuario to pay respect to their patron saint. The square in front of the church turns into a village fiesta. Food lovers can savour *buñuelos*, a Mexican type of doughnut. The party peaks with *castillos*, traditional Mexican fireworks.

Guadalajara's points of interest include the **Panteón de Belén** ★★★ *(Mon to Fri 9am to 4pm and 4pm to 6pm; Calle Belén no. 684)*, the **Civil Hospital** ★★★ *(Calle Hospital no. 278)* and its surroundings, and the **Iglesia de Belén** ★★★ *(Calle Hospital)* is worth special attention. Take Avenida Alcalde northward and turn right at the corner of Calle Eulogio Parrra, which will lead you to the main entrance of the remarkable Panteón de Belén, once the Pantheon of Santa Paula. This cemetery, which was opened in 1848 and closed 50 years later, is a remarkable part of the city's historical and cultural heritage. Its facade, crowned by **three neogothic spires**, is adorned with a **lovely relief** of two children in tears. Its interior features two **colonnades** sustaining a vault that covers the niches of important *tapatías* individuals buried here. Despite having been partially vandalized, the **funerary monu-**

Exploring

Fiestas de Octubre

Every October, during the traditional Fiestas de Octubre (October fiestas) Guadalajara comes alive with activity and excitement. Created in 1965 and likened to Germany's famous Oktoberfest, these fiestas attract tourists and Tapatians alike. The festivities consist of a spectacular series of shows, dances, **corridas**, fireworks, feasts and entertainment, which stretches over the entire month of October. The fiestas also feature traditional *charreadas*, *verbedas* (evening fairs) and *fútbol* matches, as well as cultural events, which include classical music concerts and operas presented throughout the city. The historic part of town comes to life at this time of year, when it becomes the setting for a number of events. Each day of the month is devoted to one of Mexico's states or two territories. Children and adults alike will have fun at the fair, which includes traditional carrousels, Ferris wheels and bungee jumping. If you are planning a trip to Guadalajara in October, you will be able to take advantage of all these activities for 31 consecutive days. Signs posted throughout the city list schedules for the various activities.

ments inside illustrate the influence of Romanticism, which had been at the forefront in the 19th century. The variety of styles— Egyptian, Roman, baroque and Gothic Revival—will surely catch your eye. The **mausoleum of famous men** that stands in the middle of the cemetery merits a close look.

Keep walking down Calle Belén and turn left onto Calle Hospital to see the Hospital Civil de Belén, one of the most important works of the city's great benefactor, Fray Antonio

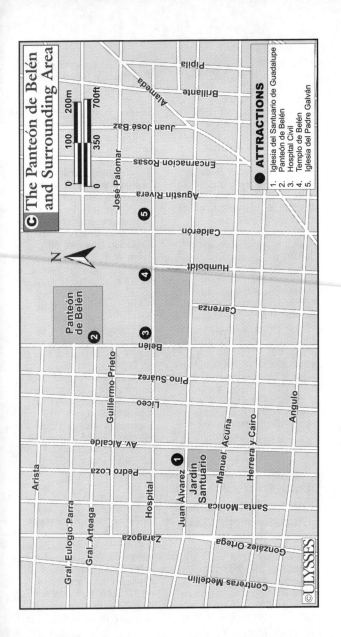

C The Panteón de Belén and Surrounding Area

ATTRACTIONS

1. Iglesia del Santuario de Guadalupe
2. Panteón de Belén
3. Hospital Civil
4. Templo de Belén
5. Iglesia del Padre Galván

Panteón de Belén

0   100   200m
0   350   700ft

© ULYSSES

N

Streets: Gral. Eulogio Parra, Arista, Gral. Arteaga, Zaragoza, Hospital, Pedro Loza, Av. Alcalde, Guillermo Prieto, Liceo, Pino Suárez, Belén, Carranza, Humboldt, Calderón, Agustín Rivera, José Palomar, Encarnación Rosas, Juan José Baz, Alameda, Brillante, Pípila, Juan Álvarez, Manuel Acuña, Herrera y Cairo, Angulo, Santa Mónica, González Ortega, Contreras Medellín, Jardín Santuario

Alcalde. This hospital, opened in 1794, still provides important medical services. Its facade, with its Ionic columns and pediment, is worth a look.

Next to the hospital stands the Templo de Belén, built at the same time. A **sculpture of St. Michael**, the patron saint of Guadalajara, taken from the city's first hospital and dating from 1545, is featured above the door, which is framed by Ionic columns.

A little farther down the street stands the impressive **Iglesia del Padre Galván** ★★★. The facade of this original building, built in a modern gothic style in 1960, will catch your attention. Around the high reliefs representing the birth of Christ, 56 angels dressed in mariachi costumes and playing traditional instruments celebrate the event.

Tour D: Analco, Las Nueve Esquinas and Parque Agua Azul

Analco and Nueve Esquinas, the old, popular districts of Guadalajara, have managed to preserve some of their charm of yesteryear. This tour will allow you to relive the daily life of the area's inhabitants of centuries past. Your tour begins in the Jardín de San Francisco on Avenida 16 de Septiembre, four streets south of the Plaza de Armas.

The charming **Jardín de San Francisco** ★★★ is located on the left side on the corner of Avenida 16 de Septiembre and Avenida Prisciliano Sánchez. The **Iglesia San Francisco de Asís** ★★★ stands at the end of the garden and is one of Guadalajara's oldest churches, a jewel of baroque architecture. Built in the 17th century where the first church had once stood, this superb temple is worth special attention. Its admirable facade is adorned with rococo columns and five magnificent sculptures. If richly decorated interiors appeal to you, go inside to discover wonderful colonial paintings and an impressive golden rococo altar. Do not miss the Gothic-like ribs that adorn the vault.

Cross Avenida 16 de Septiembre to get to the **Capilla de Nuestra Señora de Aranzazú** ★★★. The facade of this 18th century chapel features a very simple style, as the classic towers of old Spanish churches are missing. The **belfry**, however, may surprise you: its contours are reminiscent of old

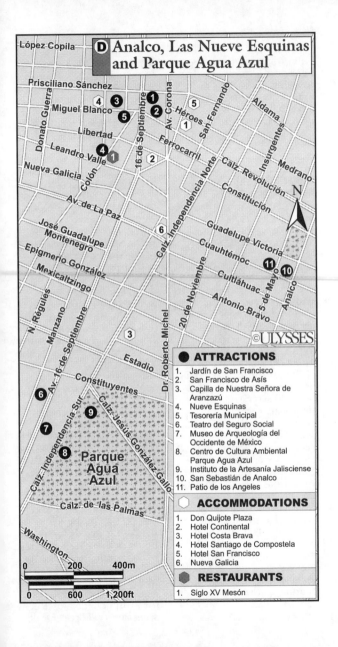

D Analco, Las Nueve Esquinas and Parque Agua Azul

López Copila

Prisciliano Sánchez

Miguel Blanco

Libertad

Leandro Valle

Nueva Galicia

Donato Guerra

Colón

Av. de La Paz

José Guadalupe Montenegro

Epigmerio González

Mexicaltzingo

N. Regules

Manzano

Av. 16-de-Septiembre

Constituyentes

Parque Agua Azul

Calz. de las Palmas

Washington

16-de Septiembre

Av. Corona

Héroes

San Fernando

Aldama

Ferrocarril

Calz. Revolución

Insurgentes

Medrano

Calz. Independencia Norte

Constitución

Guadalupe Victoria

Cuauhtémoc

Cuitláhuac

Antonio Bravo

20 de Noviembre

Dr. Roberto Michel

Estadio

Calz. Independencia Sur

Calz. Jesús González Gallo

5-de-Mayo

Analco

N

©ULYSSES

0   200   400m

0   600   1,200ft

● ATTRACTIONS

1. Jardín de San Francisco
2. San Francisco de Asís
3. Capilla de Nuestra Señora de Aranzazú
4. Nueve Esquinas
5. Tesorería Municipal
6. Teatro del Seguro Social
7. Museo de Arqueología del Occidente de México
8. Centro de Cultura Ambiental Parque Agua Azul
9. Instituto de la Artesanía Jaliscience
10. San Sebastián de Analco
11. Patio de los Angeles

⬡ ACCOMMODATIONS

1. Don Quijote Plaza
2. Hotel Continental
3. Hotel Costa Brava
4. Hotel Santiago de Compostela
5. Hotel San Francisco
6. Nueva Galicia

⬡ RESTAURANTS

1. Siglo XV Mesón

Californian missions. Its interior is a truly sacred art museum. Take the time to admire its churrigueresque altar, which survived the damage caused by the political turmoil of the 19th century.

Your tour continues with a walk through the **Nueve Esquinas ★ ★ ★**, one of Guadalajara's most pleasant districts. Its criss-crossed streets were once part of the famous suburb of Mexicoltzingo, located a little farther south. The Nueve Esquinas district, once the site of the city's slaughterhouse, is characterized by **lovely residences dating from the 19th century**. To get there, take Calle Colón, to the left just behind the Aranzazú chapel. Admirers of the Edwardian style will no doubt notice the facade of the **Tesorería Municipal ★ ★** on the corner of Calle Miguel Blanco, to the right. One street down, visitors will feel as if they have entered a late 19th-century Mexican village. Take the time to wander around a little to discover its alleys and squares adorned with old stone fountains. The numerous printing shops set up along the streets, with their old presses, provide an additional retro feel to this charming area.

If you are in the mood for local cuisine, make sure you taste *birria*, the local specialty. This traditional dish—meat seasoned with agave leaves and spices, cooked overnight—has made the neighbourhood famous. In addition to small popular eateries, a series of quality restaurants have opened for business since the recent renovation of Nueve Esquinas.

By heading farther south on Avenida 16 de Septiembre, at the corner of Avenida Constituyentes, you will reach the district of **Agua Azul**, which features important cultural sites and institutions. To get there, you can take a bus on Avenida 16 de Septiembre, since it is a long walk to Agua Azul. Still on Avenida 16 de Septiembre, you will pass a set of modern buildings on the right, which belong to the Instituto Mexicano del Seguro Social. Drama lovers should not miss the **Teatro del Seguro Social (Teatro IMSS)** *(Avenida 16 de Septiembre s/n, ☎619-4121, see p 209)*. One of the city's most important theatres, it produces excellent plays. On the left stands the **Casa de la Cultura**, home of the state's cultural radio, and the tower of the **Biblioteca Pública del Estado**. In the middle of a small garden just behind the tower stands the **Museo de Arqueología del Occidente de**

he Palacio de Gobierno displays a lovely baroque facade with wrought-iron balconies and a hint of rocaille ornamentation. - *Tibor Bognár*

The Catedral de Guadalajara, one of seven Mexican cathedrals that date back to the 16th century, is topped by two blue- and yellow-tiled steeples, which have become the town's symbol.
- *Tibor Bognár*

Behind the flowing waters of a fountain stands one of the city's most beautiful monuments: the Teatro Degollado, inspired by La Scala in Milan and designed in an Italian neoclassical style.
- *Tibor Bognár*

México ★ *($3; Tue to Sun 10am to 2pm and 4pm to 7pm; video presentation; Avenida 16 de Septiembre no. 889, ☎825-3821)*, built in a style reminiscent of a pyramid base. This small museum features a collection of archaeological items from Jalisco, as well as from other regions in the **Culturas de Occidente** area. The objects on display will provide fans of pre-Columbian antiquities with greater insight into the various aspects of daily life for Western Mexico's first inhabitants.

If you are seeking quiet and greenery, all you have to do is cross Calzada Independencia on the other side of the museum, to take a walk in the extraordinary **Centro de Cultura Ambiental Parque Agua Azul** ★ ★ ★ *($4; Tue to Sun 10am to 6pm; Calzada Independencia Sur no. 973, ☎619-0333)*, one of the most important urban ecological renewal projects in Latin America. This park has been part of Guadalajara's personality since the end of the 19th century. A lovely building from that period, adorned with an arcade, is located at the extreme southern part of the park.

In 1991, a group of prestigious *tapatíos* architects began work on an ecological interpretation centre in the park in order to protect the environment and promote its importance. With the work finished, the new Parque Agua Azul opened its doors. The natural attractions that follow one after the other in this marvelous place are impressive. A biosphere holding thousands of butterflies, unique to Mexico, stands in the middle. Sit down for a moment and these small winged creatures will appear before your eyes in no time at all. The number of species varies depending on the season, but it is sure to be an unforgettable sight.

An enormous aviary that is home to around 250 birds belonging to 53 different tropical species is just a stone's throw away. A little farther stands an orchid greenhouse of reinforced glass, built in the shape of a pyramid, that will no doubt catch your eye. Inside, you will be able to enjoy the large variety of these beautiful flowers growing in a controlled humid environment. We suggest you visit in March or October, when most of the orchids are in bloom. Gardening enthusiasts can visit the tree nursery by taking the alley to the right, halfway between the orchid wall and a small lake. With its fishponds, research labs, a library and an exhibition room, the Parque Agua Azul is an important educational cen-

Exploring

tre for locals and visitors alike.

If you enjoy crafts, walk along the Parque Agua Azul past the important **Teatro Experimental de Jalisco** *(Calzada Independencia Su s/n, Núcleo Agua Azul, ☎619-3730)* to Calzada González Gallo to reach the **Instituto de la Artesanía Jalisciense** ★ ★ ★ *(free admission; Mon to Fri 10am to 6pm, Sat 10am to 5pm, Sun 10am to 3pm; Calzada González Gallo no. 20, ☎619-1407 or 619-4664, also see p 215).* This institution is a real pop art paradise and includes an interesting Roberto Montenegro collection and two showrooms featuring extraordinary works created by craftspeople from different regions of Jalisco. While the historic centre includes most of Guadalajara's colonial monuments, old districts, originally small villages neighbouring the city, preserve important structures that are of interest. The **Analco** district is mentioned in a historical document, dated December 10, 1560. Occu-

Mexican mask

pied by indigenous communities at that time, Analco is essentially the work of Franciscan evangelists. To get there, take Calzada Independencia, eight streets north of the Agua Azul section. Taking a bus is a wise decision. Turn right at the corner of Calla Cuauhtémoc; a little farther stands the **Iglesia San Sebastián de Analco** ★ ★ *(Calle Cuauhtémoc no. 252)* in a shaded area. The church grounds feature a cross of sculpted stones dating from the first few years of New Galicia. Built in the 17th century, the main temple's facade, which in reality covers the church and two chapels (one on each side), is adorned with a simple arch and Art Nouveau reliefs. Its interior features a curious decor, a mix of baroque and neoclassical gildings.

If you continue to your left, you will discover the famous **Patio de los Angeles** ★ ★ ★ *(free admission; Mon to Fri 9am to 8:30pm, Sat 9am to 2pm; Calle Cuauhtémoc no. 250, ☎619-2886, ≈619-5479),* an important cultural centre marked by history and legends. The current building features a harmonious, modern style, but the patio's arches and columns, which were sculpted 250 years ago, were part of the former cloister of the Santa Mónica convent (see p 86). Legend says this cloister was built by young, particularly enthusiastic masons. When they had finished their work, the convent's nuns sought to pay the young masons, but they had disappeared. And so, convinced that angels had in fact built the cloister, the nuns baptized the building *el Patio de los Angeles*. The convent was demolished following the Reform War in the 19th century. The cloister's stones, which had been miraculously spared from destruction, still embellish the cultural centre. You will no doubt enjoy its columns, featuring Ionic capitals and arches adorned with flower reliefs reflecting an innocent charm.

Tour E: Chapultepec and Las Antiguas Colonias

Your tour begins at the Rectoría de la Universidad de Guadalajara, located a stone's throw from the Parque Revolución on Avenida Juárez. To get there, you have to take a bus on Juárez or get off at the Parque Revolución subway station.

Built in 1918, the **Rectoría de la Universidad de Guadalajara** ★ ★ ★ *(free admission; Mon to Sat 9am to 8pm; Avenida Juárez no. 975)*, is an important Edwardian building, a style that was popular in the early 20th century. Originally built to house the new courthouse, it has housed the university rector's office since it opened in 1925. While its facade is interesting, its main attraction lies inside: two large, powerful **frescoes**, painted by José Clemente Orozco, under the cupola and behind the **Paraninfo** stage (seance room). By walking along the Rectoría to enter by the back doors, photography and graphic art enthusiasts will discover the **Museo de las Artes** ★ *($10; Tue to Thu and Sat 10:30am to 6:30pm, Fri 10:30am to 8pm, Sun noon to 6pm; Calle López Cotilla no. 930; ☎825-8888).* The museum's small boutique sells books, souvenirs, silver objects, and CDs and videos produced by the folkloric ballet of the University of Guadalajara for Mexican dance lovers.

Keep walking on Calle Escorza to reach the Jardín Cuauhtémoc. The northern side of the garden features the **Templo**

Exploring

Expiatorio ★★★, the work of Adamo Boari, architect of Mexico's famous central post office. Notice how this church is built according to Middle Age tradition, without steel or cement structures. Its Italian gothic **façade**, featuring mosaics made in the Vatican, mesmerizes those who stop to admire it. Its sculpted wooden doors beautified by bronze facings are also of interest. If you visit the church at 9am, noon or 6pm, you will be charmed by the German clock from which apostles file out, marking the hour to the rhythm of the chimes. The church's interior should not be missed. With light filtering in through multicoloured stained glass designed by master French craftsmen, you will discover an atmosphere reminiscent of centuries past. Do not miss the gilded bronze altar, built in Barcelona and adorned with enamel icons.

The district located between the Templo Expiatorio and Avenida Unión mainly developed in the early 20th century. If you are not pressed for time when exploring this neighbourhood, you will be able to discover **lovely bourgeois residences** once belonging to the upper echelons of

● ATTRACTIONS

1. Rectoría de la Universidad de Guadalajara
2. Templo Expiatorio
3. Av. Chapultepec
4. Galería de Arte Moderno
5. Centro Cultural Jaime Torres Bodet
6. Museo del Ferrocarril

◐ ACCOMMODATIONS

1. Hotel del Parque
2. Hotel Laffayette
3. Hotel-Suites Bernini
4. Posada Cameleón

◕ RESTAURANTS

1. Bistro de Thérèse
2. Circuló Francés
3. Copenhagen 77
4. Delfín Sonriente
5. El Che
6. El Espeto
7. El Globo
8. El Pargo
9. Famosa Gardens
10. Habana
11. Karne Garibaldi
12. La Paloma
13. Le Grand Bordeaux
14. Los 4 Gatos
15. Los Itacates
16. Ma come no
17. Maximino's
18. Mondo Café
19. Monique
20. Peña Cuicalli
21. Riscal
22. Sacromonte
23. Santo Coyote
24. Suehiro
25. Veneto Café
26. Vida Leve

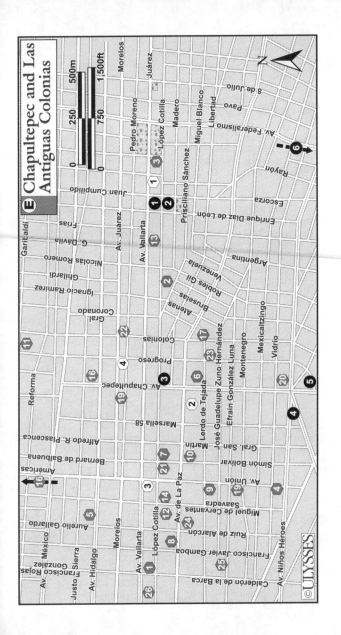

Chapultepec and Las Antiguas Colonias

| 0 | 250 | 500m |
| 0 | 750 | 1,500ft |

society. We recommend that you take the tour long offered by *calandrias* drivers (see p 78), who offer rides along the prettiest streets in this part of the city. Among other residences, do not miss the **Casa de los abanicos** (the house of fans), at 1832 Avenida Libertad.

Antique lovers should go to the **Plaza de la República** ★, located on Avenida México between Avenida Chapultepec and Avenida General San Martín, on a Sunday morning. Guadalajara's second-hand-furniture and antique dealers gather at this charming spot, known as **El Trocadero** ★★, once a week to offer an interesting array of beautiful items. Even if you aren't a devoted trinket collector, a visit will delight your eyes and put a smile on your face.

Keep walking on **Avenida Chapultepec** ★ to explore this boulevard embellished by a series of fountains and lush green trees. Take the time to stop at one of the café terraces to treat yourself to a cappuccino and a piece of cake (see p 172).

Lovers of modern art will definitely want to visit the **Galería de Arte Moderno** ★ *(free admission; Tue to Fri 10am to 7pm, Sat and Sun 10am to 2pm; Avenida Mariano Otero no. 375,* ☎*616-3266)*, located a block from the **Monumento de los Niños Héroes** traffic circle, at the intersection of Avenida Chapultepec, Avenida Niños Héroes and Avenida Mariano Otero. For 30 years, this gallery has featured temporary exhibits of paintings, sculptures, engravings and photography of contemporary artists. Finally, the city's cultural life has a special place in the **Centro Cultural Jaime Torres Bodet** *(Avenida Chapultepec Sur y Avenida España,* ☎*615-1209)*, located a stone's throw away, behind the gallery. This beautiful modern structure houses a concert room renowned for its excellent acoustics. It offers a great program of plays and quality concerts.

Train buffs will be excited to hear of the opening of the **Museo del Ferrocarril** *(Parque del Deán, corner of Avenida Lázaro Cárdenas and Calle Ramal del Ferrocarril, right in front of the Siderúrgica Guadalajara)*. Visitors can admire the beautiful steam locomotive, *Niagara*, built in Schenectady, New York in the 1940s, as well as a diverse collection of wagons and other items once used in rail transportation in Mexico. This exhibition is certainly one of the museum's most interesting attractions.

Tour F: Minerva and el Iztépete

Among the symbols that identify the city of Guadalajara, the **Fuente Minerva** ★★ is without a doubt one of the most representative. This monumental sculpture stands 8m (26ft) tall in the middle of a traffic circle at the intersection of Avenida Vallarta, Avenida López Mateos, Circunvalación Agustín Yáñez and Avenida Golfo de Cortés. To get there, take the Par Vial 400 bus on Avenida Independencia at the Rotonda, next to the cathedral. Emerging from moving clouds (an optical illusion produced by fine jets of water), Minerva, the goddess of wisdom of ancient Greeks and Romans, proudly guards the western entrance to the city. The spot is a privileged meeting place after victories of Las Chivas, one of the city's soccer teams. Today, thousands of fans invade the rotunda after matches.

Just a stone's throw from here, to the right towards the centre of town, stands the **Casa Museo José Clemente Orozco** *(free admission; Mon to Fri 9am to 5pm; Avenida Aurelio Aceves no. 29, ☎616-8329)*, the muralist's residence during his time in Guadalajara. An enormous window that provided his studio with natural light, dominates the facade. The museum houses temporary exhibits, Orozco's personal library, as well as a fresco, painted in Mexico City in 1945, that can be dismantled.

Strolling down on Avenida Vallarta, you will be able to enjoy the famous **Arcos de Vallarta** ★, built in a style reminiscent of Antiquity's Arch de Triomphe. This monument, which commemorates the 400th anniversary of the founding of Guadalajara, is adorned with yellow tiles, as are the towers of the cathedral, and is flanked by fountains on each side.

Still on Avenida Vallarta, one street past the Arcos, you will come to the **Observatorio Astronómico** ★ *(admission and guided tour in Spanish $5; Tue and Thu 10am to 1pm; guided tour in French, English, German or Russian on request $5; library: Mon to Fri 10am to 6pm; "Viernes Astronómico" conferences and telescopic view of the sky the last Friday of the month from 7pm to 8:15pm; Avenida Vallarta no. 2602, ☎616-4937)*, founded in 1926. Those who appreciate the celestial vault will certainly not want to miss the oppor-

Exploring

tunity to study Guadalajara's sky with a telescope, an activity run by this important astronomy and meteorology research centre belonging to the Univeristy of Guadalajara.

The neighbourhood surrounding the Fuenta Minerva features several large shopping centres, which you might want to explore. The latest one, **Centro Magno** ★, bordered by Avenida Vallarta, Avenida López Cotilla, Fco. de Quevedo and Avenida Lope de Vega, attracts attention for its architecture, which is both ultramodern and retro, blending cozy corners with a futuristic setting. The centre is bent on entertainment: Centro Magno houses 20 movie theatres, offering the best selection in town.

As you come back toward the Fuenta Minerva, take Avenida López Mateos heading south. By walking southward on Avenida López Mateos, four streets down, horse lovers will enjoy the *Estampida* ★, a magnificent set of bronze equestrian sculptures, located in the traffic circle at the corner of Avenida Niños Héroes. The movement of galloping horses that is reproduced is impressive.

You don't have to be a history buff or an archaeologist to appreciate the **El Iztépete** ★ ★ ★ *(free admission; Tue to Sun 10am to 6pm; Prolongación Mariano Otero s/n)* excavation site, located at the intersection of Prolongación Mariano Otero and Periférico Sur, southwest of the city. To get there, take a bus on Avenida Mariano Otero. These interesting pre-Columbian ruins, which

---

● ATTRACTIONS

1. El Iztépete

○ ACCOMMODATIONS

1. Hotel Guadalajara Plaza Expo	5. Posada del Sol
2. Hotel Guadalajara Plaza López Mateos	6. Posada Guadalajara
3. Hotel Margarita	7. Presidente Inter-Continental
4. Motor Hotel Américas	8. Vista Plaza del Sol

● RESTAURANTS

1. Bon's Café	7. Lüsherly
2. Dragón de Oro	8. Mr. Bull
3. El Gordo Steak	9. Roma Antica
4. El Sorbo de café	10. Si como no
5. Hostería del Arte	11. Tacón Galleta
6. Las Palomas	

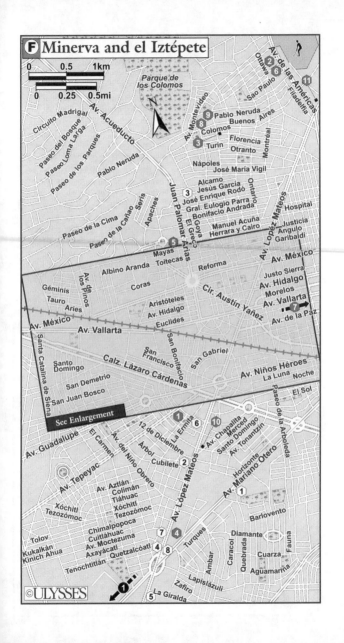

according to experts probably date from the sixth century, once made up the heart of an important ceremonial centre and elite residential neighbourhood. In observing the entire setting, you will notice how simple the style was. The main structure, a mix of clay and stones, is 6m (20ft) tall. It originally served as the base of four temples that have disappeared over the years. The four staircases next to the walls once led to the temples. The site also features a set of elite residences and a square bordered by two small structures. El Iztépete is espe

cially interesting for its historical significance. It was built by the Aztecs, during their long pilgrimage to Tenochtitlán (today Mexico City), a place identified by the gods as their definitive homeland. It is in western Mexico, in the states of Jalisco, Colima and Nayarit that they developed the basic aspects of their culture, notably their graves, "partitioned" ceramics and metallurgy. After a tour of Guadalajara, visiting El Iztépete will let you discover a different world that is as far from New Galicia as it is from modern Mexico.

● ATTRACTIONS

1. Fuente Minerva
2. Casa Museo José Clemente Orozco
3. Arcos de Vallarta
4. Observatorio Astronómico
5. Centro Magno
6. Estampida

○ ACCOMMODATIONS

1. Camino Real
2. Fiesta Americana
3. Holiday Inn Select
4. Hotel del Bosque
5. Hotel Nuevo Vallarta
6. Hotel Patricia
7. Hotel Puerto Vallarta
8. Hotel Plaza Diana
9. Hotel Plaza Los Arcos
10. Hotel-Suites Fuente del Bosque
11. Hotel Windsor
12. Las Pergolas
13. Malibu
14. Motel Guadalajara

● RESTAURANTS

1. Café Martinique
2. Dalí Café
3. Estancia Gaucha
4. El Arca
5. El Italiano
6. El Libanés
7. Hacienda Navarro
8. La Calle
9. La Destilería
10. La Pianola
11. La Squina
12. La Trattoria
13. Los Otates
14. Lüsherly
15. New York New York
16. Oliveto
17. Oui Café
18. Parilla Argentina
19. Quinta Real
20. Sushi-Nori
21. Taquería de la Minerva

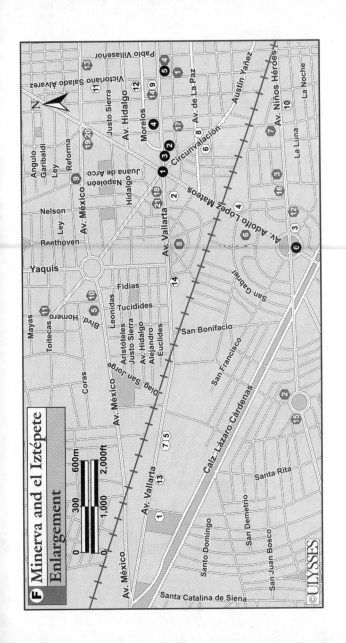

F Minerva and el Iztépete
Enlargement

ULYSSES

Tour G: Zapopan

Little is known today about **Zapopan** ★★ during the pre-Columbian period. Nevertheless, vestiges prove that it was the ceremonial centre of northwestern Mexican peoples between the fourth and sixth centuries. With the arrival of the Spanish, Zapopan became a place of little importance. The city was nevertheless founded in 1541, and the Franciscans began evangelizing inhabitants. One year later, Fray Antonio de Segivia offered a small sculpture of the Virgin Mary made from corn paste by indigenous peoples in Michoacán, to these newly converted to Christianity. Since that time, miracles have been attributed to the Virgen de Zapopan, and today the city attracts pilgrims from all over Mexico.

By following Calzada Avila Camacho around 8km (5mi) north of the centre of Guadalajara, you will reach the village's remains. The welcome arches mark the beginning of an important pedestrian area, the Paseo Teopilzintli. This *paseo* is integrated into the Plaza de las Américas, a pretty esplanade featuring a traditional Mexican stand in its centre.

Before you stands the symbol of Zapopan, the **Basílica de la Virgen de Zapopan** ★★★. The basilica and its magnificent facade date from the 17th century and were built by Franciscan monks, founders of the adjacent convent. This elegant temple houses a venerated picture of the Virgin Mary, made from corn paste. This picture was brought here by monks, who, it is said, succeeded in pacifying belligerent indigenous inhabitants simply by showing them the picture. Hence its name, *La Pacificadora* (the peacemaker). In 1606, the entire temple collapsed, but fortunately, the picture sustained no damage.

Bandstand in the Plaza de las Américas

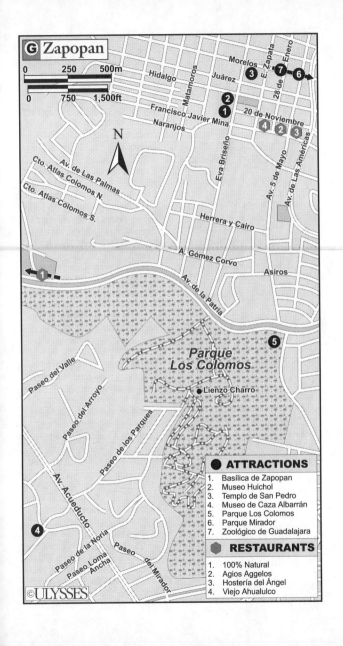

G Zapopan

0   250   500m
0   750   1,500ft

Hidalgo
Morelos
Juárez
Matamoros
3
E. Zapata
28 de Enero
7 **6**

Francisco Javier Mina
2
1
20 de Noviembre
4 **2** **3**

Naranjos
Eva Briseño

N

Av. de Las Palmas
Cto. Atlas Colomos N.
Cto. Atlas Colomos S.

Av. 5 de Mayo
Av. de Las Américas

Herrera y Cairo

A. Gómez Corvo

Av. de la Patria
Asiros

1

Parque Los Colomos
5

Paseo del Valle
Paseo del Arroyo
Paseo de los Parques

• Lienzo Charro

Av. Acueducto

4

Paseo de la Noria
Paseo Loma Ancha
Paseo del Mirador

● **ATTRACTIONS**
1. Basílica de Zapopan
2. Museo Huichol
3. Templo de San Pedro
4. Museo de Caza Albarrán
5. Parque Los Colomos
6. Parque Mirador
7. Zoológico de Guadalajara

⬡ **RESTAURANTS**
1. 100% Natural
2. Agios Aggelos
3. Hostería del Ángel
4. Viejo Ahualulco

©ULYSSES

Miraculous cures and other marvels were attributed to the picture, including curtailing a lethal epidemic that would have ravaged Guadalajara. The virgin was thus named Guadalajara's patron saint against storms and epidemics. Since then, tradition has held that the Virgin visit the 130 parishes of the metropolitan area for six months and that she return to her temple on October 12. She is currently followed by over one million believers who welcome her. Attentive visitors will surely notice the many replicas of the Virgin sold in the city's small souvenir shops.

You can therefore see the picture inside the basilica from mid-October to mid-April. Though the picture of the Virgin Mary is small and rather humble, a series of enrichments adorn it, including a silver cup decorated with pearls. To pay homage to her title of Reina de Jalisco (queen of Jalisco), she holds a gold cane and a blue ribbon. A small chest, also made of gold, underlines her role as the patron saint of commercial travellers.

Those interested in the traditions of indigenous peoples will certainly want to stop at the **Museo Huichol** ★ ★ *($6; Tue to Sun 9am to 2pm and 4pm to 7pm)*, located to the right of the main entrance of the basilica. Here you will discover a fascinating showroom of crafts and clothes made by natives from the northern part of the state of Jalisco.

Your tour continues down Calle Morelos. A little farther stands the **Templo de San Pedro Apóstol** ★, a small neoclassical church that dates from the end of the Spanish regime. Inside, art lovers will be able to enjoy a painting by Juan Correa, an important 17th-century painter. Zapopan's **city hall** is just a stone's throw away. This neoclassical building blends in well with the district's architecture.

No hunting enthusiast will want to miss the **Museo de Caza Albarrán** ★ *($20; Sun 10am to 3pm, other days by appointment, Paseo de los Parques no. 3530, corner Circuito Madrigal, Colinas de San Javier, ☎641-5122)*. This hunting paradise features the extraordinary private collection of hunter Benito Albarrán, a renowned taxidermist. The magnificent trophies that are exhibited come from five continents and are mounted in settings simulating the animals' natural habitat. The museum's facade, which is a reproduction of a Sudanese home, is unique to Mexico.

If you want to take a break during your tour, we recommend you head to the **Parque Los Colomos** ★★ *($3, every day 6am to 6pm; horse rentals; Avenida Patria, near the intersection with Avenida Alberta, ☎641-3804, see p 129)*. This spacious park features the streams that supplied Guadalajara with water in the early 20th century. Three old buildings, **El Castillo, El Colector Curiel** and **La Torre del Vigía**, are great examples of the public-works style that was popular at that time. El Castillo, a quaint structure embellished with two small crenellated towers, currently houses an important cultural centre *(☎642-0132)*. Nature lovers will especially enjoy the attractions of the Parque Los Colomos. Serenity and simplicity, traits characteristic of the Far East, also characterize the **Jardín Japonés**, a gift form the city of Kyoto to Guadalajara, its

twin city, in 1994. The **Lago de las Aves** features several bird species and the **Reino del Sol** features an interesting botanical garden specializing in cacti.

Among the natural attractions surrounding Guadalajara, the **Parque Mirador Dr. Atl** ★★★ *($2; every day; Carretera a Saltillo Km 15)* is no doubt one of the most impressive. By crossing through the small garden next to the entrance, you will come to an enormous overhanging balcony that seems to be suspended in mid-air. From this belvedere, you can view the majestic **Cola de Caballo** ★★★ waterfall, which falls 150m (490ft) into the Río Santiago. Though it flows year-round, it is most abundant during the rainy season. Take the time to enjoy this long cascade and the surrounding scenery, which features exuberant tropical vegetation.

Parrots

If you are pressed for time or wish to enjoy another lovely view from a different angle, take advantage of the belvedere at the **Parque Mirador Independencia** ★★★ *($2; every day 6am to 7pm; Calzada Independencia Norte s/n)*, better known as the **Barranca de Huentitán**, which is located at the end of Calzada Independencia. This canyon, 550m (1,800ft)

Exploring

deep, runs along the Río Santiago and takes the name **Barranca de Oblatos** a little farther. We recommend that the bravest explorers take advantage of guided tours in the Barranca, offered by the municipal police force, in co-operation with forest rangers *(free admission; Policía Municipal de Guadalajara, Departamento de Relaciones Públicas, ☎638-0683)*. By leaving from Camino de Herradura, a cobblestone road used in the 16th century by mule-drivers to transport goods, you will discover pre-Columbian vestiges, plants unknown outside of the Barranca and a bridge built in the style that was popular around 100 years ago.

Your tour of Guadalajara finally ends north of the city on Calzada Independencia, just before the Parque Mirador. This perfect spot of many discoveries includes Guadalajara's zoo, a recreational park and the planetarium. At the **Zoológico de Guadalajara** ★★★ *($22; Wed to Sun 10am to 6pm; restaurant, souvenir shop; Calzada Independencia, corner Paseo el Zoológico, ☎674-4488)*, which is home to over 500 animals, you can enjoy an aviary that is home to tropical bird species, another one housing birds of prey, and the biggest herpetorium (snake vivar-

ium) in Latin America. Do not miss the *nocturnario*, set up in a building next to the Barranca de Huentitán. In this natural setting, which recreates nocturnal wildlife, you can observe animals in Barranca's natural habitat. If you don't feel like walking, a small train is available which tours this big zoo. If you decide to take it, you won't be disappointed.

Tour H: San Pedro Tlaquepaque and Tonalá

San Pedro Tlaquepaque

Indigenous peoples have lived in Tlaquepaque since the 13th century, yet there are no traces of this period. The Spanish arrived in 1530 and three years later, the Franciscans began to evangelize the inhabitants. Considering its strategic location on the road between Mexico City and Guadalajara, Tlaquepaque quickly became a mandatory transit point for important figures at the time. Travelling civil and ecclesiastical authorities were greeted by elaborate processions featuring lively

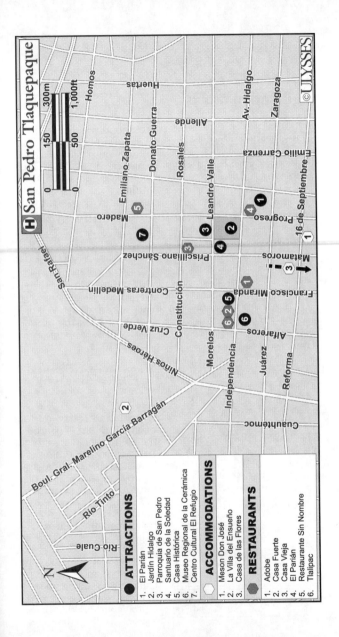

San Pedro Tlaquepaque

ATTRACTIONS

1. El Parián
2. Jardín Hidalgo
3. Parroquia de San Pedro
4. Santuario de la Soledad
5. Casa Histórica
6. Museo Regional de la Cerámica
7. Centro Cultural El Refugio

ACCOMMODATIONS

1. Meson Don José
2. La Villa del Ensueño
3. Casa de las Flores

RESTAURANTS

1. Adobe
2. Casa Fuerte
3. Casa Vieja
4. El Parián
5. Restaurante Sin Nombre
6. Tlalipac

© ULYSSES

Tapatian Crafts

During a visit to Tlaquepaque or Tonalá, you cannot help but notice the abundance and variety of local crafts. Various types of crafts developed in Jalisco several centuries before the arrival of the Spanish. Clay, leather, bird feathers, and precious stones and metals were commonly used by indigenous peoples to create beautiful objects for everyday use, ornamentation or religious practices.

These ancestral traditions were transformed and enriched by new elements, techniques and customs brought by the Conquista. Today, Jalisco has a great craft tradition and its talented craftspeople produce every item imaginable. Their art features a variety of materials and objects such as ceramics, blown glass, papier maché, lumber, leather, wrought iron and silver.

musicians, who accompanied them from there to the capital of New Galicia. Since then, Tlaquepaque has maintained a festive atmosphere. The neighbourhood was named San Pedro Tlaquepaque in honour of Pedro Gómez de Maraver, the first bishop of the diocese of Guadalajara. At the end of the colonial regime, the document proclaiming New Galicia's independence was signed in Tlaquepaque on June 13, 1821. The first stagecoach from Mexico City passed through the village in 1855, and at the end of the century, the bourgeois of Guadalajara chose to build a number of beautiful secondary residences in Tlaquepaque.

Tlaquepaque, nicknamed *villa alfarera* (potters' village), is located 7km (4mi) southeast of downtown Guadalajara. Today, this old neighbourhood is part of the metropolitan area, but being true to its calling, Tlaquepaque is still inhabited by craftspeople. A picturesque setting surrounds this small city where tradition is lived daily and a bohemian atmosphere reigns.

To enter Tlaquepaque, one of Mexico's most important craft centres, take Calle Juárez to Calle Herrera y Cairo. Your exploration of the area begins with a walk around **El Parián** ★ (see p 183), an interesting building housing restaurants around a large central garden.

Your visit continues on Calle Independencia. You will find an interesting selection of shops under the **arcades** of this pedestrian street. The **Jardín Hidalgo** ★ is just a stone's throw away. This pleasant green space is especially busy on Sundays. At Christmastime, locals organize traditional *pastorelas* (jokes or comedies alluding to the birth of Christ, introduced by the Spanish in the 16th century).

Though the neighbourhood has few extraordinary attractions, it is fascinating to stroll about to discover its traditional Mexican charm. Take some time to explore the streets, and you will be surprised to discover magnificent gardens and craft workshops hidden behind the facades of houses that seem to hold little interest. **Parroquia de San Pedro** ★, a church built at the start of the 20th century, is located on the same side as Calle Morelos. Its extremely simple facade is adorned with a few baroque elements and is crowned with a statue of St. Peter. A little farther on Calle Morelos stands the **Santuario de la Soledad** ★, a church featuring a mix of styles characteristic of the 19th century. You can then return to Calle Independencia, which is a great place to wander; those who appreciate handmade crafts will be in heaven. The street is lined with beautiful bourgeois homes that were converted into elegant shops offering an endless variety of quality goods. If you would like to visit a blown-glass workshop, you can get in touch with craftspeople at no. 163 Casa Camarasa, to make an appointment (the workshop is located outside Tlaquepque's town centre). At no. 208, the facade of the **Casa Histórica** ★ (the house where the patriots of Jalisco proclaimed New Galicia's independence), is worth a visit. Those who appreciate ceramic will no doubt want to stop at the **Museo Regional de la Cerámica** ★★ *(free admission; 10am to 6pm Tue to Sun; Calle Independencia no.237, ☎635-5404).* This museum houses a collection particularly rich in works produced according to Tlaquepaque tradition, as well as the ancient cuisine of the residence, which dates from the 19th century. You can also visit the **Museo del Premio Nacional de la Cerámica Pantaleón Panduro** ★, located inside the **Centro Cultural El Refugio** *(free admission; Tue to Sun*

Exploring

*9am to 7pm; Calle Donato
Guerra no. 160, ☎635-1089),*
a lovely building built in
1859 to house a hospital.
Today, the Centro Cultural
offers a wide range of interesting cultural activities.

While visiting Tlaquepaque
is pleasant any time of year,
we recommend you go
between June 15 and early
July, during the village's
fiesta. Among the many
events organized for the
occasion, folklore shows, a
mariachi festival, craft exhibits and especially a national ceramic contest, are
not to be missed.

Tonalá

Tonalá was an important
trade area well before the
arrival of the Spanish. Its
inhabitants produced all
sorts of clay objects that
they traded for vegetables
and grains. In the 16th century, Tonalá became the
county seat of Tonallan, the
seigneury that ruled over
the Atemajac Valley. In
1530, Queen Cihualpilli
greeted conquistador Nuño
de Guzmán, the president
of the Audience of New
Spain and founder of the
Kingdom of New Galicia. At
the same time, another
group of Spaniards first
founded Guadalajara on
Cascane territory, on the

spot of Nochistlán (100km
or 62mi from the current
city), but later moved it to
Tonalá in 1533, site of
Guadalajara's second founding, since they were being
watched by the native in-
habitants. The city was finally moved to its current
location in 1542 and Tonalá
lost its political and strategic
importance.

Today, Tonalá is an important suburb of Guadalajara,
located 14km (9mi) south-
east of the town centre.
Despite its proximity, this
picturesque historic place
has maintained its rural
charm. In addition to some
mining, Tonalá's economy
revolves around crafts, notably the production and
marketing of an extraordinary variety of clay goods.
On Thursdays and Sundays,
the village's streets come
alive with a large craft market (see p 219).

The road linking
Guadalajara and Tonalá
turns into Avenida
Tonaltecas at the entrance
to the village. Follow this
route, which is bordered by
workshops and boutiques,
until you reach Calle Pedro
Moreno, where you will
turn right. It will lead you
to the main square, a pleasant garden embellished by
a lovely stand with stone
arches. To the left stands
the **Santuario del Sagrado
Corazón ★**, an interesting

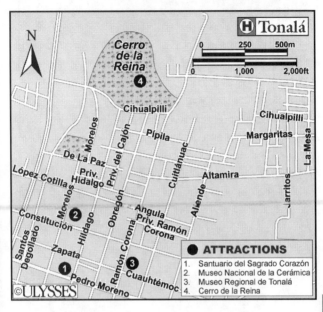

Tonalá

N		0	250	500m
		0	1,000	2,000ft

Cerro de la Reina ④

Cihualpilli

Cihualpilli

Pípila

Margaritas

De La Paz

Morelos

Priv. del Cajón

Cuitláhuac

Altamira

López Cotilla

Priv. Hidalgo

Allende

La Mesa

Jarritos

Constitución

Morelos

Obregón

Angula

Priv. Ramón Corona

Ramón Corona

② Hidalgo

Santos Degollado

Zapata

③

Cuauhtémoc

① Pedro Moreno

©ULYSSES

● **ATTRACTIONS**

1. Santuario del Sagrado Corazón
2. Museo Nacional de la Cerámica
3. Museo Regional de Tonalá
4. Cerro de la Reina

example of the Gothic revival style that was popular in Mexico towards the end of the 19th century. You will no doubt notice that the contours of its facade are reminiscent of those of the gothic cathedrals of Europe, though simplified and adapted to a semi-tropical climate. This place's charm is crowned by the **Presidencia Municipal**, a neo-colonial building, and the **Parroquia de Santiago Apóstol** ★, a lovely 17th century church.

Those interested in the architecture of religious buildings can stop at the former convent next to the church.

Inside, you will discover Medieval-like gargoyles that crown the cloister. From here, you can take any street to continue your visit. The pleasure of exploring Tonalá lies in discovering the heart of western Mexico's craft production through pure chance. By strolling along its streets, bordered by workshops and small boutiques, you may meet craftspeople at work in their homes.

Though you don't need an itinerary to visit the village, you can always visit the two museums exhibiting interesting collections: the **Museo Nacional de la**

Exploring

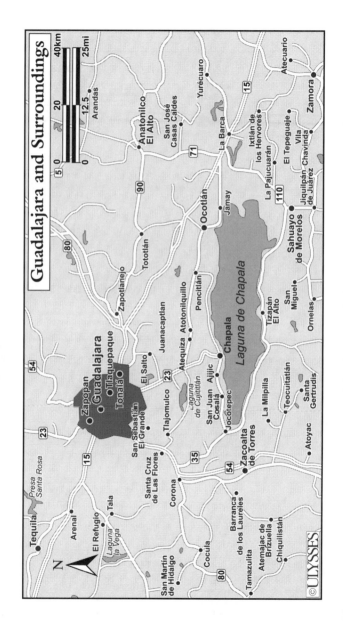

Guadalajara and Surroundings

40km
25mi

20
12.5

5 0
0

Arandas

Anatonilco
El Alto

San José
Casas Caldes

Yurécuaro

15

La Barca

Ixtlán de
los Hervores

Zamora

Atecuario

El Tepeguaje

Vila
de Juárez

71

Jiquilpán
de Juárez

110

Sahuayo
de Morelos

Ornelas

90

Ocotlán

Jamay

La Pajucuarán

Chavinda

Tototlán

Zapotlanejo

80

Juanacaptlan

Pencitlán

Chapala
Laguna de Chapala

Tizapán
El Alto

San
Miguel

54

Zapopan
Guadalajara
Tlaquepaque
Tonalá

El Salto

23

Atequiza Atotoniquillo

laguna
de Cujitlán

San Juan Ajijic
Cosalá

Jocótepec

La Milpilla

Teocuitlatán

Santa
Gertrudis

San Sebastián
El Grande

Tlajomulco

Zacoalta
de Torres

23

15

Santa Cruz
de Las Flores

Corona

35

54

Atoyac

Presa
Santa Rosa

Tequila

Arenal

Tala

Laguna
la Vega

El Refugio

San Martín
de Hidalgo

Cocula

80

Barranca
de los Laureles

Atemajac de
Brizuella

Chiquilistán

Tamazulita

N

© ULYSSES

Cerámica ★ *(free admission, Tue to Sun* 10am to 5pm; *Calle Constitución, between Hidalgo and Morelos no. 110,* ☎*683-0494)*, which has 10 rooms devoted to the exhibition and sale of clay and ceramic objects from all the regions of Mexico, and the **Museo Regional de Tonalá ★** *(free admission, Tue to Sun 10am to 5pm, Calle Ramón Corona, between Cuauhtémoc and Constitución)* a rustic village residence built with sun-dried clay bricks. This house, which was converted into a museum reflecting a traditional Tonaltec atmosphere, features an interesting showroom of local goods. Finally, if you enjoy walking and want to take in a magnificent view of the Atemajac Valley, we suggest you make a detour on **Cerro de la Reina ★★★**, located at the end of Calle Hidalgo. The summit of this hill is crowned with a small stone church and a monument to Queen Cihualpilli commemorating the battle between Tonaltec rebels and the army of conquistador Nuño de Guzmán in 1530. This belvedere, from where visitors can grasp the complexity of Greater Guadalajara, should not be missed.

While Tonalá attracts visitors year-round, visiting the city on July 25 is particularly fascinating because this is the day St. Jacques,

the village's patron saint, is celebrated. On this day, visitors will enjoy a multitude of activities. The **danza de los Tastoanes ★★★**, is worth special attention. This dance, which dates from the conquest of New Spain, represents the battle between the Spanish and the Tastoanes rebels. Under the leadership of St. Jacques, who mounts a horse brandishing a sword, the army of Nuño de Guzmán fight against the natives, who sport masks and wigs. After several hours of fighting, the natives win the battle and elect the person who will have the honour of interpreting the role of St. Jacques the following year. The fiesta ends with *castillos* (traditional Mexican firecrackers).

Tour I: Laguna de Chapala

The shores of Laguna de Chapala, Mexico's largest lake, were one of the first regions inhabited in the western part of the country. Arrowheads found near the lake indicate that nomadic peoples arrived here around 6,000 years ago. It was only in the 12th century, however, that non-nomadic inhabitants settled here. At the time, indige-

Exploring

nous peoples of Aztec origin founded the seigneury of Chapallan on the north shore. When the Spanish arrived in the 16th century, Franciscan chronicler Antonio Tella described the region as quite populated. Monks began evangelizing natives and built churches and convents at Chapala and Ajijic. Towards the end of the 19th century, Mexican and immigrant bourgeoisie discovered a lovely spot by the lake that was surrounded by hills. They built beautiful residences in Chapala and this peaceful fishing village developed little by little. It grew rapidly as a vacation destina-

tion when President Porfirio Díaz spent his vacations here, from 1904 to 1909. The inauguration of the railway linking Chapala and Guadalajara contributed considerably to the city's growth.

Located 48km (30mi) south of Guadalajara, Chapala has been a source of inspiration for poets, musicians and painters since the 19th century. Its natural setting, enhanced by a year-round spring-like climate, makes it a prized vacation spot. It has seduced a large number of foreigners who have settled on the banks of this big lake, measuring

1,690km² (652 sq mi).
Among the historic figures
who have lived in Chapala
is English writer D.H. Law-
rence, who wrote *Plumed
Serpent* here. According to
the U.S. consulate's archives
in Guadalajara, one thou-
sand Americans lived in
Guadalajara by the begin-
ning of the 20th century.
There are currently 30,000
Americans, 13,000 Cana-
dians and a certain number
of Europeans who list their
permanent residence as
Guadalajara. The commu-
nity of expatriates doubles
in winter.

The presence of a number
of artists at the heart of the
community has fuelled the
region's cultural life. The
Music Appreciation Society
organizes a concert season
in winter in the concert
halls of **El Auditorio del Lago**
in Ajijic, and offers a bus
service to the Teatro
Degollado in Guadalajara
during opera season. **The
Lakeside Little Theatre** has
regularly performed
English-language shows for
more than 20 years. Several
painters, engravers,
sculptors and
photogra-
phers organize
exhibits and
internships in
associations
such as the
Ajijic Society of the Arts
and the CABA (Centro
Ajijic de Bellas Artes).

★★
Chapala

Your tour of Chapala begins
at the **Presidencia
Municipal ★**, an interesting
building on the corner of
Calle Madero and Calle
Hidalgo, featuring a style
popular at the beginning of
the 20th century. A stone's
throw away, still on Calle
Madero, stands the **Hotel
Nido ★★**, built in 1902,
whose facade blends in
with that of the Prese-
dencia. There is an extraordinary collection of ancient
photographs mounted on
the walls of the lobby. You
will be surprised to discover
sailboats sailing on the lake
at a time when Chapala was
considered a fishing port.

The **Parroquia de San Francisco de Asís**, which dates
from the 18th century,
stands a little farther
down, on the other
side of the street. Its
asymetrical towers,
crowned with a
pointed roof cov-
ered in tiles, are
reminiscent of
Guadalajara's
cathedral. Don't
miss the famous **Casa
Braniff ★** (today the
Restaurant
Cazadores), an an-
cient European-
looking villa which

Pelican

Exploring

The Resorts of Lago de Chapala

Guadalajara's climate, which is exceptionally hot year-round, is a true blessing for Mexicans living there. It is not uncommon for temperatures to reach 35°C (95°F).

Lago de Chapala's aquatic parks will help you cope with the intense heat. These *balnearios* offer a number of activities for the whole family, including water slides, thermal springs and aquatic sports. The village of San Juan Cosalá has a long tradition of attracting visitors seeking fresh air. Since the beginning of the 20th century, this resort has accommodated visitors drawn by its therapeutic waters. The villages of Acatlán de Juárez, Villa Corona and Ajijic are also great destinations for swimmers.

As for thermal springs, water slides and other nautical activities, **Chimulco** (*$3.50, every day 8am to 6pm; 0.5km or 0.3mi from Camino Real Estipac, Villa Corona,* ☎778-0014) and **Agua Caliente** (*$2; every day 8am to 6pm; 58km or 36mi on Barra de Navidad, Villa Corona,* ☎778-0022) in Villa Corona, are interesting. **Tobolandia** (*$4; every day 10am to 6pm; 57 Boulevardo Ajijic, Chapala,* ☎766-2120) has heated pools and gigantic water slides and is the largest resort of its kind in the region. **Las Alberquitas** (*$1.20; every day 9am to 7pm; Prolongacíon Zaragoza, Acatlán de Juárez,* ☎772-0065) is another option and features pools, a forest and a campground.

has become a symbol of Chapala, on the corner of Calle Madero and Calle Ramón Corona.

Calle Madero begins at the **Malecón** ★ (promenade) and the quay, which is 130m (39ft) long. Located between a small beach and the **Parque Ramón Corona**, this district definitely has its charm. If you love boat tours, sailors offer various options. We recommend that history buffs not miss the outing to the **Isla de Mezcala (Isla del Presidio)** ★★★, located around 25km (15.5mi) east of Chapala. A **penal colony** was built on this island (the lake's largest) towards the end of the colonial regime. With the island having been turned into a **fortress** during the War of Independence, Mexican patriots defended it valiantly for four years, but were defeated following a long siege. You can study the parapets, defensive walls and neo-classical portal of this historic building, which is covered by exuberant semi-tropical vegetation. Just a stone's throw from here lie the ruins of a small stone church, which will surely catch your eye.

Continue your tour of Chapala with a pleasant stroll down Calle Ramón Corona. By leaving Calle Madero, you will be able to enjoy a few **beautiful French-style hotels**, reminiscent of a time when Chapala attracted a cosmopolitan bourgeoisie. Finally, your visit ends at the **former train station** ★★, located at the intersection of Avenida Cristianía and Avenida de la Estación. This interesting

building, located by the lake and built at the end of the First World War, had a dual role: it housed a port for small steamships put into service between different ports in the region in 1885, as well as a train station serving the Chapala-Guadalajara line. Its facade, which is a mix between the Edwardian and Art Deco styles, is worth the detour. The area's two biggest traditional fiestas are the **carnival** and **St. François**, the city's patron saint, celebrated between late September and October 4.

Ajijic

This picturesque riverside village, with paved roads and colourful houses, is located 7km (4mi) from Chapala. When you arrive, take Calle Colón, the village's main artery, which leads to the **main square** ★★. The bandstand is surrounded by iron benches shaded by huge, leafy trees. Take a minute to sit down and enjoy the change of scenery offered by this traditional village, which brings you back to the Mexico of old. The **Capilla del Rosario**, a 17th century chapel, can be viewed on the northern side of the square. One street down stands the **Parroquia** de San Andrés ★★ on Calle Marcos Castellanos. It dates from the same century as the chapel. The front of the church, which is built in stone and features a white facade decorated with yellow contours, serves as the setting for the portrayal of Jesus's trial and crucifixion, during the last three days of the Holy Week. Come back towards Calle Colón and go down a few streets towards the Lago. You will reach the **Malecón ★** (promenade) and the quay which offer a magnificent view of the lake. The peaceful life of Ajijic undergoes a dramatic transformation during the fiesta of **St. André**, the village's patron saint. These nine days of *fiesta* hit their peak on November 30 with the *castillos*.

Tour J: Tequila and Surroundings

Tiquiles, a people of Aztec origin, founded a native seigneury in the region of Tequila before the arrival of the Spanish. Many clay and stone tools found at Teochichán, their capital, illustrate the life of these inhabitants. In 1530, Cristóbal de Oñate conquered the natives, while the Franciscans took care of their evangelization. At the time, the region's economy was based on agriculture and cattle breeding. In 1600, Don Pedro Sánchez de Tagle, marquis of Altamira, set up the first tequila distillery. This industry quickly became the main activity of local *haciendas* and the hills were covered with blue agaves (*agave azul tequilana weber*), The main ingredient in tequila. Elegant colonial residences were built and this small city's profile developed little by little. At the start of the War of Independence, Tequila was the main district of the region's operations.

Today, Tequila attracts visitors from around the world. This home of the famous drink of the same name, located at the foot of the extinct Tequila volcano, 50km (31mi) northwest of Guadalajara, is an attraction not to be missed.

Tequila

The pleasure of discovering Tequila lies in exploring its streets and uncovering its charm. The main square features the **Templo de Santiago Apóstol ★**, which was

Tequila Distilleries

A day in Tequila would not be complete without visiting one of the city's many distilleries. Guided tours of distilleries other than those offered by the *Tequila Express* (see p 53) are available. They include a visit to the blue agave fields and cover distillation and the maturation process, as well as the history of Mexico's national drink. Guided tours in Spanish and English, subsidized by the State of Jalisco, leave from the tourism bureau on the hour *($2.50; every day 10am to 5pm)* and head directly to the distillery. Tours organized by distilleries begin at their respective plants on the hour. **José Cuervo** and **Sauza** *($2; Mon to Sat 9am to 2pm; duration: 1hr,* ☎742-0050*)*, the two largest distilleries, stand side by side, two blocks north of the Plaza. Each visit ends with a tasting of the best the city has to offer.

built in the 17th century with opal stones from the mines of the neighbouring village of Magdalena, and is adorned with a baroque facade. An amusing natural phenomenon can be witnessed from the front of this church every day: just before sunset, at around 5pm, the **Volcano de aire ★**, tiny whirlwinds caused by the unique configuration of the buildings on the square, begin to stir up. Right across from here stands the **Capilla de los Desamparados**, a neo-colonial church built towards 1950.

By continuing to the left of the Templo de Santiago, you will reach the **Plaza de Armas**, a pleasant square adorned with a bandstand of French design. To the northeast, you will notice a colonial hotel which houses the **Museo Recinto Javier Sauza Mora ★** *(voluntary donation; Mon to Sat 10am to 2pm, Sat and Sun 10am to 5pm; craft shop; Albino Rojas no. 47,* ☎742-0247*)*. This museum features an interesting exhibit on the Sauza distillery. A mural featuring old French-made stills and tools that were used in the past, helps visitors understand the process and development of the tequila industry. The superb wooden desk of the former distill-

Exploring

ery, dating from 1870, is worth special attention.

A little farther lies the **former producers' district ★**, as well as important distilleries, which makes for an interesting stroll. Visitors will immediately notice the smell of cooked agave. Take the time to admire the beautiful facades of the residences that border its streets. At 7am, 3pm and 8pm, you will hear the *silbato*, the whistle that indicates the changing of distillery worker shifts. At night, the neighbourhood lights up for the pleasure of strollers and the atmosphere is relaxed. The tourist information office (☎742-1819), located on the Plaza de Armas, at the entrance to city hall, offers a choice of guided tours (in Spanish, French or English) of distilleries, including tastings. If you want to visit an agave plantation, stop at the **Rancho El Indio ★★**, located on the road to Magdalena, at the exit of the city. Finally, we recommend you visit Tequila with the **Tequila Express** (see p 53).

Magdalena

Located 30km (19mi) west of Tequila, Magdalena is especially known for its opal production. In addition to the 17th century Franciscan church **El Señor de los Milagros ★**, Magdalena's main attraction lies in the possibility of visiting an opal mine. You will be handed a hammer and should you find a pretty stone, it is yours to keep. If you are looking for a different kind of experience, a detour through Magdalena is for you. **Ópalos de México ★★★** *(free admission; Mon to Sat 9am to 8pm, Sun 9am to 2pm; guided tours of a mine in Spanish or English by appointment; Independencia no. 115, ☎/≈744-0447)* features an extraordinary selection of products worth a close look, which can be purchased.

The Aztecs appreciated this semi-precious iridescent stone, which they named *vitzitziltecpatl* (hummingbird stone). The Aztec sun god, an extremely large opal from the pre-Columbian period, was part of the famous collection of precious Hope stones, which was purchased by the Chicago Museum of Natural History in 1881 and later integrated into the Tiffany collection. Magdalena's mining activity ceased during the colonial regime, but was renewed towards 1840. There are currently 200 opal mines in the region, as well as turquoise and agate mines.

Tour K: Tapalpa and the Mountain

The sierra was inhabited well before the arrival of the Spanish and even that of the Aztecs. The huge stones engraved with prehistoric symbols located at the entrance to Tepec confirm that humans lived here around 6,000 years ago. At the current location of Tapalpa, natives of Aztec origin founded the village of Tlacpacpan towards the 12th century. The region was conquered by Alonso de Ávalos in 1523 and, shortly thereafter, Franciscan monks began to shape the spiritual life of the natives.

During the colonial regime, gold and silver mines in the Sierra de Tapalpa drew adventurers seeking riches, but the mines were quickly exhausted. Iron was then exploited, as can be attested by Ferrería de Tula, a smelting works dating from that period.

Following independence, La Constancia, the first pulp and paper factory of its kind in Latin America, was built near the village. Opened in 1840, this industrialization attempt was managed by an Englishman from Manchester. Today, the region's economy is based on cattle breeding, dairy products and tourism.

The picturesque village of **Tapalpa** ★ ★ ★, "the land of colours" according to Aztec etymology, is 90min south of Guadalajara. Located at the heart of the western Sierra Madre mountains 2,560m (8,400ft) above sea level, this charming village of 5,000 residents, is surrounded by green woodlands and gurgling brooks.

Upon your arrival on the main square, you will be surprised to discover its beautiful white residences with wooden balconies decorated with geraniums, reminiscent of Swiss villages. You can begin your stroll, in this setting where tradition lives on, from the ancient parish church, **San Antonio de Padua** ★. Its plateresque facade, built by Franciscan monks at the end of the 17th century, features two columns and an arch: an extremely simple, though very elegant design.

Right across from here stands a new brick church, whose traditional style blends in well with the local architecture.

Go up the stairs to Calle Hidalgo and take a right. After a few minutes of walking, you will come

Exploring

upon **La Pila del Pescado ★**, the first of five small *pila* fountains dating from the end of the 19th century, that feature a patch with the image of a sculpted animal. The quaint fountains, which are enveloped in colourful legends, identify each region of Tapalpa. Go down Calle Zarapoza to reach the small **Plaza El Fresnito ★**. Another fountain, **La Pila Las Culebras ★**, lies to your right. Walk down Calle Vicente Guerrero a few metres, then down Calle Madero, near **La Pila Colorada ★**, to the **Nuestra Señora de la Merced ★** church, whose style is a mix between neo-classical and baroque elements. Trek back to the main square to explore the local shops.

Outdoor enthusiasts will not want to miss hiking in Tapalpa's surroundings. Secluded in magnificent scenery a few kilometres from the village, lie the imposing ruins of a structure reminiscent of the English industrial revolution. This unexpected discovery is **La Constancia ★**, an old pulp and paper factory built in the 19th century. It is easily accessible on horseback (horse rentals in Tapalpa around the main square),

but it is also pleasant to get there on foot. **Las Piedrotas ★**, the gigantic stones chiselled by the elements of nature and mysteriously dropped in an open field, lie a little farther.

For those who are more daring, reaching the remains of **La Ferrería de Tula ★**, located 23km (14mi) from Tapalpa, is a good hiking challenge. During the winter, amateur ornithologists should make sure to take a trip to the **Canada goose observation station** *(Chen caerulescens)* organized by the university of Guadalajara at Atoyac *(upon reservation with the Departamento de Ciencias Ambientales, laboratorio de Sayula, ☎682-0374, ext. 152, ⊶682-0072, g_barba@yahoo.com).*

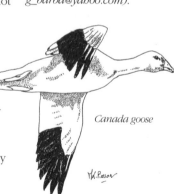

Canada goose

Outdoors

W ith its urban complexity and pervasive pollution, Jalisco's metropolis hardly lends itself to outdoor activities.

C ycling and in-line skating are not only difficult here, they are downright dangerous in the infernal traffic that clogs the city's streets. Fortunately, the city has many parks, primarily concentrated in the beautiful northwestern districts, where sports can be enjoyed readily enough. But as a general rule, sports enthusiasts will have to rely on one of the various fitness centres, most of which are located in Minerva's major hotels, or golf courses and nature reserves outside the city.

Parks

Tour F: La Minerva

Parque Los Colomos *(access via Calle Chaco no. 3200 or*

Avenida Patria no. 1805, Col. Providencia), located in the very heart of the Providencia district, is considered one of the city's "green lungs." As far back as 1597, this natural area was exploited by the building of the Castillo, a water tower that supplied the city's aqueduct with water. Reforested and laid out as a park in 1902, this huge oasis of relaxation (140ha or 346 acres, of which 40ha or 99 acres are wooded) is still home to the Castillo (Casa de las Bombas), as well as a cultural centre and an artificial lake. The south part of the park features many trails ideal for lovely strolls or a brisk morning jog. To the north, a wilder area offers year-round urban camping.

Tour G: Zapopan

Parque Mirador Independencia *(every day 6am to 7pm; last stretch of Calzada, Independencia)* is a huge nature reserve made up of a 500m-deep (1,640ft) canyon carved out by the Río Santiago. The park features many footpaths that will introduce you to extraordinary flora, such as beautiful jasmine, daisy and rose gardens. A circuitous route links seven lookouts that offer unobstructed views of the whole canyon, and a

Roses

1,900m-long (6,234ft) cableway gives you a unique opportunity to enjoy a bird's-eye view of the ravine and marvel at the surrounding wilderness. Pleasant picnic areas have been laid out, some of which feature a barbecue and restaurants, while others boast an outdoor theatre.

Providing a nice change from the usual Sunday stroll and, above all, delighting young and old alike, **Parque Alcalde** *(access via Calle Mariano Bárcenas, near Calle Jesús García)* and the **Zoológico de Guadalajara** (see p 112) both offer year-round funfair facilities.

Located on the northern confines of Zapopan, the **Bosque de la Primavera** *(access at Km 20 on Carretera Guadalajara-Tepic-Puerto Vallarta, Hwy. 15)* is considered another one of the city's "green lungs." The conifer forest that covers practically its entire hilly territory is a beautiful place for lovely strolls or a day of picnicking in the great outdoors. The forest is also home to the Universidad de Guadalajara's sports facilities, which means you can play volleyball or swim for a minimal fee. What's more, you can also enjoy a wonderful dip in the hot springs, at a steady temperature of 40°C (104°F).

Tour H: San Pedro Tlaquepaque and Tonalá

Inaugurated during the first Iberian-American Summit, **Parque de la Solidaridad'Iberoamericana** *(Mon to Fri 10am to 5pm, Sat and Sun 8am to 6pm; Avenida Malecón, Tetlán)* is one of the largest parks in Latin America, with its 110ha (272 acres) of greenery. In their spare time, hundreds of Tapatios flock here in the afternoon to practise sports or simply relax. Moreover, the park also features a soccer stadium, a motocross track and even a train with panoramic windows.

Tour I: Laguna de Chapala

Today, Chapala looks like a slightly outdated seaside resort where old, once-prestigious hotels and mansions bear witness to the lakeside town's heyday. On the road that separates the town from Ajijic is a still very vibrant former seaside resort, the **Tobolandia** water park *(20 pesos; every day 10am to 6pm; Boulevard Ajijic no. 57, Chapala, ☎ 766-2120)*, whose scores of pools and water slides will delight one and all on sweltering summer days.

Tour K: Tapalpa and the Mountain

Located about 1.5hrs from Tapalpa, near the village of Las Moras, the **Salto de Nogal** *(from Tapalpa, take the road to Atacco, then to Cafradía and finally to Barranca, where excursions start)* is the highest waterfall in the entire state of Jalisco. The trail leading to the falls will introduce you to the treasures of the local flora. Be careful, though, as this trail is relatively difficult; it is therefore advised that you be accompanied by a guide. North of Tapalpa lies **Las Piedrotas** *(from Tapalpa, take the road to Chiquilistlán for a few kilometres)*, also known as Valle de los Enigmas ("valley of the enigmas"), a strange field strewn with enormous stones whose origins remain a mystery.

Outdoor Activities

Sports Clubs

There are many sports clubs in the metropolitan area and it's no secret that Jaliscans are great *fútbol* fans. In fact, every neighbourhood has its own soccer field. In Guadalajara,

Outdoors

perhaps even more than in the rest of the country, this sport has a large following. Every year, the Chivas, the local professional soccer team, ranks among the most serious claimants to the national title. Visitors looking to stay in shape during their stay will have a difficult time of it, however, as there are still very few facilities catering to their needs. Listed below are a few clubs where you can practise various sports.

Club Deportivo Universidad de Guadalajara
Francisco de Quevedo no. 175
☎*615-6725*

Squash Club & Gym
Avenida México no. 2530
☎*616-4577*
Squash, judo, body-building and gymnastics.

Club Olympia
Calderón de la Barca no. 129
between La Paz and L. Cotilla
☎*615-7859*
Swimming, squash, aerobics, karate and body-building.

World Gym
Jesús García no. 804
at Miguel Angel de Quevedo
Col. Providencia
☎*640-0704*
Gymnastics, aerobics and body-building.

Golf

Much like elsewhere, golf has become a very popular sport here, and the metropolitan area offers a host of world-class golf courses. Unfortunately, several are private and so off-limits to visitors. We have therefore selected a few that are noteworthy either for their interesting links or exceptional setting.

Located in a residential development at the foot of the mountains surrounding the city, the **Club de Golf Santa Anita** will delight avid golfers. The 18-hole golf course is varied and most pleasant to roam.

Information and reservations:
Club de Golf Santa Anita S.A. de C.V.
every day 7am to 5pm
Carratera Guadalajara–Morelia
Km 6.5
Tlajomulca de Zúñiga
☎*686-1431*

In addition to being located in an urban area, the **El Palomar Country Club** boasts an 18-hole golf course in a mountain setting at 2,000m (6,562ft) above sea level. While perfecting your golf swing, you will be treated to spectacular views of the city of Guadalajara and the Nevado de Colima. Reservations can be made through the Camino Real (see p 149) and Presidente Inter-Continental (see p 149).

Information and reservations:
El Palomar Country Club
Paseo de la Cima no. 437
Fracc. El Palomar Country Club
☎ *684-4434*
≈ *684-2411*

Tennis

Tenis del Bosque
☎ *122-0283*

Accommodations

Guadalajara offers visitors several types of accommodation, from modest *posadas* to luxurious *Gran Turismo* hotels, including many hotels suitable for business travellers.

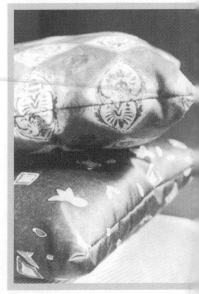

In Mexico, budget accommodations do not always offer very good value for the money. On the other hand, those willing to pay $20 to $40 a night can find very comfortable lodgings that are charming and offer excellent value for the price. **Breakfast is only rarely included in the price of the room.** In the few cases that it is, we have mentioned it. Generally speaking, hotel-reception employees speak at least a modicum of English. It is customary to leave the porter $0.50 to $0.60 per suitcase.

Seasons have little influence on hotel rates. With the exception of most hotels hosting conventions, prices vary little during the year. Several business hotels even advertize discount rates on weekends to boost their weekly occupation. It's up to you to make the most of it.

Rates

The rates mentioned in this guide apply to a standard double-occupancy room year-round, including 15% tax (IVA) but not breakfast.

$	$20 or less
$$	$20 to $40
$$$	$40 to $70
$$$$	$70 to $100
$$$$$	$100 or more

Hotels

There are scores of luxury hotels in and around Guadalajara, including a few with extraordinary charm, though many are only extravagant when it comes to their rates. This guide provides details of each hotel's perks and drawbacks, diligently eschewing establishments that don't offer good value for the money. Almost all rooms come with a television, a telephone and a private bathroom, whatever the rate.

In Mexico, local calls made from hotels are very costly. Calling abroad is also very expensive, particularly since long-distance rates in Mexico are the highest in North America. It is therefore best to use a direct-dial service (such as Canada Direct): in general, no fees are charged to your hotel account and charges are just slightly higher than in your home country.

Posadas

Posadas are hotels of all categories, which have a more human, friendlier cachet than the major chain hotels. Establishments that bill themselves as *posadas* generally offer a congenial atmosphere and predominantly feature warm, Mexican-style colours.

Camping

Campgrounds are an extremely rare commodity in Guadalajara, but you'll find two worthwhile places below nonetheless.

Ulysses's Favourites

In this guide, we've attempted to choose the best establishments in each category.

For Business Travellers

For History Buffs

Tour A: The Cradle of Guadalajara

Accommodations

Hotel Las Américas
$
pb, tv, ⊗
Avenida Hidalgo no. 76
C.P. 44100
☎*613-9622*
In a rather uninviting, noisy environment right next to the Hidalgo-tunnel exit, the Hotel Las Américas courteously welcomes visitors in a lobby with sombre, heavy furniture in a style reminiscent of Spanish lounges. This hotel deserves consideration for its location, just three blocks from the cathedral.

Hotel Francés
$$
pb, tv, ℜ, ⊗
Maestranza no. 35
C.P. 44100
behind the Palacio del Gobierno
☎*613-1190*
≈*658-2831*
www.hotelfrances.com
Hotel Francés is a veritable Guadalajara landmark. Built in 1610 to provide short-term shelter for traders, the hotel witnessed the entire development of the city and modern Mexico. Over the years, it has welcomed many of the Republic's powerful historical figures. It was also one of the shooting locations for *The Evil That Men Do*, starring Charles Bronson, who actu-

ally stayed at the hotel. Today, the city's oldest hotel is designated a national historic monument and so protected from any modifications. And for good reason: indeed, its colonial heritage is immediately felt upon entering the lobby, where both guests and pigeons hang about! Those with an appreciation for gleaming floors and artwork will not be disappointed by the corridors on the upper floors, though unfortunately, the dim lighting makes it difficult to fully appreciate their splendour. The rooms also exude old-world charm, but are rather lacking in modern conveniences and hardly sound-proof at all (light sleepers, you've been warned).

La Rotonda
$$
pb, tv, ℜ, ⊗
Avenida Liceo no. 130
C.P. 44100
☎*614-0387*
Located right near the square of the same name, the La Rotonda hotel occupies an old mansion, now renovated with a certain style. Comfort is definitely a feature each of the 32 rooms, but at the expense of furnishings that are far from harmonious with the building's venerable age. A refreshing, airy interior courtyard serves as a meeting place for guests and,

above all, as a restaurant where patrons dine well.

🌴 Hotel de Mendoza
$$$
pb, tv, ≡, ≈, ℜ, P
Venostiano Carranza no. 16
at Calle Independencia
C.P. 44100
☎*613-4646 or 800-361-2600*
≈*613-7310*
www.mexplaza.com/dmendoza
The Hotel de Mendoza, located near the Teatro Degollado, is most definitely a classy establishment. Its decorators have succeeded in preserving some of the old building's original elements, such as the lobby and restaurant richly appointed with sculptures and Louis XV chairs. The wood-panelled corridors lead to rooms that are modestly furnished but whose bathrooms are graced with a stained-glass window. However, guests should waste no time settling on the balcony to enjoy the sun and a view of the pool. Then again, you may prefer stretching out on the rooftop terrace to take in the magnificent view of the city below. Those seeking deluxe accommodations will also have the opportunity to admire the cathedral in all its splendour from one of the suites on the top floors. Keep-fit buffs can take advantage of the exercise room, while businesspeople

have a conference room at their disposal.

Tour B: Residences and Squares of Old Guadalajara

Hotel Jorge Alejandro
$
pb, tv, P, ⊗
Avenida Hidalgo no. 656
Zona Centro
C.P. 44100
☎*658-1051*
The newly renovated Hotel Jorge Alejandro, decorated in shades of pink and white, is well kept. The rooms are clean and the hotel gets a good grade for its gracious staff and discount rates for stays of three days or more.

Hotel Maya
$
pb, tv, P
López Cotilla no. 39
C.P. 44100
☎*614-5454*
On a small street located a stone's throw from the cathedral, Hotel Maya offers 55 rather plain, soberly laid-out rooms. Although its central location is a major asset, the hotel is especially noteworthy for its budget rates. Some rooms come with four large beds.

Posada Regis Guadalajara
$
pb, tv, ℜ, ⊗
Avenida Corona no. 171
Juárez district
C.P. 44100
☎/≈*613-3026*
The Posada Regis Guadalajara has been welcoming visitors to the "Pearl of the West" since 1870. The lobby, covering the entire second floor of an 18th-century colonial building, looks surprisingly like a peaceful garden. Set up all around this oasis, the 18 small rooms feature elegant period furnishings and the building's original high ceilings. By way of welcome, the charming elderly owner will proudly reel off everything the hotel has to offer, including a dining room, laundry room, big-screen TV, the rooms' amenities and, above all, her own personalized attention.

Posada San Pablo
$
sb, ⊗
Avenida Madero no. 218
C.P. 44100
☎*613-3312*
On the third floor of a historic building in the heart of the city, the Posada de San Pablo is accessible by way of a large period wrought-iron staircase from which you can admire a pretty stained-glass window that adorns the high ceilings. The restored hacienda now offers 10 rooms furnished

with considerably less elegance and that could use a serious facelift. Backpackers will admittedly find a simple boardinghouse here, but one whose more-than-affordable price will banish from their minds the unpleasantness of the shared shower and Spartan surroundings.

🏨 Posada Tapatía
$
pb, ⊗
Avenida López Cotilla no. 619
between Pavo and 8 de Julio
C.P. 44100
☎**614-9146**

Located near the historic centre, the Posada Tapatía offers a few guestrooms within the old rooms of a period villa still graced with high ceilings and several original decorative details. With a warm decor and a welcome that does credit to Mexican hospitality, the atmosphere here is positively spring-like every day of the year.

Hotel Fénix
$$$
pb, tv, ≡, ℜ
Avenida Corona no. 160
C.P. 44100
☎**614-5714 or 800-361-1100**
⊷**613-4005**

While strolling along Avenida Corona, you'll soon notice one of the district's only modern-looking buildings that utterly clashes with its surrounding architectural environment,

and whose 250 dowdy rooms hardly justify its high nightly rates. Exhibitors of various Guadalajara fairs are offered special rates: it's worth inquiring about. The rooms on the north side of the upper floors offer a fine view of the cathedral. Other noteworthy perks include large-capacity meeting facilities and the establishment's location, just steps away from Plaza de Armas.

Tour D: Analco, Las Nueve Esquinas and Parque Agua Azul

Hotel Costa Brava
$
pb, P, ⊗
Calz. Independencia Sur no. 739
at Avenida Los Angeles
C.P. 44100
☎**619-2327**

The new Hotel Costa Brava invites you to spend the night amidst the warm colours of the coast. Youth-hostel regulars will find here the same basic comfort, simple welcome and low prices that they're accustomed to.

Hôtel Continental
$$
pb, tv, P
Avenida Corona no. 450, at Calle Libertad
C.P. 44100
☎**614-1117**

Built during this district's 1970s heyday, this large

128-room hotel has remained unchanged since its inception. The lobby and rooms feature outdated, even kitschy, furnishings, but remain comfortable and quiet. If the hotel's jarring shades of orange and lime-green don't leave you overly unsettled, this is a decent place for its equally retro rates.

Don Quijote Plaza
$$
pb, tv, ≡, P, ℜ
Avenida Héroes no. 91
C.P. 44100
☎658-1299
≈614-2845

"Good value for the money" sums up the Don Quijote Plaza in a nutshell. The hotel occupies an old colonial building that managed to avoid the wave of modernization that hit the district in the 1960s. It is one of the few successfully refurbished historic hotels combining bygone charm and modern comfort. The interior courtyard, surrounded by dozens of plants, is a tranquil haven and the rooms, though rather small, are impeccable.

Nueva Galicia
$$
pb, tv, P, ℜ
Avenida Corona no. 610
at Calle La Paz
C.P. 44100
☎614-8780

Besides gracious service with a smile, the Nueva Galicia hotel has nothing to distinguish it from its rivals. Once again, arresting orange seems to have been the decorator's colour of choice, which does little to make the place attractive. This hotel will suit budget-conscious families who wish to steer clear of *posadas* or youth hostels.

Hotel San Francisco
$$
pb, tv, ℜ, P, ⊗
Calle Degollado no. 267, at
Priscilliano Sánchez
C.P. 44100
☎613-8959
≈613-3257

Located on a bustling street, Hotel San Francisco occupies a former colonial home with typically characteristic architecture. Inside, you'll encounter the spirit of those times by wandering the corridors organized around two small, lushly flowered interior courtyards. Adding to the place's lively atmosphere, the ground-floor Don Quijote restaurant serves varied meals from morning to night. As for the rooms, though it's rather disappointing to note that they haven't been designed with as much care as the rest of the place, their large size and comfort ensure a good night's sleep.

 **Hotel Santiago de Compostela**
$$$
pb, tv, ≡, ≈, P, ℜ
Calle Colón no. 272
C.P. 44100
☎*613-8954 or 800-365-5300*
≈*658-1925*

With its magnificent neo-Renaissance facade prominently displayed across from the Jardín de San Francisco, Hotel Santiago de Compostela offers noteworthy cachet near the lovely Nueva Esquinas district. Large windows flood the clean, supremely comfortable rooms with natural light for a good part of the day. A refreshing rooftop swimming pool is the perfect spot to enjoy the city's mild climate. In short, a great choice for this category of hotel.

Tour E: Chapultepec and Las Antiguas Colonias

Posada Cameleón
$
pb, tv, ℜ, ☉
Avenida Morelos no. 1613
C.P. 44130
☎*825-0584*

Located in the Zona Rosa, said to be the quietest area in metropolitan Guadalajara, Posada Cameleón will primarily interest budget travellers. This former family home converted with little effort (perhaps to retain more authenticity) offers transient guests a courteous welcome. Note that, with only 10 rooms, the *posada* fills up quickly, so it's best to get here early to reserve a bed for the night.

Hotel-Suites Bernini
$$
pb, tv, K, ℝ, P
Avenida Vallarta no. 1881, at Unión
C.P. 44160
☎*616-0858 or 800-362-8200*
≈*616-7274*

This imposing 16-storey tower was designed with finesse marked by 1920s Italian modernism. Perfect for those enjoying an extended stay in Guadalajara, the suites are rented out by the night, the week or the month, with daily rates getting lower the longer you stay. Each of the one-to two-room suites includes a kitchen and living room with furnishings that are also in line with Italian modernism. Opt for one overlooking Avenida Vallarta, so as to avoid the "greenhouse effect" that warms up the rooms exposed to noontime sun.

Hotel del Parque
$$
pb, tv, ℜ, P, ⊗
Avenida Juárez no. 845, near Federalismo
C.P. 44100
☎*825-2800*
⇝*826-6648*
Though located next to a pleasant and all-too-rare city park, Hotel del Parque is a little far from the downtown area, about 15min walking distance from the cathedral. The hotel's decor is confined to the essentials and the furniture, though still in good condition, is becoming somewhat dated. Friendly service with a smile.

Hotel Lafayette
$$$$
pb, tv, ≡, ℜ, ≈
Avenida La Paz no. 2055, at Avenida Chapultepec
C.P. 44140
☎*615-0045 or 800-362-2200*
⇝*630-1112*
A stone's throw from Avenida Chapultepec stands another giant of the business-hotel industry. Hotel Lafayette features several

large meeting rooms and lounges set up on the two first floors, a major asset that makes the establishment a very popular convention venue. The rooms, with standardized decor, occupy the remaining 11 floors. An appreciable asset for weekenders, the hotel offers near-half-price rates on Friday, Saturday and Sunday, which greatly improves the establishment's quality/price ratio.

Tour F: Minerva and el Iztépete

Hotel Puerto Vallarta
$
pb, tv, ⊗, P
Avenida Vallarta no. 4003, at Calle Don Bosco
C.P. 45049
☎*121-7361*
For low-priced accommodations, head to Hotel Puerto Vallarta, one of the few small hotels in this commercial area. The welcome is simple and the rooms unpretentious, with modest furnishings limited to the essentials.

Hotel Windsor

$

pb, tv, P, ⊗

V. Salado Alvarez no. 131,
between Avenida México and Calle
Justo Sierra
C.P. 44130

☎*615-7790*

Marked by a large sign,
Hotel Windsor is amazingly
peaceful thanks to its location in the heart of a quiet
residential district. In this
former one-family home
you can rent one of several
rooms of varying sizes,
some of which come with a
television. Opt for a room
with a window, which al-
lows the prevailing humid-
ity to escape. Ring to enter.

Hotel Nuevo Vallarta

$$

pb, tv, ℜ, ⊗, P

Avenida Vallarta no. 3999, at Gran
Plaza
C.P. 45049

☎*629-8610*

≈*121-1086*

Located next to Guadala-
jara's chamber of com-
merce, Hotel Nuevo Vallarta
welcomes guests in a lobby
that is rather cold, but fortu-
nately, warmed up by the
friendliness of the staff. The
simple, white-stucco rooms
in shades of brown are well
kept, if not exactly attrac-
tive. A decent place for
which reservations are rec-
ommended.

Hotel Patricia

$$

pb, tv, P, ⊗

Cir. Augustín Yañez no. 2745-C
C.P.44120

☎*630-0117*

≈*616-4136*

This small hotel with 18
clean rooms is housed in a
nondescript modern build-
ing whose only asset is its
proximity to La Minerva.
Note that not all rooms
have a window, so be sure
to ask for one.

Hotel del Bosque

$$

pb, tv, K, ℝ, P, ≈, ℜ, ⊗

Avenida López Mateos Sur no. 265
at Calle Inglaterra, C.P. 44100

☎*121-4020*

≈*121-1955*

Offering a range of worth-
while services and reason-
able prices, Hotel del
Bosque is a solid choice.
The lovely interior garden is
a haven of peace, a rare
commodity in the area. The
rooms are tastefully deco-
rated, incredibly quiet and
recent renovations now
ensure near-infallible clean-
liness. Moreover, for those
enjoying an extended stay
in Guadalajara, the hotel
offers a few rooms with
kitchenette. Good value for
the price.

Motel Guadalajara
$$
pb, tv, ≡, ≈, P, ℜ
Avenida Vallarta no. 3305
C.P. 44100
☎**647-8489**

Motel Guadalajara deserves a mention for the number of services it offers for its affordable rates. Although the decor hardly merits the term and cleanliness is in short supply, this motel will suit those on a tight budget.

Motor Hotel Américas
$$
pb, tv, P, K, ≈, ℝ, ≡, ℜ
Avenida López Mateos Sur no. 2400
C.P. 45050
☎**631-4415**
≈**631-4048**

Located right across from the Plaza del Sol shopping centre, the large Motor Hotel Américas offers 96 very moderately decorated but particularly well-kept rooms. A few rooms afford a pretty view of the mountains that surround the city. What's more, not one but two outdoor swimming pools make up a considerable asset.

Posada del Sol
$$
pb, tv, ℜ, ≈, ⊗, #
López Mateos Sur no. 4205, at La Giralda
C.P. 44550
☎**631-5205**

For those who enjoy being surrounded by the greenery and rural peace and quiet of *posadas*, the Posada del Sol constitutes a good choice. The rooms are simple but charming, and the dining room with its congenial atmosphere deserves a mention. Lastly, the large swimming pool, open year-round, and the vast verdant lawn make for a pleasant stay.

Las Pergolas
$$-$$$
pb, tv, ≡, ℜ, ≈, P, △
Avenida Morelos, C.P. 44130
☎**630-1727**
≈**630-0576**

Despite a somewhat depressing facade, from the time when concrete was favoured by architects, Las Pergolas offers 158 modern and nicely laid-out rooms. This decent establishment offers a multitude of services for businesspeople, and several packages temper the already reasonable prices. Although the decor was hardly the subject of intense research, this quiet, unpretentious place will suit a fair share of visitors.

Hotel Plaza Los Arcos
$$-$$$
pb, tv, P, K, ⊗, ℝ
Avenida Vallarta no. 2452
at Francisco de Quevedo
C.P. 44100
☎*615-1845*
≈*616-3817*

Suites Moralva
$$$
pb, tv, P, K, ⊗, ℝ
Avenida Vallarta no. 2477
C.P. 44100
☎*615-4804*
≈*615-4805*

Hotel Plaza Los Arcos and its counterpart Suites Moralva, located just opposite, both offer the advantageous apartment-hotel formula. In fact, most units feature a kitchenette that gives guests the illusion of staying in an apartment. The former offers a cheaper version with a suitable decor and an Art Deco-style lobby. The second, newer hotel offers rooms of various sizes, each with its own balcony. Lastly, both are conveniently located, across from the posh Centro Magno shopping centre.

Hotel-Suites Fuente del Bosque
$$-$$$
pb, tv, ≡, K, ℝ, ⊗, ℜ, P
Avenida Niños Héroes no. 2655
at López Mateos
C.P. 44520
☎*122-0214 or 800-366-4700*
≈*122-1667*

As its Spanish name indicates, Hotel-Suites Fuente del Bosque greets guests with a charming, refreshing fountain. Located in the breezy neighbourhood of the Jardínes del Bosque, the establishment offers the practical apartment-hotel formula, and the various suites are remarkably similar to fully equipped apartments. Moreover, the rooms are decently and comfortably furnished, the service is gracious and prices are reasonable.

Malibu
$$$
pb, tv, ≈, #, ℜ, ⊗, P, ≡
Avenida Vallarta no. 3993, next to
Gran Plaza
C.P. 45120
☎*121-7676 or 800-365-2500*
≈*122-3192*

Once past the arches of the Malibu hotel, you'll be glad to have swapped the noisy traffic for the sweet chirping of birds in the interior garden. Featuring a large fountain and a 25m (82ft) swimming pool, this is a great place to relax. The business centre, two restaurants and banquet hall will optimize a business stay. As for the rooms, they are standard and somewhat Spartan-looking. For an interesting view, opt for a room on the upper floors overlooking Avenida Vallarta.

Hotel Margarita
$$$
pb, tv, $\mathfrak{S}$, ⊗, P, ≈, K, $\mathbb{R}$
Juan Palomar y Arias no. 283
Fracc. Monraz, C.P. 44670
☎*673-1176*
≈*673-2508*

At the very back of a park lined with small Mexican houses stands Hotel Margarita. This new hotel complex rents out 38 rooms for short or long stays. The establishment's clever layout, putting a natural small valley to good use, makes it ideal for those who like to combine comfort, quiet and relaxation.

Hotel Plaza Diana
$$$
pb, tv, ≡, $\mathfrak{R}$, P, ≈, ⊘, $\mathbb{R}$
Avenida Circunvalación Agustín Yañez
no. 2760, at La Paz
C.P. 44100
☎*615-5510*
≈*630-3685*

Located near the Minerva Fountain, Hotel Plaza Diana is another great lodging choice for business travellers. Both the lobby, illuminated by gorgeous stained-glass windows, and the devoted staff deserve a mention. Irreproachably kept rooms ensure the requisite comfort, while the double-glazed windows provide the necessary quiet. A good, all-day restaurant will delight gourmets and a piano bar open until the wee hours of the morning will enchant night owls.

Posada Guadalajara
$$$
pb, tv, $\mathfrak{R}$, ≈, ≡, P
Avenida López Mateos no. 1280
C.P. 45046
☎*121-2022*
≈*122-1834*

Graced with a facade that conveys a sustained interest in decoration, the Posada Guadalajara distinguishes itself by its tasteful lobby and luxuriant interior courtyard. The Mexican style of decor is manifested in all its splendour in the courtyard's magnificent fountain, arcade and varied flora. Unfortunately, what has cachet outside the rooms becomes of dubious taste once inside. Indeed, the spacious rooms tend to be somewhat kitschy by dint of wanting to dazzle guests. Also regrettable is the sloppiness of the service, though by and large this *posada* does offers good value for the money. Reservations required.

Vista Plaza del Sol
$$$
pb, tv, $\mathfrak{R}$, ≡, ≈, P
Avenida López Mateos Sur no. 2375
C.P. 45050
☎*647-8890*
≈*647-8565*
www.vistahotel.com

Located at the junction of Avenidas López Mateos and Mariano Otero, the Vista Plaza del Sol is part of a nationwide hotel chain. Made up of twin towers encompassing 357 rooms and suites, the hotel seems a little expensive, even though the many services offered partly justifies the price. Note that the hotel is home to an American-Canadian Club office, which offers packages to retired North American expats spending their sunset years in sunny Jalisco.

Hotel Guadalajara Plaza Expo
$$$$
pb, tv, ≈, ≡, P, ☺, ℝ
Avenida Mariano Otero no. 3261
at Topacio
C.P. 44550
☎**669-0215 or 888-223-7646**
≈**122-2850**
The sleek Hotel Guadalajara Plaza Expo boasts a choice location. Indeed, it is only seconds away from the Expo-Guadalajara convention centre and a few minutes from the Guadalajara World Trade Center. As its location implies, everything here is set up for business travellers. For rare moments of relaxation between meetings, a lovely rooftop swimming pool will definitely lower your stress level.

🖼 Hotel Guadalajara Plaza López Mateos
$$$$
pb, tv, ≈, P, ℜ, ≡
Avenida López Mateos Sur no. 2128
at Cubilete
C.P. 45050
☎**647-5279**
≈**122-1842**
Part of the same chain, Hotel Guadalajara Plaza López

Mateos is practically a carbon copy of its counterpart described above. The service here is just as impeccable, as is the level of comfort. A notable difference, however, is that this branch offers attractive, quiet, well-priced suites arranged around the swimming pool.

Holiday Inn Select
$$$$-$$$$$
pb, tv, ≡, ☺, 🔲, #, ≈, ℝ, ℜ, △, P
Avenida Niños Héroes no. 3089
at López Mateos
C.P. 44520
☎**122-2020 or 800-HOLIDAY**
Built just a few years ago to meet the high increase of well-heeled business travellers, this world-class hotel with eclectic decor can easily make you believe you're in Chicago or Hong Kong. The lobby, restaurant, bar and each of the rooms are designed with the allure of the 1990s, very different from what this famous chain has accustomed us to. The hotel caters exclusively to business clients, who will feel comfortable with the great number of services at their disposal, including some unusual ones like non-smoking floors, a telephone in every bathroom and a panoramic elevator. An exceptional feature, a heated rooftop swimming pool provides a 360° view of the whole city. Lastly, the staff is, as they say, at your service.

Camino Real
$$$$$
pb, tv, ≡, ⊛, ⊘, ◙, ≈, ℝ, ℜ, △, *P*
Avenida Vallarta no. 5005
at Niño Obrero
C.P. 45040
☎*647-8000*
≈*647-6781*

Among the plethora of ho-
tels that line Avenida
Vallarta, many have a modern and impersonal appear-
ance that is enough to de-
press you. But there are still
some very inviting, note-
worthy ones such as the
Camino Real. Indeed, the
sprawling hotel's series of
two-storey buildings gives it
a warmer, country-club-like
feeling. The rooms are
adorned with tasteful, contemporary furnishings, and
each of the conference
rooms is designed along
attractive, eclectic lines. The
Aquellos Tiempos restau-
rant serves breakfast, lunch
and dinner on a terrace
facing expansive manicured
lawns or inside, for a more
refined dining experience.
A real gem for those who
can afford it.

Fiesta Americana
$$$$$
pb, tv, ≈, ≡, ⊘, ℝ, ℜ, △, *P*
Aurelio Aceves no. 225 Glorieta Minerva
C.P. 44100
☎*825-3434 or 800-504-5000*
≈*630-3671*

The huge bunker-like building that dominates the entire La Minerva area houses
one of the largest hotels in

the city. Fortunately, the
Fiesta Americana's interior
features a more welcoming
aspect, with a spacious
lobby (especially height-
wise) and a bar-terrace perfect for relaxation. Each of
the 390 delightful rooms
offers all North American
modern conveniences and a
stunning view of the city.
The hotel also offers guests
meeting facilities, a tennis
court and a pleasant out-
door swimming pool. A few
shops round out the range
of in-house services, and
the Canadian Consulate
even conducts business
here. Last but not least, the
staff's welcome, much like
the price, is true to what
one would expect from a
five-star establishment.

Presidente Inter-Continental
$$$$$
pb, tv, ≡, ⊘, ◙, ≈, ℝ, ℜ, △, *P*
at Avenida López Mateos and Calle
Montezuma
C.P. 44050
☎*678-1234 or 800-9-0444*
≈*678-1222*

True to its world-famous
reputation, the Presidente
Inter-Continental offers luxury and quality to those
with deep-enough pockets.
Beyond its sparkling glass
facade lie no less than 420
rooms with a wide choice
of furnishings in line with
the great number of suites.
Everything is provided to
meet all the needs and desires of the wealthiest international business class. The

Accommodations

resort boasts a dizzying list of services and a very amenable staff. Don't miss the only part of the hotel with a certain appeal, the La Moreña Mexican restaurant, a replica of the Hacienda de la Barca, a very picturesque village near Guadalajara. All in all, a good choice for those with the wherewithal to appreciate very high standards of quality.

Tour G: Zapopan

Hotel Primavera
$$
pb, K, ≈, ⊙, ℜ, P, ⊗
Carretera A Nogales, Km 24
Zapopán
☎*616-6673*
Nestled in the hills of Zapopán, the modern Hotel Primavera was designed for those who have had enough of the austere urban landscape. Its location in the heart of peaceful woodlands, the Bosque de la Primavera, is indeed a welcome change from the city's noisy traffic. The 99-room resort appears as a spa equipped with a heated swimming pool, a volleyball court and a few footpaths. Reservations are made through the Oficina Corporativas Hoteles Universidad de Guadalajara (*Francisco de Quevedo no. 175,* ☎*616-1689,* ≈*615-0600*).

Tour H: San Pedro Tlaquepaque and Tonalá

San José del Tajo campground
Km 15, Hwy. 15 toward Morelia, Guadalajara
☎*686-1495*

Hacienda Trailer Park
Ciudad Granja
☎*627-1724 or 121-5084*

Mesón Don José
$$$ bkfst incl.
pb, tv, ≈, P, ⊗
Avenida Reforma no. 139
between Progreso and Matanoros
C.P. 45500
San Pedro Tlaquepaque
☎*639-3085*
≈*659-9315*
Tucked away on Avenida Reforma, a few minutes' walking distance from the village centre, the Mesón Don José is a country-style inn located in an enchanting villa setting. All rooms are carefully decorated with old-world charm, reminding us that this is a city of artisans. Furthermore, the small number of rooms creates a quiet family atmosphere. Lastly, the small verdant courtyard where breakfast is served particularly lends itself to lazy holiday mornings.

La Villa del Ensueño
$$$ bkfst incl.
pb, tv, ≈, ⊗, ℑ, P
Avenida Florida no. 305
C.P. 45500
San Pedro Tlaquepaque
☎*635-8792*
≈*659-6152*
www.mexonline.com/ensueno.html

Located on a quiet little village street a few minutes from the town centre, La Villa del Ensueño proves to be an exceedingly charming bed and breakfast. Everything is done to make guests feel at home: small balconies off the rooms upstairs, rustic common areas and 10 individually decorated rooms. Birds in the courtyard and flowers in the fountain and swimming pool are little treats that make all the difference. A small marvel, were it not for its price rivalling those of major downtown hotels. In short, one of those places where you'd want to live year-round.

Casa de las Flores
$$$ bkfst incl.
pb, ⊗, P
Santos Degollado no. 175
C.P. 45500
San Pedro Tlaquepaque
☎/≈*659-3186*
www.casadelasflores.com

Casa de las Flores is another bed and breakfast located on a street forsaken by the hordes of tourists who swarm the town centre. This establishment will please those in search of Tlaquepaque's unique character, as the owners have decorated the well kept rooms with pieces from local artisans, to create a comfortable setting. Personalized guide and translation services are offered.

Hotel Casa Grande
$$$$$
pb, tv, ⊗, ≈, ℜ, △, P
Aeropuerto Internacional Miguel Hidalgo
C.P. 45640
☎*678-9000*
≈*678-9002*

Connected to the adjacent Guadalajara International Airport by a covered walkway, this establishment offers a host of services and facilities, including a business centre, free shuttle service to the downtown area and a large-capacity restaurant. The decor of both the rooms and large lobby is modelled after that of an air terminal, but everything is fortunately soundproofed against the continuous air traffic. The hotel's convenient location predictably inspires its rather steep rates.

Tour I: Laguna de Chapala

Villa Montecarlo
$$$
pb, ℜ, ≈, P, ⊗
Avenida Hidalgo no. 236, Chapala
☎615-3998
Reservations: **Oficina Corporativas Hoteles Universidad de Guadalajara**
Francisco de Quevedo no. 175
☎616-1689
⇝615-0600
Like the Hotel Primavera (see p 150), the Villa Montecarlo is run by the University of Guadalajara. This time, Chapala is the place to enjoy a healthy stay at a lakeside spa amidst palm trees, while being soothed by the lake's legendary mild climate. The two swimming pools and 46 sober but comfortable lake-view rooms form a setting conducive to the serene relaxation of seaside resorts.

Nido de Chapala
$$
pb, tv, P, ⊗ ℜ
Avenida Madero no. 202, Chapala
☎765-2116
With its splendour of yesteryear, the Nido de Chapala hotel reminds us that Chapala was a very prosperous town in the early 20th century. In addition to its colonial facade, the lobby is of historical interest and the photographs dis-

played throughout attest to the many floods that have marked the local footnotes of history. Old-fashioned and somewhat sombre but inexpensive rooms are available here.

Real de Chapala
$$$
pb, tv, ≡, ≈, ℝ, ℜ, P
Paseo del Prado no. 20, Ajijic
☎/⇝766-0021
The imposing Real de Chapala hotel is the height of luxury in the area. The 82 convenient, comfortable lakeside rooms will satisfy the most demanding of travellers.

Villa Buenaventura
$$$
pb, tv, ℜ, ⊛, ≈, △, ⊗
Carretera Chapala-Jocotepec, Km 13.5 San Juan Cosalá
☎761-0303
San Juan Cosalá has long been renowned for its curative hot springs, which have attracted pilgrims from around the world over the years. Today, Villa Buenaventura still delights guests with services like a sauna, swimming pool, slide, steam bath and hot springs.

Nueva Posada
$$$
pb, tv, ℜ, P, ≈, ⊗
Avenida Donato Guerra no. 9
C.P. 45920, Ajijic
☎766-1444
Run by a genial Canadian who built the hotel himself

in 1986, the Nueva Posada hotel exudes a great deal of charm. While the architecture evokes the beautiful houses of the Pacific coast, the interior is marked by the traditional colonial style. The 19 rooms and four villas of a questionable pink colour, decorated somewhat ponderously, all feature a balcony. Some are even laid out for the physically handicapped. The place is very popular with North Americans. The restaurant's reputation, which preceded the hotel's, attracts gourmets who appreciate its excellent international cuisine served in the same welcoming setting.

Tour J: Tequila and Surroundings

Nuevo Hotel Colonial
$
pb, tv, ⊗
Avenida Morelos no. 52, at Sixto Gorjón
Tequila
☎742-0355
As the sign reads at the entrance, "Services, morality and hygiene" are the watchwords of the Nuevo Hotel Colonial. Services for those who want to be in the heart of the action, guaranteed morality despite the low price of 80 pesos a night, and hygiene that ensures a modicum of cleanliness. But better to be forewarned that

this price allows for no extravagance when it comes to the furnishings and guests must be heavy sleepers to remain undisturbed by the surrounding activity.

Hotel Abasolo
$
pb, tv, ⊗, P
Calle Abasolo no. 80
Tequila
☎742-0195
The modest Hotel Abasolo rents simply laid-out rooms lacking in decor, but at very worthwhile prices. Friendly welcome.

Las Delicias
$$$
pb, tv, ⊗, ≈, P
Carretera Internacional no. 595
Tequila
☎742-1094
For those seeking a quality hotel in a peaceful Agave country setting, the Las Delicias hotel proves to be a good choice. Its only major drawback is its distance from downtown, which means visitors need a car to get around.

Tour K: Tapalpa and the Mountain

Posada La Hacienda
$
pb, ⊗, K, P
Avenida Matamoros no. 7, Tapalpa
☎432-0193
Despite the unpleasant feeling of walking into a bank

when greeted at the reception, the Posada La Hacienda has a lot to offer, including good value for the money. Housed in a former hacienda across from the central town square, the *posada* still exudes charm. The 32 rooms, spread over two floors and linked by a lovely staircase, have retained a beautiful style characteristic of Tapalpa. Moreover, some rooms have a kitchenette (a formula known as bungalow) and a beautiful view of the valley at the back. Otherwise, the standard rooms are sparsely decorated, rather small and slightly set towards the back, but will suit those averse to spending a fortune.

Casa de Maty

only open on weekends
$$
pb, ℜ, P, ℑ
Avenida Matamoros no. 69, Tapalpa
☎432-0189

Rustic style is at its near ultimate at the Casa de Maty, a pleasant *posada*. Housing an inn and a restaurant under the same roof, this place will perfectly suit those seeking charm, quiet and relaxation. Cool in summer but somewhat cold in winter (use the fireplace), the 14 individually named and decorated

rooms are veritable havens of peace redolent of pine. At the back, a communal whirlpool with a view of the valley promises hours of pleasure. However, the prices are somewhat high, which is regrettable.

Cabañas La Frontera

$
pb, tv, ℑ, K, P
7km before arriving in Tapalpa
☎637-4768

Cabañas La Frontera is an accommodation classic in the area. Its log cabins, set in the midst of a pine forest, are a great place to get back in touch with nature. Each cabin sleeps two to six people.

Hotel Las Margaritas

$$
pb, K, P, ⊗
16 de Septiembre no. 18
Tapalpa
☎432-0799

A *posada* of modest size, Hotel Las Margaritas is set up in a small house typical of Tapalpa. At the entrance, a small shop displaying the owners' beautiful creations sets the tone for the rest of the establishment. In fact, particular attention is given to each of the rooms' decor. Rooms for one to eight people are available with or without kitchenette.

Restaurants

There is a wealth of excellent restaurants in the Guadalajara area specializing primarily in traditional Mexican cooking, but also in a great variety of other cuisines.

Although tacos, quesadillas and *moles* are menu staples, Mexican cuisine is by no means limited to these dishes. In fact, a renewed interest in the national cuisine allows one and all to savour *nueva cocina mexicana*, which revives an excellent culinary tradition of old. Moreover, Guadalajara boasts several ethnic restaurants, offering something for everyone.

As a general rule, restaurants are open from 1:30pm to 4:30pm and 8pm to 11pm. Lunch is traditionally the most important meal of the day in Mexico, so don't be surprised by the generous portions served at this time of day.

The long lunch hour, which stretches from 2pm to 4pm, indicates that Mexicans are in the habit of taking extended lunches. As a result, you will not only have to ask for your bill (*la cuenta, por favor*), but will also have to be patient when waiting for your change. It's a question of politeness; they don't want to rush you.

In this guide, we have endeavoured to provide the best possible selection of restaurants for all budgets.

It should be noted that most restaurants feature *música en vivo* in the evening, particularly on weekends. Diners are thus serenaded with live music performed by local talent. Though the quality tends to vary from one place to the next, these small shows provide a pleasant accompaniment to your meals.

Prices

Prices listed below apply to a meal (taxes included) for one person, including soup, main course, coffee and dessert. Drinks and service are not included.

$	$5 or less
$$	$5 to $8
$$$	$8 to $12
$$$$	$12 to $16
$$$$$	$16 or more

Tipping

The term *propina incluida* means that the tip is included in the price. However, this is not usually the case; instead, it must be calculated and given to the server by the diner. It is customary to leave a 10% to 15% tip, depending on the quality of the service. Unlike in Europe, service and tip are one and the same in North America.

Mexican Cuisine

Tortillas, tacos, empanadas, enchiladas, so many terms can be confusing to those encountering Mexican cuisine for the first time. Since prejudices die hard (dishes are too spicy, for example), too often visitors faced with new, unfamiliar flavours opt for international cuisine. Although some local dishes can prove particularly spicy, Mexican cuisine offers an infinite variety of dishes, from the mildest to the hottest.

Mexican dishes are often served with rice *(arroz)* and black or red beans *(frijoles),* and a basket of hot tortillas is placed on your table. Of course, the hot sauce *(salsa)* is never very far away and there are many varieties. Traditionally, salsa is prepared by mashing tomatos, onions, coriander and different types of hot pepper together with a mortar.

Breakfast is *desayuno* in Spanish, *almuerzo* means lunch and *cena* is dinner. The *comida corrida* is served in the late afternoon, until 5pm or 6pm, and it consists of a daily menu, which is usually reasonably priced. Mexicans tend not to eat a lot in the evening, so don't be surprised if you go to a village restaurant after 6pm and it's closed.

As a guide through the delicious meanderings of Mexican cuisine, we have assembled a gastronomic glossary below.

Ceviche

Raw fish or seafood marinated in lime juice. In Mexico, onions, tomatoes, hot peppers and coriander are added.

Chicharrón

Fried pork rind, usually served with an apéritif.

Chile

Fresh or dried peppers (there are more than 100 varieties) that are prepared in a thousand different ways: stuffed, or as stuffing, boiled, fried, etc.

Empanadas

Turnovers stuffed with meat, poultry or fish.

Restaurants

1. Cayenne Pepper
2. *Mirasol colorado*
3. Small Cayenne Pepper
4. Dwarf Cayenne Pepper
5. *Pequín*
6. *Hontaka*
7. *Ancho*
8. *Güero*
9. *Mulato*

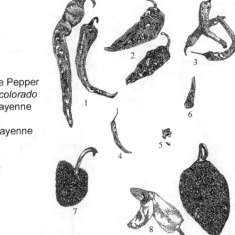

Enchiladas
Rolled and baked tortillas (see further below), which are generally stuffed with chicken, covered with a spicy sauce, sliced onions and cream, and sometimes sprinkled with cheese.

Fajitas
Strips of marinated chicken grilled with onions. Fajitas are usually served with tomato sauce, cream and vegetables, and can be wrapped in a tortilla.

Guacamole
Salted and peppered purée of avocado mixed with diced tomatoes, onions, fresh peppers and a bit of lime juice. Even when this dish is not on the menu, do not hesitate to ask for *guacamole con totopos* (with corn chips), a very common dish that makes a refreshing appetizer or snack.

Huevos Rancheros
Two or three fried eggs served on a corn tortilla and often covered with a spicy tomato sauce.

Machaca
Sun-dried meat.

Mole
This term designates a category of creamy sauces composed of mixtures of spices, nuts, cocoa, tomatoes, tortillas, peppers, onions, and other foodstuffs varying by region. The most famous of these are Mole Poblano and Mole Negro Oaxaqueno, both made with a base of cocoa and spices. These sauces accompany poultry and meat.

Nopales
Cactus leaves (without the spines, of course!) cooked in water or served in a soup or salad. The juice of these is also offered at breakfast.

Pozole
A corn and pork stew with radishes, onions, coriander and lime juice. There are two varieties, red and green. The red is hotter.

Quesadillas
Stuffed, refolded tortillas that are reheated on the stove, usually with cheese.

Sopa de Lima
A hot soup made with chicken, lemon or lime, and mixed with pieces of corn tortillas.

Tacos
Tortillas garnished with different ingredients and eaten wrapped. Stalls on the street make tacos with marinated, grilled meat which is served on a tortilla with your choice of salsa and vegetables.

Tamales
Corn husks stuffed with meat, poultry, or fish. Many vegetables and spices are also added to the

Mexican Recipes

Carne en su jugo (meat stewed in its own juice)

500g beef sirloin, sliced
250g red or green tomatoes, finely chopped
500g onion, minced
250g salted bacon, sliced
250ml water
1 garlic clove
1 Tbsp. coriander (cilantro)
1 lime, squeezed
salt and pepper

Line the bottom of the cauldron with sliced bacon.
When cooked to golden-brown, add beef, salt and
pepper. Brown, then add garlic, tomatoes and water.
Bring to a boil, reduce heat and let simmer. Just before
serving, add onion, lime and coriander.

Jericallas (Mexican custard)

1L milk
5 eggs
1 cinnamon stick, ground
250g sugar
salt

Heat milk to a simmer. Add sugar. Remove from heat.
Beat eggs lightly and add salt. While mixing, slowly
blend milk in with the eggs. Add ground cinnamon.
Pour mixture into buttered Pyrex moulds. Arrange
moulds in a dripping pan half-filled with lukewarm
water and cook at medium heat (180ºC, or 350ºF) for
about 75min or until knife blade comes out clean.
Refrigerate.

Restaurants

stuffing, varying according to region. Tamales are cooked wrapped in banana-tree leaves.

Topos

These are a rough equivalent to North American potato chips. Made with corn here, they may be round or triangular.

Tortillas

The bread of Latin America. Tortillas are flat pancakes with a corn-flour base, cooked on an unoiled griddle. Generally they accompany other dishes. Traditionally made by hand, today tortillas are mass produced in food-processing factories. Tortillas are also increasingly being made using white flour. Not to be confused with Spanish tortillas (a dish made with eggs and potatoes).

Mexican Drinks

Beer

Those looking for a beer with "character" should opt for **Bohemia** or **Indio**. These amber brews have much more taste than the blonde varieties and make for a great early evening drink. For those who prefer blonde beers, the famous **Corona** and **Sol** or the lesser-known **Lager**, **Don Esquis** and **Modelo** are pleasantly refreshing. Fans of local products should also note that **Estrella** is brewed in Guadalajara.

Wines

In general, the least expensive wine served in restaurants is domestic. Half bottles are very rarely featured on wine lists. Expect to pay $7.50 for a bottle of Mexican *vino*, $9.50 to $11 for a Chilean wine and $18 to $30 for a French wine. Given storage conditions and the climate, drinking domestic rather than imported wine is advised. Besides, this will give you the opportunity to sample local products.

Cocktails and Liqueurs

The queen of cocktails, the margarita will quickly make you lose your head if not enjoyed in moderation. It is a cocktail made up of tequila, Cointreau, lime juice and sugarcane syrup, mixed with crushed ice and served in salt-rimmed glasses. Tequila, made right here in Guadalajara, is derived from the bulbous base of the agave (a succulent indigenous to Mexico). The juice collected is then slowly fermented and distilled, producing a dry, clear alcohol. Tequila is usually drunk straight up with a pinch of salt and a bite of lemon or lime. A variety of

Giggling schoolgirls express their joy as classes end.
- *M. Daniels*

There is an incredible wealth of crafts in Mexico. In Guadalajara, where folklore and traditions live on, you will find crafts in a rainbow of colours.
- *M. Daniels*

The Instituto Cultural Cabañas, a UNESCO World Heritage Site, house one of the most important cultural centres in the country. - *T. B.*

other drinks derived from this same *bebida nacional* caters to all tastes.

Restaurants by Type of Cuisine

Restaurants

Ulysses's Favourites

Tour A: The Cradle of Guadalajara

Pollo-Chicken
$

Plaza Guadalajara no. 17

If you're ravenous after visiting the Guadalajara Cathedral, you'll be forgiven for stopping by Pollo-Chicken. Prices here are absolutely unbeatable: $1.60 for a breast of chicken, two tacos and a drink—now there's something to satisfy budget travellers. Although the dining room is as hot as an oven, at these prices, you really can't ask for too much!

La Rinconada
$$

Avenida Morelos no. 86
Plaza Tapatía
☎613-9914

La Rinconada occupies a singular colonial building that is one of only two buildings, to have remained unchanged since its construction in the 18th century (the other being the tourist office). The interior courtyard, colonial arcade and lovely stained-glass windows remind us of the great care for detail that was taken by erstwhile builders of centuries past. Unfortunately, the current owners have not put all its potential to good use, contenting themselves with unfortunate comprises. The ceiling fans,

background music and faux-chic furnishings seem to attract tourists nonetheless.

Las Sombrillas del Hospicio
$$

Paseo Hospicio, Suite 110
opposite the Instituto Cultural
Cabañas
☎618-6966

After visiting the Intituto Cultural Cabañas, it's a good idea to stop in for a drink or a meal on the parasol-dotted terrace of Las Sombrillas del Hospicio, which actually consists of four restaurants in one: Los Lauretes, which serves traditional Mexican fare, Casa de los Moles, predictably offering *moles*, El Jimador, with *molcajetes* and seafood, and Uriger, which dishes up international fast food. This place will satisfy all tastes while offering a magnificent view of the Intituto Cabañas's facade as a bonus.

Antigua
$$-$$$

*Sun to Wed 8am to midnight,
Thu to Sat 8am to 2am*
Morelos no. 371
small entrance on Plaza Guadalajara
☎614-0648

Set up on the third floor of a colonial building, Antigua offers one of the best views in the city, right on the cathedral. Patrons here savour old Mexican cuisine that, for lack of originality, is

Restaurants

100% authentic. Very
friendly service.

Sandy's
$$-$$$
Plaza Guadalajara
Sandy's terrace is a great
place to take a breather, in
the shade of the forest-
green parasols on the very
touristy Plaza Guadalajara.
Considering its prime location across from the cathedral, this eatery serves
good-quality, relatively inexpensive fare. A tourist hot
spot.

Cafés and Bakeries

Café Madrid
$
every day 7:30am to 10:30pm
Avenida Juárez no. 264
☎*614-9504*
At the Café Madrid, you can
take the time to sip your
delicious morning coffee
while having breakfast
before starting a day of
sightseeing downtown. As
evidenced by the furnish-
ings and Santa Fe—style
coffee machine, out-of-
towners and regulars have
been getting their java fix
here at retro prices since
the 1950s.

Tour B: Residences and Squares of Old Guadalajara

Sanborn's
$$$
every day 7:30am to 1am
Juárez, corner 16 de Septiembre
Sanborn's restaurant is cer-
tainly not unfamiliar to
those know Mexico. The
chain, which has branches
in every strategic point in
the city, is renowned for
both the quality of its food
and the efficiency of its
service. The menu features
international and Mexican
cuisine. What's more, every
outlet boasts a first-class
pharmacy, perfume shop,
and music and book sec-
tion.

Fonda San Miguel
$$$-$$$$
Donato Guerra no. 25
☎*613-0809*
The owners of Fonda San
Miguel have made the most
of the beauty of the former
convent (1690) in which
their restaurant is housed.
Indeed, the interior court-
yard that serves as a dining
room abounds in beautiful
handicrafts, each more orig-
inal than the last. Even the
washroom has been deco-
rated with care. The sonic
environment is amazingly
pleasant, with cries of par-
rots, a trickling fountain and
live music. Moreover, the

menu unquestionably demonstrates that Mexican cuisine does not merely consist of tacos and palate-scorching sauces, but dishes that can prove to be very refined. Note, however, that the quality of the dishes is tends to vary.

Cafés and Bakeries

🐚 Panificadora la Nacional
$
Pedro Moreno no. 587
☎614-9489
Definitely one of the best bakeries in all of Guadalajara, the Panificadora la Nacional has been turning out delicious oven-fresh biscuits, doughnuts, bread and cakes made from the finest Mexican recipes every morning since 1915. This is why generation after generation of tourists and locals have been flocking here to savour freshly baked treats every day.

Tour C: The Panteón de Belén and Surrounding Area

🐚 La Gorda
$
every day 1pm to midnight
Juan Álvarez no. 1336, corner Gral. Coronado
☎825-2239
You guessed it, this restaurant makes it a point of honour to serve rich and nourishing fare, including enchiladas, *moles*, tacos, tamales and many other classics of Mexican cooking. Good value for the money, too.

Tour D: Analco, Las Nueve Esquinas and Parque Agua Azul

Vamos a Licuar
$
Mon to Sat 9am to 8pm
Niños Héroes no. 1560
corner E.D. de León, next to Qué Pues
It's a well-known fact that fruit juices at breakfast brighten up the day and provide the body with rich essential vitamins. At Vamos a Licuar, fresh fruit juices are prepared right before your eyes and according to your wildest tastes, giving a wake-up call to those still-slumbering taste buds.

Restaurants

Siglo XV Mesón
$$$$
Mon to Sat 2pm to 2am
Colón no. 383
☎614-4278

In 15th-century Spain, it was probably in this type of place that seafarers and merchants discussed a new route to India that would later lead to the "discovery" of Mexico. From massive wooden tables and benches, to armour, candles and wrought-iron tableware, everything here recalls great medieval banquets. The flavours of the dishes, including the famous paella, also take us back to the Middle Ages. To enjoy an aperitif or after-dinner drink in a very original setting, do not hesitate to venture down the small spiral staircase that leads to the dungeon. The barrel seats and dimly lit room recall the hostile conditions in which prisoners of the time lived.

Tour E: Chapultepec and Las Antiguas Colonias

Peña Cuicalli
$
every day 1pm to 1am
Avenida Niños Héroes no. 1988
☎825-4690

After a little shopping on Avenida Chapultepec, a stop at Peña Cuicalli ("house of song" in Nahuatl) to sample the lunch special is easily warranted. For a mere 50 pesos, you can load up on enough food to sustain you for further exploring. Come nightfall, the *cantina* turns into a cultural centre, resonating with the sounds of myriad village folk singers. With one of the many national drinks in hand, fans of local music will then appreciate the refreshingly exotic indigenous culture.

Los 4 Gatos
$-$$
every day 1pm to 1am
Avenida López Cotilla no. 1835
☎616-8277

Although Mediterranean decorative elements are in short supply here, Los 4 Gatos is a pleasant spot for lovers of Mediterranean cuisine. At lunch, an interesting daily special is offered for as little as 45 pesos, while at dinner, the ambiance is warmed up by live flamenco and *romantica* music. The Valencia paella alone is worth the trip.

Los Itacates
$$
every day 8am to midnight
Avenida Chapultepec Norte no. 110
☎825-1106

For a taste of authentic old-time Mexico, head to Los Itacates. Walls emblazoned with suns, colourfully painted wooden furniture and the friendly atmosphere tastefully and good-naturedly evoke the fascinating culture of Mexico's indigenous peoples. So, too, does the menu, featuring *tacos dorados*, rice soup with egg and *huastec* fillet. To quench your thirst, tequila has, as tradition dictates, the place of honour. Whether to eat on the premises or for takeout, this is definitely a good choice.

Karne Garibaldi
$$
Garibaldi no. 1306
corner Clemente Orozco
☎826-1286
Carne en su jugo at its finest and served in as much time as it takes to say it. In fact, this eatery holds the Guinness record for the world's fastest-served meal: 13.5 seconds!

Café Fridas
$$
Mon to Sat 8am to midnight
Marcos Castellanos, opposite Parque Revolución
Located at the same address as Copenhagen 77 (see below), but on the ground floor, Café Fridas is a good place to start the day with a wholesome French, Mexican or American breakfast, depending on your mood and appetite. The soothing *azulejos* decor, muted lighting and tranquillity of Parque Revolución, right across the street, are sure to help you start the day off on the right foot. Good value for the money at breakfast, lunch and dinner.

El Ché
$$$
every day 1:30pm to midnight
Avenida Hidalgo no. 1798
corner A.L. Gallardo
☎615-0325
Follow your nose to the Argentinian El Ché restaurant. Indeed, with the open kitchen right at the front, passersby can admire the chef at work and, above all, smell the mouth-watering aroma of meat cooking on the grill. Your appetite having been thus aroused, you can gratify your taste buds with a variety of interesting Argentinian cuts of meat. All of which can be enjoyed in an unmistakable family atmosphere in the company of regulars.

Copenhagen 77
$$$
Mon to Sat 2pm to 1:30am
Marcos Castellanos, opposite Parque Revolución
Ah, sweet, sweet jazz! Sizzling-jazz aficionados will make the detour to get their fix at Copenhagen 77, where a jazz combo captivates gourmets enjoying Spanish and international cuisine every night from 8pm to 1:30am.

Restaurants

El Espeto
$$$
Mon to Sat 1pm to 11pm
Sun 1pm to 6pm
Avenida Chapultepec no. 287
corner Lerdo de Tejada
☎*825-0392*

Nostalgic for Brazil? Then El Espeto will soon take you back to the bustling streets of Sao Paulo with its well-known hospitality and colours. This cafeteria-like eatery serves a daily buffet of refreshing salads and Brazilian-style cooked meats. So dizzying is the selection of Brazilian drinks with which to wash down this simple, hearty fare, that you'll be unable to make head nor tail of them, especially with the Portuguese labels.

Habana
$$$
every day 1:30pm to midnight
Avenida La Paz no. 2199
corner Calle Simón Bolívar
☎*616-0096*

Cuban gastronomy is on offer at Habana, one of the only Cuban restaurants in town. The decor deserves a mention for its unique marriage of images of bygone Cuba and streamlined 1990s furniture. All island specialties are offered in an atmosphere livened up by Cuban singers. Perfect for an intimate evening.

Ma Come No
$$$
every day noon to 2am
Avenida Américas no. 302
corner Calle Manuel Acuña
☎*615-4952*

Si Como No's (see p 177) little sister proves to be of an entirely different style, but with just as much character. In fact, visitors here will find the last word in Italian restaurants in Guadalajara. From floor to ceiling, terrace to bar, every inch of the place has been conceived according to good Italian taste. The equally refined menu is composed of seafood, fish, pasta and thin-crust pizzas. In short, a must-visit. And be sure to meet congenial owner Darío Pérez, who offers a glass of wine or a margarita to Ulysses readers!

Riscal
$$$
every day 1:30pm to 10:30pm
Avenida López Cotilla no. 1751
corner Calle Simón Bolívar
☎*616-8677*

Riscal offers traditional Spanish fare, including, of course, the seminal paella, but also an amazing variety of meats, fish and seafood, unfortunately prepared with little originality. The place features the atmosphere of a venerable but somewhat old-fashioned and uninviting colonial house.

🌴 Sacromonte

$$$

every day 2pm to midnight
Avenida Pedro Moreno no. 1398
☎825-5447

Sacromonte's lovely, warm-coloured house is as wonderful within as it is without. Indeed, from the covered interior courtyard and pleasant bar to the bull-themed lounge and upstairs terrace, you will see how much care the owner has put into decorating the walls. The collection on display includes photographs of bygone Guadalajara, artworks of the "fair sex" and interesting pottery. In such a Mexican setting, what else can be served but *vieja cocina mexicana* such as the San Mateo steak and *Chamorrito El Manglar*? A great place for a romantic tête-à-tête or an evening with friends to the sounds of rhythmic jazz.

Bistro de Thérèse

$$$-$$$$

every day 1:30pm to 11pm
Calderón de la Barca no. 95
corner Avenida López Cotilla
☎616-2947

In addition to offering tasteful *objets d'art* for contemplation, Bistro de Thérèse lavishes its patrons with good home-style French cooking. The soups, seafood and meats will transport you to the heart of the French countryside in the time it takes to enjoy your meal. A few false notes, such as spelling mistakes on the menu and very average value for the money, are best forgotten with the help of one of the many house wines.

El Pargo

$$$-$$$$

every day 1:30pm to 5pm
Avenida La Paz no. 2140
☎615-7465

"Afishionados" are spoiled for choice at all three El Pargo branches. *Pescado* and *camáron sarandeado* are but two dishes that grace a menu consisting exclusively of bounties of the sea. Once seated in the middle of this restaurant-cafeteria while entertained by *música en vivo* and refreshed by the bracing sea breeze, you will notice just how popular the place is at lunchtime, which is always a good sign. Reservations recommended; multilingual staff.

Circuló Francés

$$$$

every day 1:30pm to midnight
Avenida López Cotilla no. 1221
☎825-0515

This pioneer of French restaurants was founded in 1942 by the local Barcelonnette association, families of French immigrants who were responsible for several French institutions in Guadalajara (see inset, p 24). Today, the establishment continues to attract the city's francophiles in a post-war setting

Restaurants

that has likely remained unchanged since its foundation, as evidenced by the sombre dining room adorned with a period chandelier. Unfortunately, the restaurant's French essence has become somewhat diluted over time, as it serves food with international accents, perhaps to cater to a larger clientele. Somewhat overpriced.

Delfín Sonriente
$$$$
every day 1:30pm to 11pm
Avenida Niños Héroes no. 2239
☎616-0216
Ah, the sea and its wealth of delights! Delfín Sonriente is the place to go for the gustatory riches of the ocean blue, from seafood dishes and tuna salad to smoked fish. However, aside from the mounted dolphin casting an inquisitive look at patrons, there is absolutely nothing special about the decor.

🌴 Le Grand Bordeaux
$$$$
every day 1:30pm to midnight
Avenida López Cotilla no. 1002
☎825-2011
Set up in an old mansion in the heart of the French district, Le Grand Bordeaux is a place gourmets will soon call their own. Chef Frederick Berbille, originally from Bordeaux, has put together a wonderful, authentic French menu. The liver pâté, fresh marinated

salmon and fillet of beef in red wine are the best dishes on the menu. The place is resolutely European-looking, with characteristic refinement and a decor mainly composed of simple images of old French advertisements. A sure bet.

Maximino's
$$$$
every day 1pm to midnight
Calle Juan Ruiz de Alarcón no. 221
at Avenida Lerdo de Tejada
☎630-0280
Recently reopened with a more casual format than its previous incarnation, the new Maximino's remains a sophisticated establishment. Modern-art paintings and elegant wooden furnishings lay the groundwork for a choice international menu. Moctezuma crepes and Azteca soup as starters, followed by *rotelli putanesca* with shrimp and octopus as a main course and a good Amaretto parfait for dessert make for a unique culinary experience. For a more informal atmosphere, diners can sit out in the garden, a great idea on warm Guadalajara summer nights.

🛶 Santo Coyote
$$$$
every day 1pm to 1am
Avenida Lerdo de Tejada no. 2379
corner Calle Tepic
☎616-6978
Santo Coyote will undoubtedly impress you. Indeed, its decor deserves a men-

tion, consisting of every Mexican cliché and cult object, such as the Virgin of Guadalupe, country haciendas and candelabra-shaped cacti jumbled together in every section of the large terrace. You can therefore revel in a good meal of Mexican nouvelle cuisine in a replica of a western hacienda, beneath a thatched roof brightened up by a large fountain or in a cheerful village atmosphere. Menu-wise, while the delicious *huesitos en sal* starter rouses your appetite, main dishes such as *cabrito al Pastor* (the house specialty) are a real treat. For dessert, the *rollo de piña* lands the prize. After ordering your meal, be sure to keep an eye on the chef preparing your food near your table.

Formosa Gardens
$$$$-$$$$$
every day from 1pm
Calle Unión no. 322
☎615-7415

Finding a good Chinese restaurant in Guadalajara is no easy task. At Formosa Gardens, you can enjoy quality traditional Cantonese cuisine. Located in an old house of North African architecture, the dining room is appealingly elegant. Chinese vases and Moorish windows combine to give business lunches a lot of class. Comfortably ensconced in the air-conditioned dining room, you

can dig into the fried rice, refreshing salads or *Pato entero Loquedo* (the house specialty).

Suehiro
$$$$$
every day 1pm to 1am
Avenida La Paz no. 1701
☎826-0094

For a nice change from Mexican cooking, the Suehiro restaurant-bar offers Japanese haute cuisine. In an ultra-chic setting, you can first swing by the bar for sake (rice-based alcohol) or head straight to the dining room, which looks out on a charming Japanese-style garden. Once seated at the exquisite Oriental-style table, you can peruse the multi-page menu chock-full of dishes whose names are each more exotic than the last. This will give you the perfect opportunity to consult the pleasant staff, dressed in the tradition of the land of the rising sun, about the delicious house specialties. The servers will undoubtedly mention the sushi (pieces of fresh raw fish wrapped in rice), sukiyaki (thin slices of beef with vegetables sautéed in soya sauce), sashimi (thin fillets of raw fish) and delicious tempura (battered and deep-fried seafood and vegetables), all of which deserve consideration. This solemn setting is perfect for those looking to impress business clients or friends.

Restaurants

Cafés and Bakeries

El Globo
$
Avenida Lópex Cotilla no. 1749
corner Calle Simón Bolívar
☎616-6408
Avenida Rubén Darío no. 640
corner Calle Bonifacio Andrada
☎641-7849
El Globo takes pride in the fact that it has been serving its gourmet clientele scrumptious pastries since 1884. The place is especially worth the trip for its wide selection and moderate prices. Takeout only. Two outlets.

Mondo Café
$
every day 8am to 10:30pm
Avenida Chapultepec Sur no. 48
corner Avenida Pedro Moreno
☎616-2709
One of the favourite pastimes of café loafers is unquestionably to watch and exchange nonchalant glances with the steady yet ever-changing stream of passersby. And this is precisely what you can do at Mondo Café, where both a huge window and a terrace looking out on Avenida Chapultepec allow patrons to miss nothing of the passing parade. Besides the view, this café with rather cold urban decor is nothing special. The staff, as young

as the clientele, serves light fare and good iced coffee.

Monique
$
every day 8:30am to 10:30pm
Calle Unión no. 410
corner Avenida Montenegro
☎615-6851
At Monique, a renowned French bakery, you must first take the time to choose among the variety of tempting sweet treats at the counter before sitting down at a table. Once seated, you'll find out just how delicious these pastries are.

La Paloma
$
every day 8am to midnight
Avenida López Cotilla no. 1855
☎630-0195
La Paloma features a genuine Mexican terrace, which all of Guadalajara patronizes at all hours of the day for its local (if rather unstylish) cachet. Ensconced on the terrace, young consumers come to pass the time here while having breakfast and a simple drink.

Vida Leve
$
Sun to Thu 2pm to 11pm
Fri and Sat 2pm to 1am
Avenida López Cotilla no. 1580
☎616-8754
What could be more pleasant than getting together

with friends over coffee, while putting the world right through discussion? Such is the atmosphere you'll find at Vida Leve, which boasts a terrace and a decor entirely fashioned by local artists. A student crowd hangs out here, playing checkers or dominos while munching on a sandwich, bagel or house salad.

Veneto Café
$$
every day 11am to 1am
Calle Francisco Javier Gamboa no. 284-1, at Avenida Efrain González Luna
☎615-8892

A favourite with local young people and families, the Veneto Café is a pleasant, quiet little place for sipping coffee along with a dessert or a sandwich on homemade bread. While a skylight floods the white stucco walls with natural light, designer wooden furniture gives the whole place a sense of Italian refinement.

Tour F: Minerva and el Iztépete

La Calle
$-$$
every day 1pm to 11pm
Calle Autlán 2-A, corner Avenida Vallarta
☎647-7595

Facing a lovely, verdant public garden near the Fuente de la Minerva, the La Calle restaurant serves simple, unexceptional Mexican fare. Despite the neon lights around the windows and the shoe ads that cover the walls, you should not be deterred from appreciating the huge portions served here: 50 pesos for a nourishing meal including a delicious caramel pancake. A real bargain!

Roma Antica
$
Avenida Pablo Neruda no. 3006
☎641-2511

There's nothing like a good pizza to satisfy the most intense of cravings. One of the three Roma Antica outlets has been offering a wide array of pizzas, said to be the best in town, for 20 years. For a pittance, you'll get a large *mexicana*, *roma*, *picolli* or *chorizo* pizza. Whether to eat in the dining room or for takeout, Roma Antica will delight those for whom time is precious.

Taquería de La Minerva
$
24hrs
Avenida Vallarta, corner Calle Isabel la Católica

Located a stone's throw from the fountain of the same name, Taquería de La Minerva is this district's Mecca of *comidas corridas*. Open round the clock, this clean and simple little eatery features a typically popular menu. Budget travellers

Restaurants

will enjoy *tacos al pastor*
(also offered with brains,
tongue or tripe for braver
souls), quesadillas or the
healthiest of *tacos tostados*.
Perfect for a quick snack or
late-night cravings. For a
little local flavour, be sure
to ask the cook what he
thinks of the last Chivas
game!

El Gordo Steak
$$
every day 1:30pm to midnight
Avenida Terranova no. 1244
corner Calle Milán
☎*642-0127*
Located on the very high-
class Avenida Terranova, El
Gordo Steak is noteworthy
for its muted setting, shel-
tered from the scorching
rays of the sun. The menu
features deliciously pre-
pared meats of all kinds,
making them veritable
feasts for the palate.

La Squina
$$
*Sun to Thu 1:30pm to mid-
night*
Fri and Sat 1:30pm to 1am
Avenida Golfo de Cortés no. 4182-8
☎*813-0513*
Avenida Aztlán no. 3787
☎*122-3526*
La Squina can satisfy the
strongest cravings for
burgers. The menu
first invites you to
savour traditional
Mexican entrées,
then to follow up
with one of the
chef's two spe-

cialties: burgers of all kinds
and *sincrozinadas* garnished
in every way imaginable.
All of which is served on a
quiet terrace modelled after
Mediterranean bistros.
Good food and budget-
pleasing prices are available
at both outlets.

New York New York
$$-$$$
every day 8am to midnight
Avenida Guadalupe no. 1258
☎*121-8657*
Facing the Glorieta
Guadalupe is another
neighbourhood restaurant
with reasonably priced
food. Home-style cooking is
served in an unoriginal
setting. Congenial atmo-
sphere.

Oliveto
$$-$$$
every day 1pm to midnight
Avenida Niños Héroes no. 3000-A
☎*121-8364*
Oliveto is neither more nor
less than a simple neigh-
bourhood Italian restaurant.
In a laid-back atmosphere
amidst warm colours, treat
yourself to pasta garnished
with everything imaginable
or, for a little more refinement, the Chili Oliveti fillet
with mango and ginger.
Despite the quality of the
food, the menu unfortu-
nately suffers from a
definite lack of
imagination
and street
noise in-
trudes somewhat

on dining-room conversations.

🦐 Las Palomas
$$-$$$
every day 8am to 1am
Avenida Américas no. 1491
Col. Providencia
☎817-2798

Set up on the terrace of a Mexican *finca* adorned with rustic tables and chairs, Las Palomas specializes in typically Mexican cuisine. While a *leticia* (a vodka-based drink) sharpens your appetite, main dishes such as *moles*, enchiladas and *molcajete* delight your taste buds. Light meals are also available.

El Arca
$$$
every day 1:30pm to 11pm
Avenida Vallarta no. 2425
Centro Magno
☎630-0860

The El Arca restaurant opened its doors in the winter of 1999 with a very original concept. Giraffes, hippos, zebras and horses, all of which are perched in a giant ark in the middle of the dining room, make up the colourful decor here. The cow-patterned furnishings perpetuate the place's safari theme. Unfortunately, originality stops there, as the menu features unexceptional international cuisine.

Dragón de Oro
$$$
every day 1pm to midnight
Avenida Américas no. 1637
☎817-1655

Set up within a Chinese temple, Dragón de Oro predictably offers Cantonese, Mongolian and Schezuan food, in addition to a few international dishes. The two floors with Asian decor feature a piano whose ivories are tinkled nightly. Although the city's pioneer of Chinese restaurants seems to have a little trouble drawing customers, this should in no way prevent you from enjoying it all to yourself.

Hacienda Navarro
$$$
every day 1pm to 11pm
Avenida Arcos no. 588
☎121-1179

Hacienda Navarro is a veritable temple for carnivores. "Meat" is the watchword when ordering from the menu, although seafood and salads are also featured for less carnivorous types. Your everyday steakhouse.

El Libanés
$$$
every day from 1pm
Avenida López Mateos no. 550
☎121-3009

For a touch of exoticism, visitors can drop by El Libanés, one of the few Lebanese restaurants in town. For starters, the *taboule* and kebabs will

Restaurants

prime you for the delectable *shish taouk* or *wara arich* (stuffed vine leaves) to follow. And, for a satiating finale to a fine meal, nothing beats the sweet treats whose secrets only the Lebanese are privy to. As for the rest, the only decorative element consists of a series of Moorish arches that do not do honour to the elaborate architecture of the Near East. Nightly pianist.

Mr. Bull
$$$
Mon to Sat 1pm to 11pm
Sun 1pm to 6pm
Avenida Buenos Aires no. 3090-A
corner Avenida Pablo Neruda
☎641-2734

Dark parquet floors, stuffed heads of cattle and wagon wheels will draw ranch and Far West enthusiasts to Mr. Bull, a restaurant specializing in barbecued meat. While enjoying the reassuring smell of charcoal, patrons sample the culinary specialty of the West. Try one of the excellent domestic wines, so little known north of the Rio Grande. And for an after-dinner drink, move on to the adjacent bar with authentic saloon decor.

Los Otates
$$$
every day 1:30pm to midnight
Avenida México no. 2455-2
☎630-2855

Good traditional Mexican food awaits you at Los Otates. The menu, slightly more elaborate than average, offers a selection of tacos, *tacos tostados*, meats and seafood. Sharing the very generous Los Otates platter, a combo of the best house dishes, is also a good idea. Since the establishment was founded in 1951 by two influential local families, the decor has continuously been enriched with adornments made by indigenous people, including the *barra negra* and other fine paintings and woven pieces.

Oui Café
$$$
every day 8:30am to 2:30am
Avenida López Cotilla no. 2171
☎615-0614

Coffered ceilings, omnipresent stained-glass windows and classic artworks make up the decor of the Oui Café. Whether enjoying the terrace on sunny days or seated beneath the enormous skylight in the dining room, patrons here are continually impressed by the Art Nouveau–style decorative elements reminiscent of early-20th-century restaurants. For lack of originality, the international menu caters to all tastes. But patrons here are duty-bound to try the *cappucino l'amour*, made from a top-secret Italian recipe, as all the servers will enjoy telling you.

Parilla Argentina
$$$
Mon to Sat 1:30pm to midnight
Sun 1:30pm to 7:30pm
Avenida Fernando Celada no. 176
near the Minerva
☎615-7361
Those who feel like sinking their teeth into a tender steak should make a beeline for Parilla Argentina, which offers a whole range of delicious imported meats, mostly straight from Argentina. From the ranch-style cow hides and wagon wheels to red-tiled roofs, everything here aims to reproduce the atmosphere of the legendary Patagonia prairies. Wine-lovers will also be pleased to note that the restaurant has a wide variety of Chilean and Argentinian red wines.

La Pianola
$$$
every day 7:30pm to midnight
Avenida México no. 3220A
☎813-1385
La Pianola proudly shows off its colours, Mexican-village cachet and multicoloured garlands. Indeed, the place thrives on Mexican traditions. Perhaps a little too much so, with the *equipales* furnishings, flower-covered terrace and pastel colours on the verge of spilling over into kitsch. The menu features the standard Mexican fare and a lunch buffet.

Si Como No
$$$
every day 1:30pm to midnight
Avenida Chapalita no. 120
☎122-5926
Rather unexotic international fare garnishes your plate at Si Como No, to the great comfort of more timid palates. It is rather in the decor that all the originality of this garden-like restaurant-bar lies. Indeed, patrons here dine in an astounding, huge greenhouse blooming with exotic flora and dotted with colourful massive-wood tables and chairs. This "green lung" offers a delightful change from the neighbourhood's austere urban landscape.

Sushi-Nori
$$$
Sat to Thu 1:30pm to 11:30pm
Fri 1:30pm to 1:30am
Avenida México no. 2705
corner Avenida López Mateos
☎615-2323
Located on the corner of Avenidas México and López Mateos, Sushi-Nori not only offers sushi, but also a whole variety of unique Japanese dishes. Whether seated at the bar or a table facing a lovely fountain, you can enjoy *teparyakis* and *makis* with equal refinement. The Japanese decor is elegant, but the presence of a television is unfortunate.

Restaurants

La Trattoria
$$$
every day 1pm to midnight
Avenida Niños Héroes no. 3051
☎*122-4425*

The city's large Italian community may explain the existence of yet another good Italian restaurant, La Trattoria. For a reasonable price, patrons are entitled to top-notch fare such as traditional pasta (10 varieties), tender escalopes and pizza, all prepared from original recipes flavoured with olive oil. It's enough to make your mouth water, isn't it? Those in a hurry can order this hearty cuisine to go.

La Destilería
$$$-$$$$
Mon to Sat 1pm to midnight
Sun 1pm to 4pm
Avenida México no. 2916
corner Calle Nelson
☎*640-3110*

What could be more Jaliscan than the national drink, tequila? The La Destilería chain makes it a point of honour to showcase the agave-distilled nectar, the pride of all Jaliscans. The restaurant-cum-tequila-museum also makes a point of instructing its customers about the three stages of the tequila-making process (baking or steaming, fermentation and distillation) with the help of numerous original pieces that make up the decor. What's more, several dishes are made with tequila, including the seafood-lime soup, three-cheese fondue and breast of chicken. Perfect for those with no time to visit Tequila.

Hostería del Arte
$$$-$$$$
Mon to Sat 2pm to 1am
Avenida Manuel Acuña no. 3141-B
☎*641-6936*

Hostería del Arte regulars surely return again and again for the always-charming environment. The art gallery, brick walls and *azulejos* create a very appealing setting in this charming little Mexican house. Opt to dine in one of the many lounges with different atmospheres, rather than on the cold terrace, in order to fully appreciate the Italian and French cuisine, offered for a rather less-satisfying price.

Estancia Gaucha
$$$$
every day 1:30pm to midnight
Avenida Niños Héroes no. 2860-A
☎*122-6565*

For a successful business lunch, arrange to meet at Estancia Gaucha, one of the best Argentinian culinary embassies in the city. The restaurant's designers have judiciously taken advantage of the natural light filtered by stained-glass windows and skylights. Even a few shrubs benefit from such refreshing brightness. The menu is decidedly Argentinian, with specialties

1such as *chamorro de ternera* and *alsado de costilla*.

El Italiano
$$$$
every day 1pm to 11pm
Avenida México no. 3130
☎813-2984

At El Italiano, you'll have the impression of walking into one of those highly exclusive places frequented by the Sicilian diaspora. Meals are served on lovely checkered tablecloths surrounded by various objects dear to the owner, including a string of plates autographed by famous clients. The great classics of Italian cuisine are served in a rather formal manner. Reservations recommended.

Lüsherly
$$$$
Mon to Sat 1pm to midnight
Sun 1pm to 7pm
Calle Duque de Rivas no. 5
corner Avenida Morelos
☎615-0509

A 20-year-old standby set up in a charming half-timbered cottage in a residential neighbourhood, Lüsherly brings Swiss-German and Italian specialties to your table. The red-checkered tablecloths, piano and tables on the balcony overlooking the interior courtyard fairly successfully recreate the ambiance of a Swiss inn. The menu is composed of the not-to-be-missed cheese fondue, singular sauerkraut and

Zurich-style *émincé*, all skillfully prepared by Swiss-born chef Lüsher. Unfortunately, the prices do not break with Helvetic tradition.

Quinta Real
$$$$$
every day 7am to midnight
Avenida México no. 2727
corner Avenida López Mateos
☎615-0000

Those who appreciate a sophisticated atmosphere and polished service will enjoy the Quinta Real hotel's restaurant, where patrons can eat well at any time of day. Business people and well-heeled travellers rub elbows in a sumptuous setting inspired by ornate Spanish castles. Those with well-padded wallets can uncompromisingly enjoy the many specialties of a thematic Spanish menu that changes every three weeks.

Cafés and Bakeries

Bon's Café
$
every day 8am to midnight
Avenida Tepeyac no. 455
Chapalita
☎122-0601

For variety, Bon's Café is a must. The 23 flavours of coffee and 14 varieties of homemade pastries will introduce those who claim to have seen and tried it all to unknown flavours. With that in mind, you must try the Café Diablo (coffee, brandy and *contry*) or the Sara García (hot chocolate, coffee and tequila) to understand just how wide the definition of "coffee" is here. The term "variety" hardly applies to the rather gaudy yet humdrum decor, however. Business clientele in the morning, preppy crowd at night.

Café Martinique

$

every day 8am to midnight
Avenida López Cotilla no. 2071
opposite the Centro Magno
☎*616-0413*

Connoisseurs of Guadalajara coffee will invariably recommend Café Martinique, named in honour of this French overseas territory. Coffee here is elevated to cult status. From the wild plantations of Veracruz to the cup, by way of grinding and filtration by authentic Italian machines, everything is controlled to guarantee the best coffee in the city. Three explanatory brochures enlighten java junkies about the famous beverage's production process. Such seriousness in the cultivation of good coffee cannot but be reflected in this most sophisticated of places. International dishes are served as an accompaniment. An absolute must.

Dalí Café

$

Mon to Thu 8am to midnight
Fri and Sat 8am to 1am
Sun 9am to 11pm
Avenida Guadalupe no. 1144
opposite the Glorieta de Guadalupe
☎*122-5655*

The Dalí Café features a decor inspired by the works of Catalan painter Salvador Dalí. At breakfast, you can enjoy home-style cooking in the company of business people. In the afternoon, you can relax alongside hip students while sipping one of the many libations on the menu, including the one-of-a-kind Café-Dalí, a cappucino with Bailey's Irish Cream. Pity, though, that the constant noise of traffic along Avenida Guadalupe disrupts this relaxing interlude.

El Sorbo de Café

$

Plaza del Sol, suite 21
☎*122-8228*

Those who are tired of window shopping around the Plaza del Sol can take a break at the refined El Sorbo de Café. Hot or cold, long or short, the coffee here is always good. To tell the truth, it is sheer pleasure to sample a new flavour each time, while reading the paper and savouring the sweet smell of ground coffee that wafts by your nose. Judging by the variety of people that flock here, this small café is a unanimous favourite.

Tacón Galleta
$
Mon to Thu 2pm to 11pm
Fri and Sat 2pm to 1am
Calle Mar Báltico no. 2240-102
near the Country Club
☎817-5299

Coffee, pastries, salads, entrées and a variety of sandwiches are featured on the menu at the Tacón Galleta café-snack bar. The carefully designed contemporary decor is appreciated by the young professionals who patronize the place. Both upstairs and on the terrace, relaxing jazz plays throughout the day. Just one question: what is a banal television doing in such an inspired setting?

Tour G: Zapopan

Viejo Ahualulco
$-$$
Calle 20 de Noviembre
Zapopan's main pedestrian street, Calle 20 de Noviembre, is lined with small snack bars with sidewalk terraces. All serve more or less the same kind of food, generally rather unoriginal but reasonably priced seafood. Among them, Viejo Ahualulco offers a little more variety,

including soups, meats and other Mexican dishes. A good place for those who enjoy crowds.

Agios Aggelos
$$-$$$
every day 1:30pm to midnight
Calle 20 de Noviembre no. 342
☎633-1131

Agios Aggelos is further proof that Guadalajarans cultivate the world's cuisines. The only Greek restaurant in the area gratifies all five senses. Taste is fulfilled by the incomparable souvlakis, gyros and moussaka, while smell delights in the bouquet of Hellenic wine. Sight revels in the Aegean Sea–blue parasols dotting the terrace, and touch is caressed by the sweet breeze that wafts through the heart of Zapopan after sundown. Last but not least, hearing is enchanted by *música en vivo*, which gets under way in the evening. What more could you ask for?

🛶 Hostería del Ángel
$$-$$$
every day 8am to midnight
Avenida 5 de Mayo no. 295
☎656-9516

The head chef of Hostería del Ángel has brought back a strong European influence from his long culinary stint in Spain. All the food he concocts abounds in Iberian flavours, including the *Platón de Carne de la Casa*, which will definitely delight the most demanding of palates. The warm setting, flooded with bright colours, evokes the transcendent exoticism of the Mexican culture. Very attentive service and unbeatable prices.

100% Natural
$$$
every day 7am to midnight
Avenida Patria no. 714
☎673-5640

Natural food can be enjoyed at breakfast, lunch and dinner at 100% Natural, a vegetarian restaurant. This restaurant chain, primarily established on the coasts of Mexico, has now set up shop in Guadalajara. The thatched-roof eatery has built its reputation on the exclusive use of the best fresh and organic products available. The menu is most varied, ranging from Italian pasta dishes and American-style burgers to tropical juices and Mexican burritos. And you need not have any qualms about eating all these goodies with gusto, as all dishes are low in fat. Somehow, you'll even have room left after your meal for an organic brownie soaking in frozen yogurt. *¡Buen provecho!*

Tour H: San Pedro Tlaquepaque and Tonalá

Adobe Fonda
$$$
every day noon to 7pm
Calle Independencia no. 195
Tlaquepaque
☎957-2792

Set up inside the magnificent craft gallery of the same name (see p 219), Adobe Fonda is a must in the village of Tlaquepaque. The sheer abundance of crafts on display is sure to give you ideas for your next shopping spree. The menu, presented in a tin envelope, is unfortunately the only original feature of the bill of fare, which offers contemporary Mexican cuisine with international accents. The restaurant-gallery also features a front terrace.

Casa Fuerte
$$$
every day noon to 8pm
Calle Independencia no. 224
Tlaquepaque
☎639-6481

A restaurant specializing in poultry and fish, as well as Oaxaca cuisine, Casa Fuerte is a nice change of pace. After enjoying a tequila along with innovative appetizers in the European-style lounge, you will be led into the pleasant dining room set within a flowery courtyard. At dinnertime, *música*

en vivo mingles in crescendo
with the chirping of birds
nestled in the garden.

Casa Vieja
$$$
Mon to Thu 8am to 11:30pm
Fri to Sun 8am to 1am
Avenida Guillermo Prieto no. 99
corner Calle Constitución
Tlaquepaque
☎657-6250

At the end of Avenida
Guillermo Prieto stands an
excellent restaurant offering
refined cuisine. The menu
features marvellous salads
and *molcajetes* made from
Tlaquepaque recipes.

🦐 Restaurante Sin Nombre
$$$
Sun to Thu 8:30am to 9pm
*Fri and Sat 8:30am to mid-
night*
Avenida Francisco I. Madero no. 80
Tlaquepaque
☎635-4520

Set back a little from the
very touristy Calles
Independencia and Juárez,
on a quiet little village
street, Restaurante Sin
Nombre deserves a men-
tion. Indeed, this eatery is
just the place for those
seeking a little peace and
quiet in a lovely, dimly lit
interior courtyard. Whether
by the delightful shrubs
near the craft gallery or in
the courtyard among free-
roaming hens and roosters,
you can enjoy various Mexican dishes. Try the *chiles en
nogada*, which, unlike what

its name suggests, is not too
spicy for foreign palates.

Cafés and Bakeries

El Parian
$
every day 9am to 1am
Jardín Hidalgo
corner Calle Progreso
☎659-2362

Located in the heart of
Tlaquepaque, the very
conspicuous El Parian
complex is considered a
tourist attraction in itself
(see p 115). The huge café-
restaurant is, however, a
victim of its own success.
The many servers paid on
commission relentlessly
fight over potential clients.
Of course, once seated at
the *equipales* tables, all
courtesy soon vanishes. Not
to mention the incessant
solicitation by scores of
street vendors who consider
the place an extension of
the adjacent market. Ulti-
mately, if you can stand all
this chaos, you will probably enjoy being serenaded
by the mariachis who per-
form hourly in the café's
gazebo.

Tlalipac
$
every day 9am to 8pm
Calle Independencia no. 270
Tlaquepaque
☎635-0706

Whether in its lovely dining
room adorned with a host
of crafts or its pleasant

Restaurants

garden embellished with flowers and birds, lovers of Mexican *botanas* will make a point of sampling Tlalipac's guacamole. The many nibbles featured on the menu go hand in hand with a refreshing beer enjoyed among friends. You'll ask for more!

Tour I: Laguna de Chapala

In San Juan Cosalá, most restaurants are located along Laguna de Chapala and offer roughly the same fish and seafood dishes. Equally good but without much refinement, they will nevertheless suit fans of the genre.

Salvador's
$$-$$$
every day 8am to 11pm
Carretera Oriente no. 56
Ajijic
☎766-2301
The great number of "snowbirds" who spend their winters in Ajijic has spawned many restaurants offering international cuisine. Among them, Salvador's, though undistinguishable from its counterparts, is a decent place. The salads (bar), simple meat or poultry dishes and burgers are served in a space equally devoid of style.

Cozumel
$$$
Tue to Sun 11am to 10pm
Paseo Ramón Corona no. 22-A
Chapala
☎765-4606
The owners of the Cozumel restaurant have exchanged their heavenly island for the uniformly pleasant Chapala climate, but they made sure they brought along the best they had: their cuisine. As such, caviar, salmon and lobster grace the menu, but the best bet remains the *Carne a la Tampiqueña*, a combination of three Mexican-style cooked meats. The service, in Spanish or English, is friendly and the decor predominantly features photographs of the island of Cozumel, located off the Yucatan peninsula.

Mariscos Guicho e Hijos
$$$
Wed to Mon 11am to 8pm
Calle Ramón Corona no. 20
Chapala
☎765-3232
The Marisco Guicho e Hijos restaurant is a pleasant place for a good but simple meal. Upstairs, you can enjoy fish and seafood along with a lovely view of the lake; on the main floor, *molcajetes* and ceviches are served at tables draped with checkered tablecloths.

Los Telares
$$$$
Sun to Thu noon to 9pm
Fri and Sat noon to 10pm
Avenida Morelos no. 6
Ajijic
☎*766-0428*

Los Telares, Ajijic's sophisticated restaurant, meets the demand of the village's wealthy resident clientele. Opt to sit out in the garden rather than in the dining room, so as to take advantage of the lovely fountain, dazzling sunshine and the colourful crockery that adorns the tables. The menu ranges from seafood to pasta to salads.

Cafés and Bakeries

Árbol de Café
$
Mon to Fri 8am to 4pm
Sat 8am to 2pm
Calle Hidalgo no. 236
Plaza de las Palmas
Chapala

Whether on the terrace or inside, Árbol de Café is a good place to enjoy hot or iced coffee brewed from a whole variety of beans. In the afternoon, you can do so while quietly writing love letters, daydreaming or watching passersby on Calle Hidalgo. All this and, as the menu says, service with a smile!

El Santuario de Caba
$$
Calle Colón no. 43
Ajijic
☎*766-1920*

After visiting the art gallery or the printing house, a small alley at the back of the courtyard will lead you to El Santuario de Caba. Inside this peaceful flowery garden, two charming South American women run the best café in Ajijic. Fine chocolate, refined ice cream, sandwiches on French bread and Italian coffee: all these treats combine to create a feast for the senses. It's a pity that the noise of the neighbouring houses disrupts this serene oasis. Then again, such a setting is worth putting up with just about anything.

Tour J: Tequila and Surroundings

El Callejón
$$
every day 9:30am to 11pm
Avenida Sixto Gorjón no. 105
Tequila
☎*742-1037*

Among Tequila's restaurants, few stand out for their refinement. Yet El Callejón is an exception to the rule for several reasons, including a mural that proudly evokes the day-to-day life of locals and a menu featuring many dishes

Restaurants

Aïe Tequila!

Tequila, Mexico's legendary national drink, derives its name from a village located in the heart of the region in which it is produced. According to its residents, it would seem that indigenous people made a similar type of liquor in pre-Colombian times. But it wasn't until the arrival of the Spanish in the 16th century, when large *haciendas tequileras* were established in the region, that this liquor was produced through the same process used today.

The reddish soil on the slopes of the extinct Volcán de Tequila and in its surrounding area provides the necessary agricultural properties for the cultivation of the blue agave, while preserving its specific characteristics. This variety of agave, whose scientific name is *agave tequilana Weber*, in honour of the German biologist who studied it in the early 20th century, is the raw material for authentic tequila.

However, there is also another production area located east of Guadalajara, between the towns of Zapotlanejo and Arandas.

Tequila's development process is similar to that of other spirits, but the first phase is interesting to note. First, after the land is cultivated, agave shoots are selected and planted. The agave plants take eight to 10 years to mature, after which the leaves are removed and the huge pineapple-like cores (*piñas*) are taken to the distillery where they are baked or steamed for 24hrs, then cooled for another 24hrs. During this time, the sap of the agave's heart turns into a natural syrup. This liquid, which exudes a particular fragrance, is extracted by a press, then fermented for 72 to 96hrs and distilled in *alambiques* (stills). Finally, an aging period then determines if it is a *joven*, *reposado* or *añejo* tequila.

The prestige of good tequila has grown worldwide primarily since the implementation of the "guaranteed vintage" designation in the early 1970s. At present, strict quality-control standards govern everything from the growing and transportation of agaves to the production and bottling of this traditional Mexican liquor.

perked up with tequila. A four-person economy menu (*queso fundido*, guacamole, *tacos dorados*, refreshments, tacos and a bottle of tequila) is offered.

Mariscos El Mar
$$
Carretera Int. Curva de la Toma
Tequila
☎*742-1029*
At the exit from the town, on the road to Magdalena, Mariscos El Mar attracts seafood-lovers with a reputation than extends beyond the town itself. Perched at the end of an agave field, the small cottage offers a superb panorama of the whole area.

La Posta
$$
every day 8am to 2:30pm
Avenida Sixto Gorjón no. 111
Tequila
☎*742-0114*
The La Posta eatery is devoted body and soul to tequila. Indeed, no less than 27 varieties are offered as an aperitif, accompaniment or after-dinner drink. Here is your opportunity to hone your tastes and test your knowledge. The distilled agave is even used in the food: the house specialties are actually cooked with a hint of the fiery liquor.

El Marinero
$$$
every day 9am to 10:30pm
Calle Vicente A. Rosas no. 16-B
Tequila
☎*742-1674*
With "captain" Andrés Cantreras at the helm, this restaurant's exemplary cuisine has not deviated from its course since it opened five years ago. The bounties of the sea served here are always fresh. Moreover, the menu features a few stowaways, such as pizza and Japanese food, and prices are very reasonable. The musical currents that serenade landlubbers come from the seven seas.

Restaurants

Tour K: Tapalpa and the Mountain

Fonda Doña
$
every day 8am to 10:30pm
Avenida Raúl Quetinra no. 10
Tapalpa
To lunch on *comida corrida* in Tapalpa, drop by Fonda Doña, which serves decent-quality, locally flavoured food. Patrons here eat their fill of simple dishes such as *pozole*, *arrachera* and *anogada*.

Los Arcos
$$
Thu to Tue 9am to 10pm
Calle Obregón no. 123
Tapalpa
☎432-0557
The Los Arcos eatery is one of the only places that of-fers an unobstructed view of the Tapalpa valley and the Nevado de Colima, a still-active volcano. Here, meals and meats are often one and the same, and the cuts of meat are usually seasoned with Mexican spices. If you can manage it, the best time to eat here is definitely in the early evening, when the view on the terrace is complemented by pink-hued sunsets.

El Jardín de las Delicias de Antoño
$$
Calle Luis E. Bracamontes no. 249
Tapalpa
☎432-0464
If you take Calle Braeahountes on your way out of town, you'll come across a small rural farm-house that actually turns out to be an excellent res-taurant. El Jardín de las Delicias de Antoño, well run by Magdalena Villa Señor, has made it its mis-sion to sustain Mexico's somewhat endangered culi-nary tradition. Ready-cooked dishes are therefore offered here as they were in the 19th century. The menu changes on a weekly basis. Having lunch in the garden amidst trees and flowers allows visitors to appreciate beautiful Jalisco's charming countryside. All this and service with a smile offered at no extra charge!

Las Girasoles
$$$
Mon to Fri 9am to 9:30pm
Sat and Sun 9am to 11pm
Calle Obregón no. 110
☎432-0458
Las Girasoles is unquestion-ably one of the best dining establishments in the re-gion. People come here for the country-style setting, as well as the pleasure of spending a privileged mo-ment in a most soothing environment. Among the string of dishes on the

menu, many specialties tempt diners to try out new flavours. The famous *borrego* (lamb), a local specialty, is a fine choice.

Cafés and Bakeries

La Villa
$
every day 8am to 11pm
Calle Raúl Quintero no. 93
Tapalpa
☎*432-0009*
Located on the village's main square, the La Villa *cantina* is a good place to kick back after an exhausting walk through the steep streets of Tapalpa. Inside a timeless house, sports paraphernalia is strewn about the place with disconcerting anarchy. The menu, which ranges from omelets to burgers and *carne asada* to *chilaquiles*, offers all the classics of home-style cooking. The village's two specialty cocktails, the *rompompe* and *ponche*, are also available.

Entertainment

Guadalajara has it all, and weekend nights in the metropolis never seem to end, if one goes by the heavy Saturday night traffic at 3am.

A major precaution must be taken when drinking in dubious-looking, but not necessarily dangerous, bars and nightclubs. In Mexico, though ether is now illegal, this thirst-stimulant is still found all too often in the ice of drinks served in bars. Ether is not particularly hazardous to your health but gives you a nasty hangover. To avoid these migraine-inducing problems, opt for bottled alcohol rather than drinks served in glasses.

Let it be said once and for all, Guadalajara is a happening city. The list of entertainment possibilities is endless: classical-music concerts, opera and sporting events are just a few of the choices available to you.

To say nothing, of course, of the *cantinas*, bars and dance clubs of all kinds that come to life every night in the city.

This chapter offers a cursory glance at the various night-time experiences

that await you in
Guadalajara.

Bars and Dance Clubs

We have not included the
many restaurants that offer
música en vivo, but keep in
mind that you can have just
as much fun at these places.
In other respects, scores of
bars offer the *barra libre*
formula (open bar for an
extra cover charge) every
Wednesday. Lastly, our
selection includes a host of
places catering to young
people. As the average age
of the city's population is
around 25, the nightlife
scene is largely tailored to
this generation.

Tour A: The Cradle of Guadalajara

La Fuente
Mon to Sat
Calle Pino Suárez, at Avenida Hidalgo
In the past, all downtown
workers were in the habit
of going to *cantinas* (Mexican bars serving light fare)
at the end of the day to
quench their thirst. Al-
though this tradition is
largely lost today, authentic
taverns such as La Fuente
can still be found. Much
like 50 years ago, an almost
exclusively male and relatively mature clientele takes

refuge here to listen to
música en vivo and, above
all, chew the fat with
friends. The ceilings and
walls covered with the
smoky patina of time seem
to have remained un-
changed since the bar's
opening in 1925. Even the
prices harken back to the
good old days, with beer
going for a paltry $0.70, for
instance.

Tour B: Residences and Squares of Old Guadalajara

La Barra del Moreno
every day 6pm to 2am
Calle Pedro Moreno no. 1051-A
at Avenida E.D. de León
☎827-1234
La Barra del Moreno is a
good place to start off the
night. On weekends, a
huge crowd of students and
"beautiful people" flocks
here for the first drink of
the evening, paving the
way for lively conversations
and flirting with the opposite sex. As for the layout of
the place, the odd mix of
eclectic and Mexican style
works surprisingly well, and
is enhanced with good
background music inspired
by big hits.

Don Porfirio Cantina
every day 5pm to 3am
Calle Maestranza no. 70
Unlike the Maestranza (see
p 194), the Don Porfirio

Cybercafés

One of the cheapest ways to communicate with loved ones is, of course, by e-mail. Over the last few years, cybercafés have therefore become the favourite haunts of travellers wanting to stay in touch and surf the Net at their leisure. Listed below are cybercafés in Guadalajara where you can get online for 15 to 40 pesos an hour.

Café Expresso
Andrés Terán no. 478
☎826-6518

Punto.exe Cybercafe
Mon to Sat 10am to 8pm
Avenida de La Paz no. 1759, corner Calle Bruselas

La Red
Plaza Millenium, suite D26
☎133-1955

Spacio
Avenida López Cotilla no. 1500
☎616-1320

Hackers
Avenida Pedro Moreno no. 863-A
corner M. Castellanos
☎826-6762

CyberWeb
Mon to Sat 10am to 8pm
Calle Paseo Degollado no. 62-1

Entertainment

Cantina welcomes a distinctly younger and less fashionable crowd. After passing the "checkpoint" at the door (not too strict), club-goers head to the second floor of a colonial building with a certain cachet but a shockingly incongruous fluorescent-orange colour scheme that clashes horribly with the venerable building. References to famous Mexican ex-president Porfirio Díaz are especially apparent in the period paintings that hang throughout the place. Fans of hot Latin rhythms blow off steam here all night long to a smooth-flowing sequence of Mexican *ranchera*, *cubana* and *ballade* tracks.

La Maestranza

every day 1pm to 12:30am
Calle Maestranza no. 179
corner Avenida López Cotilla
☎*613-5878*

A local landmark, La Maestranza is unanimously considered the best bar in town. Founded in 1940, the famous *cantina* has made this street what it is: a hot night spot that is now looked on as a veritable institution in the historic centre. Once inside (arrive early to get a table), you can admire what founder Don Paco Jaúregui has put 30 years into collecting: over 30,000 posters, articles and cult objects related to bullfights cover the walls,

making the place a veritable museum. Moreover, you'll notice you're not alone in appreciating the place, as it fills up with 25- to 35-year-olds every night of the week. Despite its success, prices have not spiralled out of control and the music remains authentically Mexican. Not to be missed.

Rockocó

Calle Pedro Moreno no. 532
corner Avenida Donato Guerra
☎*613-5632*

Also in the area, Rockocó is set up in another beautiful colonial house downtown. And once again, historical references to the period of Spanish occupation are numerous. A series of small rooms with different ambiances follow each other, including a terrace and a dance floor where patrons strut their stuff to pop, dance and Latin music.

Tour D: Analco, Las Nueve Esquinas and Parque Agua Azul

El Archivo

Mon to Thu noon to 1am
Fri and Sat noon to 3am
Sun 5pm to 1am
Avenida Madero no. 111 corner Calle Degollado
☎*613-9758*

The El Archivo *cantina* broadcasts sporting events at all hours of the day for the benefit of male sports fans. That's right, this old colonial house has been turned into a viewing room for sacred sports games transmitted by satellite. On days of major *fútbol* matches, the atmosphere is particularly frenzied, with Chivas and Atlas fans crowding the place in droves. Fortunately, the decor is not solely confined to banal television sets, as the walls are covered with sports-related articles, plastered higgledy-piggledy. Like all bars in Guadalajara, El Archivo offers its own house drink, the Yerbabuena (a mixed drink made from *yerbabuena* plants, known for their curative effects on stomach aches), for those tired of traditional beer and tequila.

Beer Saloon
Mon to Sat 11am to 11pm
Calle Galeana no. 372
Nueve Esquinas

Upon walking through the swinging doors of the Beer Saloon, you'll find yourself immersed in Old West times alongside cowboy hats and horseshoes. No, this is not a ranch in the Mexican northwest, but another small bar patronized by students in the Nueve Esquinas district. Just the place to chug beer while nibbling on a good selection of *botanas*.

El Cubilete
every day 10pm to 2am
Calle General Río Seco no. 9
Nueve Esquinas
☎ *658-0406*

El Cubilete is well worth the trip for its warm Cuban ambiance. Located in the heart of the Nueve Esquinas district, this small bar-restaurant gets cooking every night of the week to the sounds of live Cuban music and tireless salsa and merengue dancers. During the day, the atmosphere is more relaxing, especially when the sun illuminates the photos of old-time Guadalajara on the warm-coloured walls.

La Feria
every day 1:30pm to 2am
Calle Corona no. 291, corner Héroes
☎ *613-7150*

La Feria is just the place to spend an authentic Mexican-style evening in the company of true-blue Tapatíos. While savouring the priceless classics of regional cuisine, you can take in a lively mariachi show accompanied by equally spirited entertainment. Located in the historic courtyard of a cheerfully decorated colonial building, this spot is perfect for those seeking a fun-filled evening. Live music, dance contests and karaoke will convince you to stay on until the wee hours of the morning with no thought of

Entertainment

tomorrow, as do many of the locals.

Tour E: Chapultepec and Las Antiguas Colonias

La Charla
every day 8am to 1am
Avenida Vallarta no. 1095
corner Calle Argentina
☎825-0393
Another early-evening meeting spot, the small La Charla bar is well known in Guadalajara for having spearheaded French-style terraces. You can therefore spend a wonderful evening with your sweetheart or a friend seated outside while enjoying the gentle summer-night breeze. Soft shades of blue, orange and yellow also make this a great place to end the night on a relaxing note. All in all, a good choice.

Los Famosos Equipales
Avenida de La Paz no. 2308
corner Calle Miguel de Cervantes
As its Spanish name indicates, patrons here sit in *equipales*-style armchairs. This is another *cantina* very much in keeping with *tapatios* tradition, where bull races are elevated to cult status. The music is Mexican, of course, and prices are competitive enough to cater to a wide demographic. While you're here, be sure to order the famous

house drink, *nalgas alegres* (happy buttocks)!

La Veradera
every day 2pm to 2am
Avenida López Cotilla
corner Calle Francisco Javier de Gamboa
Whether to take advantage of the wide variety of drinks available or the "2-for-1" specials at any time of day, thirsty drinkers flock to La Veradera. As early as 2pm, people come here for a drink, but also to nibble on a few Mexican specialties beneath the thatched roof. At night, the back room provides an intimate setting, with candlelight and a decor made up of local crafts.

Tour F: Minerva and el Iztépete

Botanas & Beer Bar
Tue to Sat 1pm to 10pm
Sun 11am to 5pm
Calle Privada del Niño no. 25
corner Avenida Guadalupe
☎121-7238
Featuring a very western decor, Botanas & Beer Bar is a great place to start off the night. A mixed crowd hangs out here in anticipation of an eventful evening. Although the amazingly moderate beer and tequila prices encourage elbow-bending, the quantity and variety of *botanas*, including chips, tacos, *ruedas* (wheel-

shaped chips), *tortas salgadas* and chilies, are primarily what make the place so successful. You'll also enjoy the contemporary music and ambiance.

Casa Bariachi
Mon to Sat 6pm to 3am
Sun 5pm to 2am
Avenida Vallarta no. 2308
corner Calle Lope de Vega
☎615-2706
At the Casa Bariachi, traditional Jaliscan music is front and centre. From the early afternoon, mariachis take the stage and get the joint jumping to the sounds of the biggest hits of their romantic repertoire. While some don't hesitate to kick up their heels, others prefer watching the show while comfortably seated with friends or family. Many also sing along to the music, denoting the remarkable complicity between the mariachi singers and their legions of fans in Guadalajara. This is hardly surprising, since this is the birthplace of mariachi, now well known throughout the world.

Copacabana
$4
Wed to Sat 9pm to 5am
Avenida López Mateos Sur no. 5290
corner Calle Las Águilas
☎631-4596
After submitting to required security checks at the entrance, club-goers end up in a large space in the middle

of which lies a dance floor that looks like a theatre set. And for good reason, as this is where scores of devotees of salsa, merengue and other sizzling Latin rhythms show off their dance moves. Those who pause to take a breather will notice the decor's modern lines.

D.J. London
Tue to Sun 6pm to 2:30am
Avenida Patria no. 600
☎673-1600
Fans of London bars will love D.J. London, a veritable temple of English rock. Photos of the biggest rock stars of the last 40 years (including the Beatles, Kiss and U2) adorn the walls, and an authentic jukebox plays the most popular golden oldies. Even the decor reflects this period. Karaoke provides budding singers with a perfect showcase for their talents, while more timid souls can always surf the Net at one of eight computer terminals.

La Enretradera
every day 2pm to 2am
Avenida San Ignacio no. 450-A
at La Gran Plaza
☎647-7101
La Enretradera is the perfect little bistro in which to start off an evening with friends. While seated around wooden furniture in a modern Mexican setting, patrons can indulge in animated discussions. The place will also suit lovebirds looking

Entertainment

to enjoy a casual, romantic evening. Atmosphere ensured by good *música en vivo*.

Glass House Café

Mon to Sat 8am to 2am
Sun 8am to 3:30pm
Plaza Exhimoda,
corner Avenida Vallarta
☎ *122-7501*

The Glass House Café is a good choice for those who enjoy watching videos. The modern decor made up of mirrors and green stucco is hardly original, of course, but the ambiance is relaxing, gratifying the yuppies who seek refuge here in the evening.

La Marcha

men $10, women $7
Wed, Fri and Sat
10pm to 4am
Avenida Vallarta no. 2648
corner Calle Los Arcos
☎ *615-8999*

Located at the corner of Calle Los Arcos and Avenida Vallarta, the La Marcha dance club is the first stop on what has been nicknamed the "Ruta Vallarta." This stretch of Avenida Vallarta encompasses a series of some of the most popular dance bars in town, where many make the rounds every weekend. Among these nightspots, you won't fail to notice the ornate mansion that is home to this first stop of the tour. La Marcha's setting features a series of spaces to satisfy the motley crowd of revellers here: a billiard room upstairs, outdoor terrace at the back, dance floor on the main floor, each with its own atmosphere. And yet, the potential for such a setting does not seem to have been fully exploited, several rooms being empty and somewhat dull. As for the tunes, Latin music seems to attract quite a following, as evidenced by the many couples who offer ample proof of Mexicans' talent for dancing.

Hippos

every day noon to 1am
La Gran Plaza
☎ *122-3543*
Plaza del Sol
☎ *121-0091*

After a long day of shopping, there's nothing like kicking back with a good beer while discussing your purchases. With two locations in the city's two big shopping centres, Hippos is just the place for exhausted bargain hunters. Between the stylized hippo motifs and eclectic forms, the decor here is akin to pasteboard film scenery. *Botanas* are served here.

Jimmy's
men $5, women $3
Fri and Sat 10pm to 4am
Avenida Lapislázuli no. 3467-A,
corner Calle Mariano Otero,
near Plaza Millenium

Those into rave music are sure to like Jimmy's, which features a pleasant, if slightly bizarre, atmosphere and a decor consisting mainly of curtains of all kinds. Also surprising is the wild crowd, everybody dancing frenziedly to their own drummer to dance, techno and rave beats till they drop. Introverts abstain.

Lado B
men $12, women $6
Wed, Fri and Sat 9:30pm to 3am
Avenida Vallarta no. 2451,
corner Calle Fco. de Quevedo
☎615-7170

A trendy place on the Ruta Vallarta where dancing and cruising are the main pastimes.

Hard Rock Live
Avenida Vallarta no. 2425
☎616-4560

Another place for a night out on the Ruta Vallarta, a decidedly lively area, Hard Rock Live is the latest brainchild of the British chain. Featuring an all-live formula, this embassy of English rock showcases high-calibre bands. The decor is just like its counterparts around the world, and the music is exclusively English.

This style works and is considered very "exotic" in Mexican Guadalajara. Folks come here to enjoy a drink and leave having spent less than you might expect for this type of place.

Lola Mundó
Wed to Sat 10pm to 3am
Avenida Vallarta no. 4454
opposite La Gran Plaza
☎121-9837

Lola Mundó is known in Guadalajara as the only club that does not control its customers by chicking their age upon entrance. Although age isn't an issue, only the "crème de la crème" of the crowd lined up at the door is chosen to fill the club on weekends. Inside, futuristic lines and a light show worthy of the biggest dance clubs await fans of techno music.

Métro
men $5, women $3
Wed, Fri and Sat 9:30pm to 3am
Avenida Pablo Neruda no. 3980,
corner Calle Jacarandas
☎641-5360

Anyone into Guada's hip nightclub scene is certainly no stranger to Métro. This venerable, industrial-size dance club fills up on long-awaited weekend nights. So get here early, wearing suitable attire, and don't hesitate to talk to the bouncer to ease your way in. Bouncers here handpick the best crop of "beautiful people," both foreign and local, cooling their heels at the door. Once again, the very stylized, indeed futuristic, decor attracts attention. Hipsters will be dazzled. Light fare available; rock and dance music.

Los Remedios
every day 2pm to 2am
Avenida Américas no. 1462
☎817-4410
Much like its neighbour Unducci, this bar-restaurant draws both the young and not-so-young in search of pleasure of relaxation. Just the place to start off the evening before moving on to the dance club next door.

Pixie
Wed to Sat 10pm to 3am
Avenida Vallarta no. 2503
Every bar on the Ruta Vallarta has its own clientele and Pixie is no exception, drawing a success-ful coalition of bohemians, hip-hoppers and ultra-hip stu-dents, who groove to relentless techno and house beats. The guest DJ accordingly rocks all four floors, packed with this crowd of deafening-music diehards. In an attentively-lit, stylized setting, you can drink at the ground-floor bar or head to the top-floor terrace to ad-mire the Guadalajara sky-line. Open bar every Wednesday.

¡Qué Pues!
Avenida Niñoes Héroes no. 1554, corner Avenida E. Díaz de León
Located at the junction of Avenidas E. Díaz de León and Niñoes Héroes, ¡Qué Pues! is a good place to stop in for a drink. Decked out in blue-neon lighting and low tables, this spot draws a varied crowd, in-cluding young people, cou-ples, students and business people, both gay and "straight," and a smattering of foreigners. The secret to its success: essentially Eng-lish music with trademark rock and blues. What's more, a Tuesday-night show (usually a very quiet night in Guadalajara) sets this place among La Mi-nerva's trendy ven-ues. Unusually inti-mate performances are guaranteed by the small size of the place.

Räda Lounge
Wed to Sat 10pm to 3am
Avenida de La Paz no. 2550
☎615-7636
As its name indicates, pa-trons here congregate in a large, open 1950s-style lounge (avoid casual dress). Mainly patronized by a clean-cut crowd, the place quickly becomes jam-packed on weekends. As the volume is kept at a

moderate level, you can appreciate the latest hits and European dance music while chit-chatting with fellow lounge lizards.

Rancho Grande

Avenida López Mateos Sur no. 4520
☎632-9332

Alla en el Rancho Grande, alla donde vivi... the simple lyrics of this Mexican song are enough to evoke the ambiance of Rancho Grande, a very fun, traditional nightclub. Mariachis and *bandas* share the spotlight to get their diehard fans movin' and groovin'. Many enthusiasts even hit the dance floor or the bar, where beer and tequila flow freely.

Undicci

Wed, Fri and Sat 9pm to 2am
Avenida Américas no. 1462
☎817-4410

A young atmosphere reins at Unducci, where so many students hang out it seems like an extension of the University of Guadalajara. You'll notice that, like everywhere else in the world, students here know how to party till dawn—even if tons of homework await them later on, or so they will tell you (ahem). Beer and popular English and Latin American music is all it takes to get this small bar moving in next to no time. The only false note: the place's over-capacity crowd makes it difficult to move

around. Table reservations can be made by phone during the day.

Van Go
$5

Wed, Fri and Sat 9pm to 3am
Avenida D no. 810,
corner Calle San Jorge
☎633-7719

Along with Métro, Van Go is one of the leading dance clubs in the city. Despite having been around for several years, it still draws a hip crowd, an exploit all the more notable given the fickle nature of this type of clientele. The night begins with a game of pool, chatting with regulars or watching videos flashing on the slew of television screens. But once midnight rolls around, the crowd hits the dance floor to get down to a string of dance and rock hits.

Wall Street

Avenida Américas no. 1417
corner Avenida Pablo Neruda
More cheerful than a Belgian bar, less exotic than an Australian watering hole, but as pleasant as an Irish pub, Wall Street has nothing to do with the streets of New York City. On the terrace, you can easily imagine yourself on the Pacific coast, so much does the decor recall a relaxing beach bar, with its thatched roof and paper lanterns. And the drink menu is noteworthy for its wide

Entertainment

Gay Bars and Dance Clubs

Angel's
$4
Wed to Sat 9pm to 3am
Avenida de La Paz no. 2030
☎615-2525

Angel's dance club is unquestionably one of the best gay clubs in metropolitan Guadalajara. On weekends, this hot spot fills up quickly as of 11pm with the city's young gay, lesbian and "straight" jet set, here to "shake their groove thang" to the latest dance hits. Whether with friends or solo, hipsters cruise here until 2:30am, at which time diehards move on to Mónica's.

Mónica's
$3
Wed to Sun 10pm to 5am
Avenida Obregón no. 1713

Located in a more modest part of the city, which is reflected in its clientele, Mónica's dance club packs them in every weekend. Pink neon lights, wall mirrors and a large dance floor make up the club's somewhat clichéd decor, but this in no way deters the exclusively gay clientele of all ages and types from having a great time, especially from 2am until the wee hours of the morning. Nightly drag show.

Maskara's
$3
every day 2pm to 2am
Calle Maestranza no. 238, at Avenida Pisciliano Sánchez
☎614-8103

In the Centro, Maskara's is one of the only bars in town that thankfully favours quiet conversation with a drink in hand over the blaring music of trendy nightclubs.

Though the place could certainly use a facelift, such drawbacks are soon forgotten in light of the chance of meeting your soulmate among the mixed crowd (mature men, young go-getters and professionals).

SOS Disco-Club
$2.50
Wed 6pm to 4am, Thu to Sun 10pm to 4am
Avenida de La Paz no. 1413
☎*826-4179*
The SOS Disco-Club is primarily frequented by a lesbian crowd of all ages. This club doesn't stand out for either its very dark decor or repetitive music, but gets our stamp of approval nonetheless.

selection and moderate prices. A great early-evening spot.

Tour G: Zapopan

Fonda de Doña Gavina Escolástica
Tue to Sun 7pm to 11pm
Calle Javier Mina no. 237, near the Basilica de Zapopan
Those nostalgic for the 1970s will enjoy going to Fonda de Doña Gavina Escolástica, which resurrects the authentic *fondas* (modest restaurants) so numerous at that time. Owner and patron Ángel Cervantes sought to recreate this quintessentially Mexican ambiance, which lives on in the collective consciousness. He has salvaged this architecturally unique Mexican cottage and hung relics of the 1970s on the walls. The *tapatios* dishes are equally authentic and the *música en vivo* is representative of the romantic Mexican era.

La Boca
Thu to Sat 9:30pm to 3am
Avenida Américas no. 1939
opposite Plaza Patria
☎*636-1996*
What would you say to having a drink amidst hundreds of replicas of Picasso's works, endlessly marvelling at this Spanish artist's creative genius? A temple of modern art, the La Boca dance club is, of course, prized by young hipsters, well-off professionals and curious foreign-

Entertainment

ers. A place to see and be seen.

Tour H: San Pedro Tlaquepaque and Tonalá

Salón México
Calle Mota Padilla no. 54, corner Avenida Gigantes

If you like dancing to hot, hip-swaying salsa, *banda* and *norteña* rhythms, Salón México is for you.

Tlaquepaque Histórico
Avenida Indenpendencia no. 2
☎*659-1381*

Those looking for a reason to stay in Tlaquepaque come nightfall need look no further than Tlaquepaque Histórico. The place draws the local young set and a handful of tourists—surely because of the laid-back atmosphere. Handicrafts, scores of plants and furnishings with antiquated cachet contribute to its charm and create a very appealing setting for a drink.

Tour J: Tequila and Surroundings

La Capilla
every day 1pm to 10pm
Calle Hidalgo no. 32
Tequila

La Capilla will suit those looking to mix with the good people of Tequila at the cocktail hour. The

green-stucco walls and trophies of the local *fútbol* team do not make for an inspired decor, of course, but the good-humoured Mexican clientele is a whole attraction in itself. A good old bistro that bucks current trends.

Sauzal
every day 1pm to 1am
Calle Juárez no. 45
Tequila

Besides being the title of a famous song, Sauzal is a café-bar facing the church square. In the evening, all of Tequila enjoys gathering here to make conversation while seated amidst a predominantly orange 1960s decor. The menu offers light fare and a list of locally distilled tequilas. Bohemian- and romantic-style *música en vivo*.

Tour K: Tapalpa and the Mountain

The popular holiday from January 4 to 12 is a good opportunity to visit Tapalpa, where you'll enjoy a wonderful stay far from the city in a very authentic setting.

El Callejón
every day 2pm to 1am
Calle Francisco Madero no. 37
Tapalpa

Patrons of El Callejón, a bar on Calle Madero, quench their thirst in a typical house redolent with the fresh scent of pine. The upside: the place boasts a fireplace for cool winter nights, an amazing easel plastered with business cards, and live *banda* and mariachi music. The downside: the presence of a television and the limited choice of drinks.

Cultural Activities

Guadalajara, *la ciudad de las rosas* (the city of roses), celebrated its 458th anniversary in 2000, 458 years during which Tapatios and Jaliscans have continued to express the vibrancy and richness of their culture. This cultural dynamism, now inspiring the whole region, promises visitors an exotic voyage of discovery into the soul and character of the local people. Guadalajara is home to top-notch performance halls and scores of cultural centres with no shortage of entertainment possibilities, provided you are sufficiently conversant in the Spanish language. Throughout the year, the calendar of cultural activities allows visitors to discover several facets of the Jaliscan culture, particularly in October, during the **Fiesta de Octubre**, when events are exceptionally numerous. Moreover, the biggest book fair in Latin American is held here in early November.

Given the plethora of activities offered every month, we invite you to consult the current cultural-events listings in the various publications listed below. These publications will provide you with detailed information about current programs, schedules as well as rates. You will also find the addresses and phone numbers of a few entertainment venues as well as various associations and other sources of information.

Let's Enjoy
A free bilingual (English-Spanish) monthly with tourist and cultural information. Available in most cultural and tourist establishments.

Informarte
The municipality of Guadalajara's free monthly information bulletin. Available at all cultural centres or at their offices *(Avenida Hidalgo no. 499, at Avenida Alcalde).*

Guía Guadalajara
A bilingual quarterly issued by the Jalisco tourist office *(Calle Morelos no. 102, Plaza Tapatía)*

Público
Every Friday, this large-circulation daily newspaper publishes a special section entitled "Ocio" that provides a very good description of all the cultural activi-

Calendar of Traditional Festivals in and Around Guadalajara

Mexico is known throughout the world as *fiesta* country. As in the past, traditional festivals continue to enliven the everyday life of Mexicans with folklore that has been going strong since the 16th century. Every city district and village honours its patron saint with parades livened up by typical musicians, exhilarating dancing and gastronomy reserved for the occasion. The night of the festival, the multicoloured lights of *castillos,* fireworks delineating moving animals and geometric shapes add a new, colourful dimension to revellers' gaiety.

January 5, 6 and 7
Feast of the Epiphany (Three Kings Day), in Cajititlán

January 12
Festival of the Lord of Miracles, at the San Sebastián church, Barrio de Analco

January 20
Festival of the Virgin of Guadalupe, in Tapalpa

February (variable)
Carnaval, in Chapala

February 2
Candlemas, in Santa Anita

March 19
St. Joseph's Day, at the San José church, Barrio de Analco, Guadalajara

May 3
Holy Cross Day, in Tequila and Santa Cruz de las Flores

May 15
Festival of St. Isidore the Ploughman, in Santa Ana
Tepetitlán

June 24
St. John the Baptist Day, at the San Juan de Dios
church, Guadalajara

June 29
St. Peter's Day, in Tlaquepaque

July 25
Festival of St. James the Apostle (*tastoane* indigenous
dance representing the battle of St. James against the
Moors), in Tonalá, San Martin de las Flores, San Juan
de Ocotán and Nextipac

October 4
Visit of Our Lady of Zapopan at the Mercado de San
Juan de Dios, Guadalajara (date to be confirmed with
the parish of Zapopan; ☎633.66.14 or 633.01.04)

October 12
St. Francis of Assisi Day, in Chapala

November 30
Return of Our Lady of Zapopan to the Basílica de la
Virgen de Zapopan

December 7 and 8
St. Andrew's Day, in Ajijic

December 12
Festival of the Immaculate Conception, in Tlajomulco

Festival of Our Lady of Guadalupe, Barrio del
Santuario, Guadalajara

Entertainment

There are also major civic celebrations, of which we recommend the following two: El Grito, on the night of September 15, which commemorates the beginning of the War of Independence; and the opening night of the Fiestas de Octubre (early October), featuring a parade of allegorical floats, folkloric dancers and zoo animals.

El Grito marks the beginning of Mexico's national holiday, Independence Day. On this occasion, the governor of Jalisco State steps out onto the main balcony of the Palacio de Gobierno and repeats the *"¡Viva México!"* cry of Independence while waving the Mexican flag. This is followed by several hours of festivities culminating with *castillos* illuminating the night sky in a blaze of glory.

ties organized in Guadalajara.

El Informador
A major daily that features "La buena vida," a section devoted to cultural activities in Guadalajara, every Friday.

Associations

Instituto Cultural Mexicano-Norteamericano de Jalisco
(Mexico-U.S.)
Avenida Enrique Díaz de León no. 300
☎ *825-5838 or 825-5666*
⇋ *825-1671*
Recitals, exhibitions, shows, gallery and poetry.

Goethe Institut Guadalajara
(German Institute)
Avenida Morelos no. 2080
☎ *615-6147*
⇋ *615-9717*
Exhibitions, conferences, concerts, seminars and German film club.

Casa d'Italia
Avenida Garibaldi no. 1849
☎ *615-9744*
Film club, conferences, library, concerts and gastronomic events, all in Italian.

Cinemas

Most films are screened in their original language with Spanish subtitles.

Cinepolis Centro Magno
Avenida Vallarta no. 2425
☎*630-1073*

El Cinematógrafo 1
Avenida Vallarta no. 1102
☎*825-0514*

Multicinemas Tolsa
Avenida Enrique Díaz de León no. 430
corner Calle Tolsá, col. Moderna
☎*825-2877*

Theatres, Concerts and Shows

Teatro Degollado
between Avenida Hidalgo and Calle
Morelos, on Plaza Tapatía
☎*614-4773*
The largest theatre in the city, Teatro Degollado presents various operas, concerts and ballets in a fabulous setting. Under no circumstances should you miss the best folk-dance revue in Jalisco, the University of Guadalajara's Ballet Folclórico, which performs every Sunday at 10am.

Conferences, shows, concerts and temporary exhibitions are regularly held at the following cultural centres: **Centro Cultural Casa Colomos** *(Calle El Chaco no. 3200, Col. Providencia,* ☎*642-0132)*, **Centro Cultural de la Colonia Atlas** *(Calle Río La Barca, corner Calle Río Mascota, Col. Atlas,* ☎*639-9889)* and **Centro Cultural San Diego** *(Avenida González Ortega no. 443, corner Calle M. Acuña, Barrio de San Diego,* ☎*658-1275)*.

In addition to being a remarkable building, the **Instituto Cultural Cabañas** *(Avenida Cabañas no. 8, Plaza Tapatía,* ☎*618-8135)* houses a cinema and hosts concerts and temporary exhibitions. Along the same lines, the **Ex-Convento del Carmen** *(Avenida Juárez no. 638,* ☎*613-1544)* offers a whole variety of cultural events.

Among the metropolis's well-attended venues, **Teatro Experimental** *(Calzada Independencia Sur,* ☎*619-1176)* presents many plays that are more audacious and contemporary that its counterparts. **Casa Teatro El Venero** *(Calle Gregorio Dávila no. 76,* ☎*825-9476)*, **Teatro Galerias** *(Avenida Lapislázuli no. 3445,* ☎*631-1550)* and **Teatro IMSS Guadalajara** *(Avenida Independencia, opposite Parque Agua Azul,* ☎*619-4121)* all present light comedies, classics and Mexican plays—in Spanish, of course. The latter is also renowned for its children's theatre productions.

Entertainment

Charrería

The wide-brimmed Mexican hat known as the *charro sombrero* has become a Mexican symbol throughout the world. And yet, it is no longer worn by the populace; indeed, you will only see this hat at folkloric shows, though it is still worn by mariachis and those who perform typical Jalisco regional dances.

Actually, this round, broad-brimmed hat is part of the *charro*'s costume. The *charrería* evolved from a series of complicated manoeuvres developed over time by *charros*, hacienda cowboys during the colonial regime whose arduous daily work involved taming half-wild animals, which required great strength and skill.

Now a popular national sport known as the *charreada*, a type of rodeo, the *charrería* is a series of competitive events held in *lienzos charros, fiesta-charra* arenas. According to official rules, the *charro*'s costume must be elegantly embellished with leather and adorned with silver buttons down the length of the pants. Though predominantly practised by men, *charrerías* do give women a chance to show off their skills, notably in the *escaramuza*. These mounted drill teams of young *charras*, clad in magnificent traditional *adelita* dresses, perform spectacular equestrian exercises to the great delight of *charrería* afficionados.

Very popular, colourful and genuinely Mexican, *charrerías* are held almost every Sunday, from October to April, at the **Lienzo Charro de Jalisco** *($4; Oct to Apr, Sun at noon; Dr. R. Michel no. 577, toward the stadium, ☎619-3232 or 619-0315).*

Spectator Sports

Sports fans intent on catching a *fútbol* game played by one of Guadalajara's two teams, the Chivas and Atlas, can do so at the **Estadio de Jalisco** *(Calle Siete Colonias no. 1772, Col. Independencia, ☎637-0563)*. You will thus witness the gusto with which Jaliscans cheer on the star athletes who defend the region's colours against teams from all over Mexico.

Finally, the tradition of Spanish *corridas* is equally widespread in Jalisco, as evidenced by the famous bullfights regularly held at the **Plaza de Toros Nuevo Progreso** *(Calle Pirineos no. 1930, Col. Monumental, ☎651-8506)*, to the great delight of the public. Those who appreciate this kind of explosive event and are not too squeamish will be enraptured by this oh-so-Hispanic ritual.

Shopping

S hops are generally open Monday to Friday from 9am to 8pm and Saturday from 9am to 6pm.

S hopping centres are open all day from Monday to Saturday.

H owever, some places such as supermarkets are also open on Sunday. In smaller establishments, you can always try haggling over the asking price.

T he State of Jalisco is renowned for its very colourful, exceptionally diverse crafts. Guadalajara and its surrounding area are no exception to this rule, so you'll have no trouble finding whatever your heart desires. As such, Tlaquepaque and Tonalá offer a particularly elaborate choice of all kinds of inexpensive souvenirs for those who know how to spot a good bargain.

Taxes

Mexico has a 15% sales tax known as the "IVA" (Impuesto de Valor Agregado), applicable to most goods and services. It's often included in the price of everyday purchases.

Tour A: The Cradle of Guadalajara

Food

It's always good to know of a supermarket when the time comes to stock up on inexpensive victuals. **Gigante** *(every day 8am to 11pm; Avenida Colón no. 4030, Centro Comercial El Saúz)* is a good place for its convenient location right downtown.

Market

Like every city in Mexico, Guadalajara has its own public market. With hundreds of stalls spread over three floors, the **Mercado Libertad** (also known as the Mercado de San Juan de Dios) *(every day 8am to 7pm; at Calzada Independencia and Javier Minc, see also p 82)* is Mexico's largest market. Shoppers must venture through a maze of narrow aisles lined with an abundance of merchandise, including everything from mouse pads and winter coats to silverware and food. Prices are decent and the smiling vendors are always ready to bargain.

Music

To discover a new, musical facet of the Jaliscan culture, head to Calle Mezquitan between Avenida Morelos and Calle Independencia, where you'll find a series of music stores. **Rock en español** *(Mon to Sat 10am to 2pm and 4pm to 8pm; Calle Mezquitan no. 89-A)* stocks Latino rock; **Librería Madriga** *(Calle Mezquitan, ☎613-1218)*, second-hand records; and **Discos Garbage** *(every day 10am to 8pm; Calle Mezquitan no. 46)* offers a bit of everything for all tastes.

Tour C: The Panteón de Belén and Surrounding Area

Market

To discover and purchase Jalisco's most beautiful floral specimens, be sure to stop by the **Mercado de Las Flores** (flower market) *(every day from 8am; at Federalismo and José María Vigil, opposite the Panteón)*. Every day, a barrage of colours and aromas enchants passersby who've come to admire the most exquisite offering of nature: flowers.

Tour D: Analco, Las Nueve Esquinas and Parque Agua Azul

Crafts

While strolling through Parque Agua Azul, you can drop by the **Instituto de la Artesanía Jalisciense** (*Mon to Fri 10am to 6pm, Sat 10am to 5pm, Sun 10am to 3pm; Calzada González Gallo no. 20, ☎619-1407*), which not only houses an exhibition gallery, but also sells gorgeous crafts. A wide variety of good-quality blown-glass pieces, pottery and handcrafted wooden sculptures are offered here. There is also another outlet in Chapala under the name **Casa de las Artesanias Ajijic** (*Carretera Jocotepec, Km 6.5, ☎766-0548*).

Tour E: Chapultepec and Las Antiguas Colonias

Bookshops and Stationers'

The **Gonvill** bookshop (*Mon to Sat 10am to 8:30pm; Avenida Chapultepec Sur no. 150, ☎616-3060; Avenida Morelos no. 530, ☎613-2614*), with many branches scattered throughout the city, is a good place to find the latest novel or a fine specialized work (art books, novels, textbooks). Enough to satisfy bookworms with a good command of the Spanish language.

Booklovers take note: the **Gandhi** bookshop (*Mon to Sat 10am to 10pm; Avenida Chapultepec no. 396, at Efrain Lez. Luna, ☎616-7374*) is a small complex entirely devoted to books and music. The two floors seem to literally groan under the weight of so much material. Upstairs, the store not only boasts a whole section devoted to Guadalajara's history, architecture and tourism, but also a travel-guide section allowing visitors to gather information about their next destination.

Tour F: Minerva and el Iztépete

Shopping Centres

Like most major North American cities, Guadalajara has its share of shopping centres, each more titanic than the last. Among them, **La Gran Plaza** (*every day 9:30am to 9pm; at Avenida Vallarta and San Ignacio, ☎122-3004*) is particularly worthwhile for its countless shops touching on every

Shopping

area of day-to-day life. The three-storey pentagon-shaped building is so vast that you can easily spend the entire day here. Moreover, it's also home to an entertainment centre (cinema, arcade and restaurants) that draws a good number of people.

If you enjoy roaming shopping centres but hate the idea of being cooped up inside, **Plaza del Sol** *(every day 9:30am to 9pm; at Avenida Mariano Otero and Avenida López Mateos, ☎121-5750)* is a good compromise. The mall features many stores, restaurants, supermarkets and banks in an open-air concept, so shoppers won't miss out on beautiful sunny days.

Bookshops

Británica Librería *(Mon to Sat 9am to 2pm and 4pm to 7pm; Avenida Hidalgo no. 179 6-B, between A.L. Gallardo and Amado Nervo, ☎615-5803)*. A comprehensive English-language bookshop.

Sandi Bookshop *(Mon to Fri 9:30am to 12:30pm and 2:30pm to 7pm, Sat 9:20am to 2pm; Avenida Tepeyac no. 718, Colonia Chapalita, ☎121-0863)*. Great selection of English- and French-language books and magazines. Also, a good place to find ways of learning Spanish.

Tequila

It would be unthinkable to leave Guadalajara without picking up the State of Jalisco's famous national drink, tequila. At the **Boutique del Tequila** *(Mon to Sat 10am to 2pm and 4pm to 8pm; Centro Magno Guadalajara, Avenida Vallarta no. 2425, ☎640-2262)*, no less than 273 brands of all categories are offered, and this, at extremely reasonable prices. The only problem is choosing! A dilemma that's easily solved by taking advantage of the free samples!

Shoes

Mexico boasts a thriving shoe industry and the number of shops advertising amazingly low prices provide ample proof. The **Galería del Calzado** complex *(every day 9am to 9:30pm; at Avenida México and Yaquis, ☎647-6422)* alone encompasses many stores with a wide variety of shoes for men, women and children.

Food

Located across from the lovely Parque Rubén Darío, **Bon Appétit** *(Avenida Rubén Darío, between Avenida Providencia and Rio de Janeiro)* not only houses a fine delicatessen and a refined cheese shop, but also prepares a variety of fine European sandwiches. Good, but pricey.

The **Casita Delicatessen** *(Mon to Fri 9am to 9pm, Sat 10am to 8pm and Sun 11am to 3pm; Avenida Terranova no. 594-A, ☎640-1192)* imports a selection of the best products from France, England, Italy and the United States that are not available in supermarkets. A deli and cheese shop round out the range of offerings.

Along the same lines but much bigger, the large **Goiti** deli *(every day 8am to 10pm; Avenida México no. 2850, ☎642-7512)* is well known to Tapatios. Spices, homemade jams, pastries, cold cuts, wine are but some of the offerings.

Chocolate-Makers

Chocoholics will be in seventh heaven when they set eyes on chocolate-maker **Arnoldi**'s *(every day 9:30am to 9pm; Avenida México, Plaza México)* fine selection of goodies. The enticing aroma that wafts through the shop won't fail to lead you into temptation, as you walk out with boxfuls of truffles, pralines and meringues.

Art Gallery

Galería del Bosque *(Mon to Sat 10am to 2pm and 4pm to 8pm; Avenida Salmón no. 2967, Residencia Loma Bonita, ☎631-2815)* offers stunning paintings for all budgets. The gallery features over 500 pieces, all works by Jalisco painters.

Tour H: San Pedro Tlaquepaque and Tonalá

Shopping is the main pastime in Tlaquepaque and Tonalá, two quaint little communities that are home to the best craft shops in the region and from which a good part of Mexican art is exported. Tlaquepaque encompasses lovely shops with the finest crafts. And yet, the village is now forsaken by most artisans who have fled to Tonalá to cash in on the tourist trade and gentrified shops. Prices therefore tend to be excessive nowadays, so be vigilant. You need only travel the few kilometres between

Shopping

Tlaquepaque and Tonalá to see prices drop drastically. The latter village is the Mecca for artisans who sell their wares at very worthwhile prices.

Music

For a good selection of essentially Mexican records, check out **Aguilar Discos** *(every day 10am to 8pm; Calle Independencia no. 119).*

Fabric

Mona's *(every day 10am to 6pm; Calle Juárez no. 17).* Located on the Juárez pedestrian street, this simple shop offers exclusive, very vibrant fabrics.

Jewellery

While visiting Tlaquepaque, be absolutely sure to check out the marvellous **Sergio Bustamante** shop *(Mon to Sat 10am to 7pm, Sun 11am to 4pm; Calle Independencia no. 236, ☎639-5519).* This nationally renowned artist's jewellery-store-cum-gallery offers exclusive and elegant jewellery. The artist's original pieces on display are a feast for the eyes, but prices are beyond all imagination.

Crafts

Arte Indio *(Mon to Sat 10am to 3pm and 4pm to 7pm; Calle Juárez no. 130, ☎635-6981)* will delight treasure hunters in search of crafts, piled up here in large rooms. Pottery, carved stoneware, attired skeletons and terracotta suns are found in abundance.

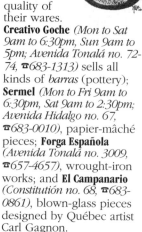

Among Tonalá's countless shops, a few stand out for the quality of their wares.
Creativo Goche *(Mon to Sat 9am to 6:30pm, Sun 9am to 5pm; Avenida Tonalá no. 72-74, ☎683-1313)* sells all kinds of *barras* (pottery); **Sermel** *(Mon to Fri 9am to 6:30pm, Sat 9am to 2:30pm; Avenida Hidalgo no. 67, ☎683-0010),* papier-mâché pieces; **Forga Española** *(Avenida Tonalá no. 3009, ☎657-4657),* wrought-iron works; and **El Campanario** *(Constitutión no. 68, ☎683-0861),* blown-glass pieces designed by Québec artist Carl Gagnon.

Home Decor

Located next to the restaurant of the same name (see p 182), **Adobe Galería** (*every day 10am to 7pm; Calle Independencia no. 195, ☎657-2792*) is unquestionably one of the finest decorative-object shops in the village. The place carries curios, carved-wood furniture and highly original crafts.

Fans of *azulejos* and wrought ironwork should not miss **Rocio Preciado** (*Mon to Sat 10am to 8pm, Sun 11am to 3pm; Avenida Francisco de Miranda no. 33, ☎635-6223*). Available here are pretty mirrors, original candles, artistic wrought-iron pieces and particularly classy Christian cult objects.

Market

During a stay in the metropolis, you owe it to yourself to set aside half a day to visit the **Tonalá craft market** (*Thu and Sun 8am to 6pm*). Local artisans set up shop on Francisco Madero, Benito Juárez, Tonaltecas and López Rajour streets to sell their wares. Rustic furniture, terracotta crafts as well as wrought-iron, papier-mâché, wood and blown-glass pieces are just a few examples of the merchandise available here, often sold for a song.

Tour I: Laguna de Chapala

Crafts

When **Galería Moon** (*Avenida Río Zula no. 4, between Avenida Ocampo and the lake, Ajijic, ☎766-1000*) first opened its doors some ten years ago, Ajijic was far from having its current reputation for quality crafts. Owner Billy Moon's determination and competence were enough to radically change the city's way of making crafts, elevating them to international standards. Today, the factory-cum-showroom remains at the forefront of the craft industry, offering some of the most elegant, striking pieces. Very pricey, but gorgeous.

Tour J: Tequila and Surroundings

Tequila

It may be cliché to buy tequila in Tequila, but what better souvenir to bring back from a trip to the area? In addition to finding good tequila in distilleries (Saúz,

Shopping

Querencia, José Cuervo, see p 125), you can head to **Martha Nuvia** *(every day 10am to 6pm; Avenida Sixto Gorión no. 102, ☎742-0139)*. A wide choice of lovely *caballitos* (shotglasses) and small wooden barrels in which to preserve the precious liquid are also available.

Tour K: Tapalpa and the Mountain

Souvenirs

Hand-woven woolen blankets with typical designs are specific to Tapalpa. Weavers live on Calle Independencia, where they also run a small co-op. Candy made from local fruit is often enjoyed, notably *pegoste*, the village specialty. Among the spirits made in Tapalpa, *rompope* (an eggnog-type drink with rum, milk and almonds) is delicious, as is *ponche de frutas* (fruit punch flavoured with rum or brandy).

Located above the hotel of the same name, the **Posada de la Hacienda** *(Thu to Tue 10am to 6pm; Avenida Matamoros no. 7)* is the most comprehensive souvenir shop in Tapalpa. Available here are many crafts made of pine (the region's main species of tree) as well as terracotta pots and tableware, among other things. On the same street, villagers sell Tapalpa's specialties: homemade jams and candy.

Glossary

Pronunciation

Consonants

b   Is pronounced **b** or sometimes a soft **v**, depending on the region or the person: *bizcocho* (biz-koh-choh or viz-koh-choh).

c   As in English, *c* is pronounced as **s** before *i* and *e*: *cerro* (seh-rroh). When it is placed in front of other vowels, it is hard and pronounced as **k**: *carro* (kah-rroh). The *c* is also hard when it comes before a consonant, except before an *h* (see further below).

d   Is pronounced like a soft **d**: *dar* (dahr). *D* is usually not pronounced when at the end of a word.

g   As with the *c*, *g* is soft before an *i* or an *e*, and is pronounced like a soft **h**: *gente* (hente). In front of other vowels and consonants, the *g* is hard: *golf* (pronounced the same way as in English).

ch   Is pronounced **ch**, as in English: *leche* (le-che). Like the *ll*, this combination is considered a single letter in the Spanish alphabet, listed separately in dictionaries and telephone directories.

h   Is not pronounced: *hora* (oh-ra).

j   Is pronounced like a guttural **h**, as in "him".

ll   Is pronounced like a hard **y**, as in "yes": *llamar* (yah-mar). In some regions, such as central Colombia, *ll* is pronounced as a soft **g**, as in "mirage" (*Medellín* is pronounced Medegin). Like the *ch*, this combination is considered a single letter in the Spanish alphabet, and is listed separately in dictionaries and telephone directories.

ñ	Is pronounced like the **ni** in "onion", or the **ny** in "canyon": *señora* (seh-nyo-rah).
qu	Is pronounced **k**: *aquí* (ah-kee).
r	Is rolled, as the Irish or Italian pronunciation of **r**.
s	Is always pronounced **s** like "sign": *casa* (cah-ssah).
v	Is pronounced like a **b**: *vino* (bee-noh).
z	Is pronounced like **s**: *paz* (pahss).

Vowels

a	Is always pronounced **ah** as in "part", and never *ay* as in "day": *faro* (fah-roh).
e	Is pronounced **eh** as in "elf," and never *ey* as in "grey or "ee" as in "key": *helado* (eh-lah-doh].
i	Is always pronounced **ee**: *cine* (see-neh).
o	Is always pronounced **oh** as in "cone": *copa* (koh-pah).
u	Is always pronounced **oo**: *universidad* (oo-nee-ver-see-dah).

All other letters are pronounced the same as in English.

Stressing Syllables

In Spanish, syllables are differently stressed. This stress is very important, and emphasizing the right syllable might even be necessary to make yourself understood. If a vowel has an accent, this syllable is the one that should be stressed. If there is no accent, follow this rule:

Stress the second-last syllable of any word that ends with a vowel: *ami*go.

Stress the last syllable of any word that ends in a consonant, except for **s** (plural of nouns and adjectives) or **n**
(plural of nouns): *us**ted*** (but *ami*gos, *ha*blan).

A Few Expressions

Greetings

Goodbye	*adiós, hasta luego*
Good afternoon and good evening	*buenas tardes*
Hi (casual)	*hola*
Good morning	*buenos días*
Good night	*buenas noches*
Thank-you	*gracias*
Please	*por favor*
You are welcome	*de nada*
Excuse me	*perdone/a*
My name is...	*mi nombre es...*
What is your name?	*¿cómo se llama usted?*
no/yes	*no/sí*
Do you speak English?	*¿habla usted inglés?*
Slower, please	*más despacio, por favor*
I am sorry, I don't speak Spanish	*Lo siento, no hablo español*
How are you?	*¿qué tal?*
I am fine	*estoy bien*
I am American (male/female)	*Soy estadounidense*
I am Australian	*Soy autraliano/a*
I am Belgian	*Soy belga*
I am British (male/female)	*Soy británico/a*
I am Canadian	*Soy canadiense*
I am German (male/female)	*Soy alemán/a*
I am Italian (male/female)	*Soy italiano/a*
I am Swiss	*Soy suizo*
I am a tourist	*Soy turista*
single (m/f)	*soltero/a*
divorced (m/f)	*divorciado/a*
married (m/f)	*casado/a*
friend (m/f)	*amigo/a*
child (m/f)	*niño/a*

husband, wife	*esposo/a*
mother, father	*madre, padre*
brother, sister	*hermano/a*
widower widow	*viudo/a*
I am hungry	*tengo hambre*
I am ill	*estoy enfermo/a*
I am thirsty	*tengo sed*

Directions

beside	*al lado de*
to the right	*a la derecha*
to the left	*a la izquierda*
here, there	*aquí, allí*
into, inside	*dentro*
outside	*fuera*
behind	*detrás*
in front of	*delante*
between	*entre*
far from	*lejos de*
Where is ... ?	*¿dónde está ... ?*
To get to ...?	*¿para ir a...?*
near	*cerca de*
straight ahead	*todo recto*

Money

money	*dinero / plata*
credit card	*tarjeta de crédito*
exchange	*cambio*
traveller's cheque	*cheque de viaje*
I don't have any money	*no tengo dinero*
The bill, please	*la cuenta, por favor*
receipt	*recibo*

Shopping

store	*tienda*
market	*mercado*
open, closed	*abierto/a, cerrado/a*
How much is this?	*¿cuánto es?*
to buy, to sell	*comprar*, vender
the customer	*el / la cliente*
salesman	*vendedor*
saleswoman	*vendedora*
I need...	*necesito...*
I would like...	*yo quisiera...*
batteries	*pilas*

blouse	*blusa*
cameras	*cámaras*
cosmetics and perfumes	*cosméticos y perfumes*
cotton	*algodón*
dress jacket	*saco*
eyeglasses	*lentes, gafas*
fabric	*tela*
film	*película*
gifts	*regalos*
gold	*oro*
handbag	*bolsa*
hat	*sombrero*
jewellery	*joyería*
leather	*cuero, piel*
local crafts	*artesanía*
magazines	*revistas*
newpapers	*periódicos*
pants	*pantalones*
records, cassettes	*discos, casetas*
sandals	*sandalias*
shirt	*camisa*
shoes	*zapatos*
silver	*plata*
skirt	*falda*
sun screen products	*productos solares*
T-shirt	*camiseta*
watch	*reloj*
wool	*lana*

Miscellaneous

a little	*poco*
a lot	*mucho*
good (m/f)	*bueno/a*
bad (m/f)	*malo/a*
beautiful (m/f)	*hermoso/a*
pretty (m/f)	*bonito/a*
ugly	*feo*
big	*grande*
tall (m/f)	*alto/a*
small (m/f)	*pequeño/a*
short (length) (m/f)	*corto/a*
short (person) (m/f)	*bajo/a*
cold (m/f)	*frío/a*
hot	*caliente*

dark (m/f)	*oscuro/a*
light (colour)	*claro*
do not touch	*no tocar*
expensive (m/f)	*caro/a*
cheap (m/f)	*barato/a*
fat (m/f)	*gordo/a*
slim, skinny (m/f)	*delgado/a*
heavy (m/f)	*pesado/a*
light (weight) (m/f)	*ligero/a*
less	*menos*
more	*más*
narrow (m/f)	*estrecho/a*
wide (m/f)	*ancho/a*
new (m/f)	*nuevo/a*
old (m/f)	*viejo/a*
nothing	*nada*
something (m/f)	*algo/a*
quickly	*rápidamente*
slowly (m/f)	*despacio/a*
What is this?	*¿qué es esto?*
when?	*¿cuando?*
where?	*¿dónde?*

Time

in the afternoon, early evening	*por la tarde*
at night	*por la noche*
in the daytime	*por el día*
in the morning	*por la mañana*
minute	*minuto*
month	*mes*
ever	*jamás*
never	*nunca*
now	*ahora*
today	*hoy*
yesterday	*ayer*
tomorrow	*mañana*
What time is it?	*¿qué hora es?*
hour	*hora*
week	*semana*
year	*año*
Sunday	*domingo*
Monday	*lunes*
Tuesday	*martes*

Wednesday	*miércoles*
Thursday	*jueves*
Friday	*viernes*
Saturday	*sábado*
January	*enero*
February	*febrero*
March	*marzo*
April	*abril*
May	*mayo*
June	*junio*
July	*julio*
August	*agosto*
September	*septiembre*
October	*octubre*
November	*noviembre*
December	*diciembre*

Weather

It is cold	*hace frío*
It is warm	*hace calor*
It is very hot	*hace mucho calor*
sun	*sol*
It is sunny	*hace sol*
It is cloudy	*está nublado*
rain	*lluvia*
It is raining	*está lloviendo*
wind	*viento*
It is windy	*hay viento*
snow	*nieve*
damp	*húmedo*
dry	*seco*
storm	*tormenta*
hurricane	*huracán*

Communication

air mail	*correos aéreo*
collect call	*llamada por cobrar*
dial the number	*marcar el número*
area code, country code	*código*
envelope	*sobre*
long distance	*larga distancia*
post office	*correo*
rate	*tarifa*
stamps	*estampillas*

telegram	*telegrama*
telephone book	*un guia telefónica*
wait for the tone	*esperar la señal*

Activities

beach	*playa*
museum or gallery	*museo*
scuba diving	*buceo*
to swim	*bañarse*
to walk around	*pasear*
hiking	*caminata*
trail	*pista, sendero*
cycling	*ciclismo*
fishing	*pesca*

Transportation

arrival, departure	*llegada, salida*
on time	*a tiempo*
cancelled (m/f)	*anulado/a*
one way ticket	*ida*
return	*regreso*
round trip	*ida y vuelta*
schedule	*horario*
baggage	equipajes
north, south	*norte, sur*
east, west	*este, oeste*
avenue	avenida
street	*calle*
highway	carretera
expressway	*autopista*
airplane	*avión*
airport	*aeropuerto*
bicycle	*bicicleta*
boat	*barco*
bus	*bus*
bus stop	*parada*
bus terminal	*terminal*
train	*tren*
train crossing	*crucero ferrocarril*
station	*estación*
neighbourhood	*barrio*
collective taxi	*colectivo*
corner	*esquina*
express	*rápido*
safe	*seguro/a*

be careful	*cuidado*
car	*coche, carro*
To rent a car	*alquilar un auto*
gas	*gasolina*
gas station	*gasolinera*
no parking	*no estacionar*
no passing	*no adelantar*
parking	*parqueo*
pedestrian	*peaton*
road closed, no through traffic	*no hay paso*
slow down	*reduzca velocidad*
speed limit	*velocidad permitida*
stop	*alto*
stop! (an order)	*pare*
traffic light	*semáforo*

Accommodation

cabin, bungalow	*cabaña*
accommodation	*alojamiento*
double, for two people	*doble*
single, for one person	*sencillo*
high season	*temporada alta*
low season	*temporada baja*
bed	*cama*
floor (first, second...)	*piso*
main floor	*planta baja*
manager	*gerente, jefe*
double bed	*cama matrimonial*
cot	*camita*
bathroom	*baños*
with private bathroom	*con baño privado*
hot water	*agua caliente*
breakfast	*desayuno*
elevator	*ascensor*
air conditioning	*aire acondicionado*
fan	*ventilador, abanico*
pool	*piscina, alberca*
room	*habitación*

Numbers

1	*uno*
2	*dos*
3	*tres*
4	*cuatro*

5	*cinco*
6	*seis*
7	*siete*
8	*ocho*
9	*nueve*
10	*diez*
11	*once*
12	*doce*
13	*trece*
14	*catorce*
15	*quince*
16	*dieciséis*
17	*diecisiete*
18	*dieciocho*
19	*diecinueve*
20	*veinte*
21	*veintiuno*
22	*veintidós*
23	*veintitrés*
24	*veinticuatro*
25	*veinticinco*
26	*veintiséis*
27	*veintisiete*
28	*veintiocho*
29	*veintinueve*
30	*treinta*
31	*treinta y uno*
32	*treinta y dos*
40	*cuarenta*
50	*cincuenta*
60	*sesenta*
70	*setenta*
80	*ochenta*
90	*noventa*
100	*cien*
101	*ciento uno*
200	*doscientos*
300	*trescientos*
1,000	*mil*
1,100	*mil cien*
2000	*dos mil*
10,000	*diez mil*
100,000	*cien mil*
1,000,000	*un millón*

Index

Index

Order Form

Ulysses Travel Guides

☐ Acapulco ..... $14.95 CAN / $9.95 US	☐ Lisbon .... $18.95 CAN / $13.95 US
☐ Atlantic Canada $24.95 CAN / $17.95 US	☐ Louisiana ..... $29.95 CAN / $21.95 US
☐ Bahamas ..... $24.95 CAN / $17.95 US	☐ Martinique .... $24.95 CAN / $17.95 US
☐ Beaches of Maine $12.95 CAN / $9.95 US	☐ Montréal ..... $19.95 CAN / $14.95 US
☐ Bed & Breakfasts $14.95 CAN / in Québec $10.95 US	☐ Miami .... $9.95 CAN / $12.95 US
☐ Belize .... $16.95 CAN / $12.95 US	☐ New Orleans .. $17.95 CAN / $12.95 US
☐ Calgary ..... $17.95 CAN / $12.95 US	☐ New York City . $19.95 CAN / $14.95 US
☐ Canada .... $29.95 CAN / $21.95 US	☐ Nicaragua ..... $24.95 CAN / $16.95 US
☐ Chicago ..... $19.95 CAN / $14.95 US	☐ Ontario ...... $27.95 CAN / $19.95US
☐ Chile .... $27.95 CAN / $17.95 US	☐ Ontario's Best Hotels and Restaurants ... $27.95 CAN / $19.95US
☐ Colombia ..... $29.95 CAN / $21.95 US	☐ Ottawa .... $17.95 CAN / $12.95 US
☐ Costa Rica .... $27.95 CAN / $19.95 US	☐ Panamá ..... $24.95 CAN / $17.95 US
☐ Cuba .... $24.95 CAN / $17.95 US	☐ Peru .... $27.95 CAN / $19.95 US
☐ Dominican .... $24.95 CAN / Republic $17.95 US	☐ Phoenix ...... $16.95 CAN / $12.95 US
☐ Ecuador and .. $24.95 CAN / Galápagos Islands $17.95 US	☐ Portugal ...... $24.95 CAN / $16.95 US
☐ El Salvador .... $22.95 CAN / $14.95 US	☐ Provence - .... $29.95 CAN / Côte d'Azur $21.95US
☐ Guadeloupe ... $24.95 CAN / $17.95 US	☐ Puerto Rico ... $24.95 CAN / $17.95 US
☐ Guatemala .... $24.95 CAN / $17.95 US	☐ Québec ...... $29.95 CAN / $21.95 US
☐ Hawaii .... $29.95 CAN / $21.95 US	☐ Québec City ... $17.95 CAN / $12.95 US
☐ Honduras ..... $24.95 CAN / $17.95 US	☐ Québec and Ontario with Via .... $9.95 CAN / $7.95 US
☐ Islands of the .. $24.95 CAN / Bahamas $17.95 US	
☐ Las Vegas ..... $17.95 CAN / $12.95 US	

☐ Seattle . . . . $17.95 CAN	☐ Vancouver . . . . $17.95 CAN
$12.95 US	$12.95 US
☐ Toronto . . . . . . $18.95 CAN	☐ Washington D.C. $18.95 CAN
$13.95 US	$13.95 US
☐ Tunisia . . . . $27.95 CAN	☐ Western Canada $29.95 CAN
$19.95 US	$21.95 US

Ulysses Due South

☐ Acapulco . . . . . $14.95 CAN	☐ Los Cabos . . . . $14.95 CAN
$9.95 US	and La Paz $10.95 US
☐ Belize . . . . $16.95 CAN	☐ Puerto Plata - . $14.95 CAN
$12.95 US	Sosua $9.95 US
☐ Cancún & . . . . . $19.95 CAN	☐ Puerto Vallarta . $14.95 CAN
Riviera Maya $14.95 US	$9.95 US
☐ Cartagena . . . . . $12.95 CAN	☐ St. Martin . . . . . $16.95 CAN
(Colombia) $9.95 US	and St. Barts $12.95 US
☐ Huatulco - . . . . $17.95 CAN	
Puerto Escondido $12.95 US	

Ulysses Travel Journals

☐ Ulysses Travel Journal	☐ Ulysses Travel Journal
(Blue, Red, Green, Yellow,	(80 Days) . . . . . $14.95 CAN
Sextant) . . . . $9.95 CAN	$9.95 US
$7.95 US	

Ulysses Green Escapes

☐ Cycling in France $22.95 CAN	☐ Hiking in the . . $19.95 CAN
$16.95 US	Northeastern U.S. $13.95 US
☐ Cycling in . . . . . $22.95 CAN	☐ Hiking in . . . . . $19.95 CAN
Ontario $16.95 US	Québec $13.95 US

Title	Qty	Price	Total

Name:		Subtotal	
		Shipping	$4 CAN $3 US
Address:		Subtotal	
		GST in Canada 7%	
		Total	

Tel: Fax:

E-mail:

Payment: ☐ Cheque ☐ Visa ☐ MasterCard

Card number_____

Expiry date_____

Signature_____

ULYSSES TRAVEL GUIDES

4176 St-Denis,
Montréal, Québec,
H2W 2M5
(514) 843-9447
fax (514) 843-9448

305 Madison Avenue,
Suite 1166,
New York, NY 10165

Toll free: 1-877-542-7247
Info@ulysses.ca
www.ulyssesguides.com